Seeds of

Book

Blood of Rome

by

K. M. Ashman

Copyright K. M. Ashman, January 2025

All rights are reserved. No part of this publication may be reproduced, stored, or transmitted in any form or by any means without prior written permission of the copyright owner. All characters depicted within this publication are fictitious, and any resemblance to any real person, living or dead, is entirely coincidental.

KMAshman.com

Prologue

Rome

The Senate was in session, which meant the noise could be heard three streets away. Inside the Curia, voices echoed off the marble walls and the wooden benches creaked under the weight of men who had grown comfortable in their positions. The air was thick with the smell of wool togas, lamp oil, and the particular staleness that comes from too many bodies packed into too small a space.

Lentulus was on his feet again, his face red and his arm gesturing wildly at nothing in particular. He was one of the consuls, which meant he had the right to speak as long as he wanted, and he was using that right to its fullest extent.

'We cannot allow this insult to stand,' he shouted, his voice cracking slightly on the higher notes. 'Caesar has been given every opportunity to comply with the Senate's lawful demands. He refuses, he mocks us and he sits in Gaul with his legions treating the Republic as if it were his personal estate.'

'Here we go again,' muttered a senator in the back row to his neighbour. 'Third time today he has made this speech.'

'Fourth,' the neighbour corrected. 'You missed the one before lunch.'

Marcellus, the other consul, stood when Lentulus finally sat down. He was younger than Lentulus, though not by much, and he had the kind of face that looked serious even when he was sleeping. He adjusted his toga with careful precision before speaking.

'The law is clear,' he said, his voice carrying better than Lentulus's had. 'A proconsul must disband his forces before entering Italy. Caesar knows this and we all know this. The fact that he chooses to ignore the law does not make the law less binding.'

Across the chamber, Pompey sat in his usual place near the front. He had been given a special seat, an honour that recognised his military victories and his importance to the Republic, though it also meant everyone could watch his face when they spoke. He was perhaps fifty-five years old, his hair still thick but greying at the temples, and had the bearing of a man who had spent most of his life being the most important person in any room he entered.

'What does Magnus say?' someone called from the benches, using Pompey's cognomen. 'He is the only one here who has actually commanded an army.'

Pompey stood slowly, letting the chamber fall quiet. He had learned long ago that silence was more dramatic than rushing to speak.

'I say that Caesar is testing us,' he said eventually. 'He wants to see if we will bend. If we do, he will push further. If we do not, he may reconsider.'

'And if he does not reconsider?' asked Cato from his bench near the back. 'What then, Imperator?'

Cato the Younger was perhaps forty years old, lean and hard-faced, with the kind of intensity that made people uncomfortable. He wore a plain tunic without any decoration, which was unusual for a man of his rank, and his hair was cut short in a style that had gone out of fashion a generation ago. He did not care about fashion.

'Then we will have war,' said Pompey simply.

'We already have war,' Cato replied. 'We simply have not admitted it yet.'

Cicero, sitting several benches away from Cato, raised his hand to speak. He was in his sixties now, his hair white and his face showing the thoughtful lines of a man who had made his reputation with words.

'Surely there is still room for negotiation,' he said. 'Caesar is a reasonable man. If we send him terms he can accept without losing face, perhaps we can avoid bloodshed.'

'Terms?' Cato turned to face Cicero directly. 'What terms? He either obeys the law or he does not. There is no middle ground here. Either we are a Republic governed by laws, or we are a kingdom governed by whoever has the largest army.'

'That is exactly my point,' said Cicero, though his voice was less certain now. 'If we force him to choose between disgrace and war, we know which he will choose. Better to give him a path that preserves both his dignity and our authority.'

'*His dignity,*' Cato repeated, making the word sound like an insult. 'The Republic is dying and you want to preserve Caesar's dignity.'

Lentulus stood again.

'Enough debate,' he said. 'We have discussed this for weeks so I call for a vote. Let the Senate declare Caesar an enemy of the state if he does not disband his legions within thirty days.'

'Seconded,' Marcellus said immediately.

The vote was called and hands went up around the chamber agreeing the proposition. Pompey, however, remained seated, watching. His face showed nothing.

Beyond the Curia, the city continued as it always had, though the tension was palpable to anyone who cared to notice. In the Forum, merchants sold their goods and farmers brought vegetables in from the countryside, but the conversations had changed. People spoke in lower voices now, and when they mentioned Caesar's name, they glanced around first to see who might be listening.

At the public baths, men argued politics whilst slaves poured water over heated stones. Some said Caesar was a hero who had conquered Gaul for Rome's glory. Others said he was a tyrant who wanted to make himself king. A few said both things were true and that was the problem.

In the taverns near the Subura, where the wine was cheap and the clientele rough, bets were being placed on what would happen next. The odds favoured war, though nobody wanted to say so out loud.

The grain merchants watched their stocks carefully and raised their prices a little each day. Not enough to cause riots, just enough to prepare for what might be coming. The bakers bought less grain and made smaller loaves, and when customers complained, they blamed the weather or the ships or anything except the truth, which was that everyone was preparing for a siege that had not yet begun.

In the wealthy houses on the Palatine, families made quiet decisions about sending their children to villas in the countryside. Not everyone, because that would look like panic, but enough that the tutors and the music teachers noticed their students disappearing one by one.

At night, the city was quieter than usual. People stayed inside after dark, and the usual noise of parties and dinner gatherings was muted. Occasionally, someone would swear they could hear something from the north, a sound like thunder or like thousands of feet marching in unison, but it was probably just their imagination…*probably!*

When the news came, it came suddenly. The Senate was in session again, still arguing about the same things they had been arguing about for weeks. Lentulus was speaking, again, and Marcellus was nodding in agreement, again, and Cicero was looking tired whilst Cato looked angry, which was how they always looked these days.

Halfway through the debate, the doors of the Curia swung open with a crash that echoed through the chamber and made everyone jump. Three men stood in the doorway, their cloaks heavy with mud from riding hard for days with little rest. One of them held a scroll in his hand and the chamber fell silent.

The rider with the scroll stepped forward. He did not bow, and he did not wait to be invited to speak.

'News from Ariminum,' he announced loudly. 'Caesar has crossed the Rubicon. He is marching on Rome.'

For a moment, nobody moved but suddenly, Lentulus stood so quickly he nearly knocked over the man beside him.

'How many men does he have?'

'One legion, Consul. Perhaps five thousand men.'

'One legion?' Marcellus glanced across at Pompey before returning his daze to the messenger. 'Is this a jest?'

'It is not a jest,' the rider said. 'He crossed two days ago, and will be at the city walls within a few weeks, maybe less.'

Pompey stood slowly, and walked towards the entrance without a word. Around him, senators were shouting questions and theories and accusations, their voices rising until the chamber was as loud as a marketplace.

Cato alone remained seated, his arms crossed over his chest. He did not look surprised, he looked vindicated, which was somehow worse while Cicero put his head in his hands and all the while, the rider with the scroll stood in the doorway, still holding the message that would change everything.

Chapter One

Northern Italia

The column halted on Marcus's order and the command rippled back through the line like a wave. Shields came off shoulders packs hit the ground, and men rolled their necks and shoulders, working out the stiffness that came from a long day's march. The road behind them stretched back towards the Rubicon, narrow and broken in places where winter rains had carved gullies through the packed earth, but the line had held and not once had a standard dipped.

Marcus rode back along the column, his cloak pulled tight against the wind that came down from the mountains. He gave signals with his hand and the cohort leaders broke away with their details, moving to begin the work of building a camp. They had done this so many times in Gaul that they barely needed orders anymore, their bodies knew the routine better than their minds did.

The tribunes hurried to carry Marcus's orders to the other cohorts, and within minutes, the first axes rang out from the nearby wood, and the smell of fresh-cut timber and pine sap spread through the air. Lines were measured, ditches marked with stakes and string, and the locations of gates chosen whilst the men of the Thirteenth took their places and began the familiar routine.

Spades bit into the hard earth, stakes were hammered in with wooden mallets, and slowly but surely, order grew from nothing.

They were not a large army by Roman standards, Marcus thought as he watched them work. Five thousand men, perhaps a little more if you counted the camp followers who had attached themselves to the legion over the years. But they were veterans, almost all of them. These were the same soldiers who had served Caesar across Gaul, who had fought the Germans and the Belgae, and who had crossed the channel to Britannia and come back alive.

They had seen half the known world under arms and they still marched to the same steady rhythm, each pace measured, each command obeyed without question. The legion was tired, but it was loyal and sure of its own abilities.

Marcus paused on a small rise to take in the view. Beyond the stream that marked the edge of their chosen campsite, the land ran south in low folds, brown and bare except for scattered patches of scrub oak. The first villages of Italia lay out there beyond the horizon, waiting for the change they knew Caesar's arrival would bring.

He turned to an optio nearby who was checking the positioning of the first tent stakes.

'Send riders along the southern road,' said Marcus. 'I want to know what lies between us and the next town. How many people, what kind of defences, and whether they have grain stores.'

'At once, Praefect,' replied the Optio, and moved off at a jog towards the cavalry lines.

By the time the first trench was squared off and the spoil piled into a neat rampart, the camp had already begun to breathe with its own rhythm. The engineers called for more men to carry dirt, while the blacksmiths had lit their portable braziers and were already working on repairs to equipment that had been damaged on the march.

The first watchfires crackled against the gathering dusk,

and the smell of smoke and lamp oil mixed with sweat and earth, creating the particular scent that Marcus had come to associate with Roman camps from Gaul to Judea.

They were few in number compared to the legions Pompey could call upon, Marcus knew that. Pompey had connections throughout the east, and he could raise armies in Greece and Asia if he chose to. But Marcus also knew what Caesar's men were worth. He had fought beside them in Gaul, had seen them hold ground that would have broken twice their number, had watched them dig defences in mud up to their knees and still make them square enough to please the most demanding surveyor. These were soldiers who no longer thought about what they were doing. Their hands knew the work before their minds gave the order.

As the rampart rose, men talked in low voices. They spoke of the march, of the road ahead, of rumours they had heard from peddlers and farmers along the way. Some said Pompey had ten legions ready, others said the Senate had already fled Rome, and a few wondered aloud how long it would take them to reach the city walls.

But none spoke of turning back. They were soldiers on the home soil of Italia now, and there was no road behind them that led anywhere except disgrace and probably execution.

Marcus moved among the working men as he always did, not to correct their technique but simply to be seen. He stopped to say a few words here and there, practical observations about spacing between tents or the placement of the watchfires, and when he picked up a spade and helped carry spoil for a while, the nearest men worked harder without needing to be told. He had learned that trick years ago from an old centurion who was dead now, killed by a British spear in a battle whose name Marcus could no longer remember.

By the time the second watch was called, the work was nearly done. The ditches stood clean and deep, the first line of sharpened stakes set at an angle to discourage attackers, and the gates were positioned to allow quick deployment in any direction. Fires burned low and steady throughout the camp, and as the trumpets sounded the call to stand down from work details, a small murmur ran through the assembled men, not joy exactly, not relief, but the sound of soldiers who knew they had done their day's work well.

The cooks began their work and the smell of food crept through the narrow streets between the tents, lentils thick with barley, pork that had been salted weeks ago and now needed long boiling to make it edible, and the sharp tang of vinegar that the men used to flavour their posca.

Soldiers gathered in groups of eight around their contubernium fires, sharing what they had and complaining about what they did not have, which was the natural state of soldiers in every army that had ever marched.

The army of Gaius Julius Caesar ate simply. There was no silver plates, no luxuries brought from Rome, only bread and salt meat and cheese.

For the common soldiers, posca that was more vinegar than wine and for the officers, slightly better wine but not much more. Caesar had made sure of that from the beginning. He dined as his soldiers dined, which was one reason they followed him across a river that made them all traitors.

In the centre of the camp, the headquarters tents had already been raised, their canvas stretched taut and pegged square to the ground. The eagle of the Thirteenth Legion stood before the entrance, its bronze wings catching the firelight and gleaming in the dusk. Beyond it, the command tent waited with its flap half open and lamplight spilling across the hard earth outside.

Marcus stepped inside without announcing himself. He did not need to, he had grown up with Caesar and was his oldest friend as well as his military advisor.

Caesar sat at the small folding table that travelled with him everywhere, his cloak drawn about his shoulders against the chill that seeped through the canvas. His cuirass lay on a wooden chest behind him, the bronze polished but showing the dents and scratches of years of campaigning. His sword belt hung from the tent pole, the gladius within reach but not on his hip.

A bowl of lentils sat on the table beside a heel of bread, but Caesar ate without interest, the mechanical movements of a man meeting a necessity rather than satisfying an appetite.

'The camp is secure,' said Marcus, unfastening his own cloak and laying it across a stool.

Caesar nodded without looking up from the map spread before him.

'Patrols?'

'Already out. I sent riders as far as the next village. They should report before dawn.'

'Good.'

Marcus took the stool opposite Caesar and poured himself a cup of watered wine from the jug on the table. He took a sip and studied his friend across the flickering lamplight. They had known each other since childhood, had grown up in the same neighbourhood in Rome, and has fought together at the siege of Mytilene where his friend had earned the Corona Civica, one of Rome's highest military honours, given for saving the life of a Roman citizen in battle.

Marcus knew Caesar's moods better than most men, and he could see the tension in the set of his shoulders.

'The men are holding well,' he said after a moment. 'No complaints. No stragglers.'

'They never complain.'

'Not where you can hear them, anyway,' said Marcus and took another sip of wine before continuing. 'I told the engineers to widen the southern ditch and they will have it finished before the second watch turns.'

Caesar's eyes flicked briefly from the map to Marcus's face, then back down.

'And the locals? Have there been any problems with the villagers?'

'Not really. Two men were found on the road this afternoon and said riders passed through yesterday but with no banners showing. They could have been scouts for Pompey or simply merchants so I sent word to the next village to keep the roads clear of civilians until we pass through.'

Caesar nodded slowly as his hand moved across the map, tracing the line of the road that led south towards Rome.

'Pompey will have word by now,' he said quietly. 'The Senate will know I have crossed the Rubicon and if Pompey is still in Rome, he will be sending out orders to raise his legions. But if he is clever, he will fall back before we arrive and let us come to him rather than meeting us at the gates.'

'He is a proud man,' Marcus observed.

'He is,' agreed Caesar. 'Which means he will make mistakes.'

The tent fell quiet except for the faint popping of the lamp flame and Marcus glanced at Caesar's bowl, which was still half full.

'You have hardly eaten.'

'I have had enough.'

Marcus broke a piece of the bread and used it to scoop up what remained of the lentils. They were bland but warm, and he chewed slowly whilst considering whether to speak again. Something in Caesar's stillness made him hesitate, but silence had never sat well with Marcus.

'Do you remember the Sambre?' he asked eventually. 'When that supply cart lost its wheel and nearly took half the baggage train with it down the embankment?'

Caesar looked up briefly.

'I remember the river. Not the cart.'

Marcus smiled faintly.

'Felix caught the mules before they bolted. I thought he would be dragged all the way to the sea before he let go of those reins.'

Caesar said nothing and the name hung in the air for a moment, heavy with memory. Felix had been more than a valued scribe. The freedman had become a close friend to both of them, and he had died in Gaul saving Caesar's life. His death was not something either of them discussed often.

Caesar returned his attention back to the map.

'The pace has been hard on the men,' he said, 'so we will stay here for a few days, just long enough to rest and resupply. Then we march again. If we stay too long in any one place, the Senate will find courage it does not have.'

The lamplight flickered as another draft found its way through the tent seams and Marcus saw Caesar's eyes catch the movement. He knew that look well. It was the same expression Caesar wore before ordering a charge, when the map became the world and nothing else existed except the problem before him and the solution he was working towards.

Marcus took another sip of his wine and tried once

more to pull Caesar into conversation.

'The scouts say the next town has a small garrison. No more than a century and probably local militia rather than proper legionaries. They may shut the gates when they see us coming, but I do not think they will stand if we actually besiege them.'

'They will open the gates,' said Caesar with certainty. 'They will see our army and decide to be loyal. Or they will see our army and decide to be pragmatic. Either way, they will open.'

'And if they do not?'

'Then they will learn what happens to towns that resist. But it will not come to that. These are Romans, Marcus. They are not going to die simply for Pompey's pride.'

The tent fell quiet again. Outside, the camp had settled into its evening routine. The low murmur of voices had faded, replaced by the steady sounds of the few men still working on the defences, the occasional challenge and the response of sentries changing watch. Somewhere nearby a horse stamped its feet, and the faint ring of iron on stone carried through the canvas walls.

'You should rest,' said Marcus, finishing his wine and setting the cup down. 'Tomorrow will be another long day.' He stood and picked up his cloak, swinging it around his shoulders and fastening it at his throat. 'I am going to walk the perimeter and check on the sentries. If the scouts return early, I will bring their report myself.'

Caesar inclined his head in acknowledgment.

'Good night, Marcus.'

Marcus paused at the tent entrance and looked back at his friend, who had already returned his full attention to the map. There was no point in trying to make more conversation, when Caesar was in this mood, thinking and planning, he was unreachable.

'Good night, Caesar,' he replied, and stepped outside into the cool evening air.

He walked the narrow streets between the tents, heading towards the eastern gate. Along the way, he stopped to check each sentry post, speaking briefly to each man on duty and asking simple questions. How far could they see in the darkness? What would they do at the first alarm? How did the wind carry sound tonight?

He corrected one man's grip on his pilum, showing him how to hold it ready without tiring his arm, and he praised another for the neatness of his post and the clear sightlines he had chosen.

When he reached the rampart, he climbed up onto the fresh-built earthwork and looked back across the camp to the command tent still glowing with lamplight in the gathering darkness. He could picture Caesar inside, still bent over that map, measuring the road to Rome not in miles but in decisions and consequences.

Marcus turned towards the dark fields beyond the camp and the road that led south. The scouts would be back before dawn, they would give their report and Caesar would decide what came next. Everything else was beyond his control.

Behind him, the camp settled down into the familiar nighttime routine as men wrapped themselves in their cloaks and lay down beside their fires or in their tents, their shields close at hand and their gladii within easy reach.

They slept the sleep of veterans, light and ready, trusting in the sentries and trusting in the man who sat awake beneath the lamplight, planning their next move.

Before them, many miles to the south, Rome waited and in the quiet of the winter night, the army of Caesar held its ground on Italian soil, no longer soldiers of Gaul, not yet conquerors of Rome, but something new and dangerous, balanced on the edge between loyalty and treason, between law and power, between what Rome had been and what it might become.

Chapter Two

Northern Italia

Marcus stood at the edge of a low ridge, watching Caesar's advance guard emerge from the treeline below and fan out across the valley floor. They moved in silence, no horns announcing their presence, no banners snapping in the wind, just the steady clatter of hobnailed caligae on frozen ground and the creak of leather harnesses. The discipline was perfect, mechanical even, and Marcus felt a familiar pride watching them work.

The road ahead curved through bare-limbed woods towards another fortified villa that served as a watch station on the northern approaches to Ariminum. Smoke rose from behind its walls, the thin grey evidence of people going about their morning routines whilst trying to pretend an army was not approaching their gates.

Beside Marcus, Balbus shifted his weight and narrowed his eyes against the pale morning light. He was a thick-shouldered man in his forties, a veteran of the German campaigns who had the kind of face that looked permanently sceptical.

'Still no signal from them?' he asked.

'Not yet,' replied Marcus.

'How many do you think they have in there?'

'Our scouts reported a few dozen at most. Local militia, probably. Nothing that should concern us.'

Balbus made a noise in his throat that might have been agreement or doubt, and adjusted the fur lining of his cloak.

'I suspect they are hoping we will march past and leave them be.'

Marcus said nothing, he already knew how this would unfold. There had been two similar outposts in the past two days. One had surrendered immediately, the small garrison falling over themselves to swear loyalty to Caesar before the first cohort even reached their gates. The second had resisted, barring their doors and shouting defiance from the walls, but after a brief assault and a few casualties, the gates had opened and the citizens inside had pretended nothing had happened. This one, though, this one was hesitating, which meant someone inside still believed Pompey might win.

A trumpet sounded from the trees ahead, and Marcus straightened, his hand moving instinctively to his sword hilt. Down below, one of the forward patrols had crested a low rise and come face to face with another unit approaching from the opposite direction and even at this distance, Marcus could see the faded Senate colours on their cloaks.

'That is no foraging party,' muttered Balbus beside him.

The two patrols clashed with sudden, terrible violence. There was no time for formation, no shouted commands, just a fast collision of iron and flesh. Marcus watched a spear catch one of Caesar's men in the throat, sending him spinning backwards with blood spraying across the frost-covered grass while another legionary tumbled into the undergrowth, his arm bent at an angle that made Balbus wince.

But Caesar's men recovered quickly and they responded with the kind of practised violence that came from years of fighting Gauls and Germans, short brutal stabs with their gladii and hammering strikes with their shield bosses that broke bones and crushed windpipes.

The Pompeian loyalists fought with desperation but they lacked cohesion, and within moments three of them were down and not getting up again. Another tried to run but was caught from behind, the pilum entering halfway down his spine and bursting out through his belly. He fell without a sound.

It was over in less than a minute. Two of Caesar's men were dead and perhaps six wounded, but almost a dozen Pompeian soldiers lay on the cold ground whilst their surviving comrades disappeared into the safety of the trees.

Marcus let out a breath he had not realised he was holding.

'First blood,' he said quietly.

'It was always going to happen,' Balbus replied. 'Better here than at the gates of Rome.'

They reached Ariminum later that afternoon. It was larger than the other towns they had passed through, not large enough to matter strategically but still one of the last real thresholds between Caesar's army and the heart of Italia. The walls were old but well-maintained, and the gates were heavy oak, reinforced with iron bands.

A delegation from the town had already gathered near the gates, six men in civic robes with purple edging, flanked by watchmen carrying torches even though it was still daylight. They stood stiffly, trying to project authority they no longer possessed.

Caesar rode forward to meet the welcoming committee. He wore his travelling armour, dusty from the road, and his red general's cloak hung simply from his shoulders without any gold embroidery or decoration.

As he neared the delegation, the leading magistrate stepped forward and bowed. The gesture was stiff and formal, the bow of a man who resented the necessity but understood the reality.

'Ariminum honours the presence of the imperator,' he

said, his voice carrying across the space between them. 'We are your loyal servants and will remain so.'

Caesar dismounted without speaking. He removed his riding gloves slowly, tucking them into his belt, then walked forward until he stood close enough to the magistrate that the man had to look up slightly to meet his eyes.

'The question,' he said eventually, 'is not whether you serve Caesar or Pompey. The question is whether you serve Rome.'

Marcus watched the magistrates exchange glances. One man swallowed visibly while another looked towards the walls as if seeking escape. None of them answered.

Caesar's expression softened slightly, though it did not quite become a smile.

'You have nothing to fear from me or my men, magistrate, the legion will be quartered outside the walls, no soldiers will be billeted in your homes and your grain stores will not be touched without fair payment.' He paused. 'But understand this. Ariminum is just the first gate. The next town will watch how you behave, and the town after that will watch them. Their fate depends entirely on what message travels down this road. Think carefully and respond by last light.' He turned away and mounted his horse before returning to the vanguard, the delegation watching him in silence as they rode away.

Balbus moved to stand beside Marcus.

'It was a good move,' he said quietly. 'They will tell the next town that Caesar was reasonable. Fair, even.'

Marcus looked back at the gatehouse and the smoke drifting up from behind the walls. Somewhere on the other side, families were listening to rumours, merchants were hiding their account books, and young men were trying to decide whether to pick up weapons or keep their heads down. The war had arrived at Ariminum, not with trumpets and battle cries, but with a quiet choice laid at every doorstep.

The gates opened fully as dusk settled over the town. A cold stillness had descended over the streets, broken only by the distant rumble of carts being moved and the cautious scrape of shutters being drawn, but Caesar's army did not surge forward. Instead, as promised, it remained encamped outside the walls, the tents arranged in perfect rows, standards planted, and watchfires already burning beneath a sky that was turning from grey to black.

Only three centuries were permitted to enter. Not enough to occupy the town, but more than enough to remind everyone of what could happen if they changed their minds about cooperation.

The citizens watched from behind shuttered windows. A few lingered on doorsteps, mothers holding children close, and tradesmen standing with their arms crossed, their faces wary. There were no cries of protest, no gestures of defiance, just quiet observation and the rhythmic sound of hobnailed caligae on stone.

Balbus rode beside Marcus in silence, chewing on what might once have been an olive stem. His jaw worked rhythmically as they passed beneath the archway and a company of civic guards stood at attention by the gate, their weapons lowered but not discarded, not quite ready to abandon their posts but no longer willing to use those weapons in defence of anything.

The town was well-kept. The market stalls had been hastily cleared, but the forum remained tidy. In one corner, a half-finished mosaic lay waiting for completion, the coloured tiles arranged to show Jupiter's victory over the Titans. Marcus caught a glimpse of it as they turned towards the basilica, the largest building in Ariminum, built from pale stone, its portico supported by thick columns and flanked by bronze statues of Romulus and Remus. It served as courthouse, grain hall, and shelter during emergencies. Today, it would serve as the seat of Caesar's authority.

Marcus dismounted and walked through the building with a detachment of legionaries, checking corners and alcoves, looking for anywhere an assassin might hide or a trap might be laid. The centurions followed his lead in other parts of the complex, spreading their men through the halls to seek anyone desperate enough to make a name for themselves.

When Marcus was satisfied that the building was secure, he nodded to the Primus Pilus, who positioned his men around the perimeter and only then did Caesar enter.

He came on foot, his red cloak sweeping behind him, the dust of the road still visible on the hem. Again, he wore no gold or carried ceremonial weapons, yet there was something in his bearing that filled the space more effectively than any display of wealth or power could have done.

Marcus had seen Caesar command in battle, had heard his voice rise above the screaming of dying men and the clash of weapons. But here, in this quiet basilica, surrounded by nervous magistrates and uncertain citizens, he was more dangerous than he had ever been on any battlefield. He looked like a man who knew the future belonged to him and was simply waiting for everyone else to realise it.

The city's magistrates arrived shortly afterwards, six of them, robed in their civic best, their hair carefully combed and their hands shaking despite trying very hard to appear calm.

They entered in pairs, flanked by attendants who carried nothing more threatening than scrolls and wax tablets.

Marcus stood to one side and watched them approach Caesar, who had taken his position on the tribunal platform at the head of the basilica.

Caesar did not rise when they stopped before him, nor did he smile. He simply looked at them and waited.

The chief magistrate stepped forward and bowed.

'We have considered your words, Imperator, and we accept your presence in the name of the Roman people.'

'Ariminum is loyal to the Republic,' another magistrate added quickly. 'And loyal to peace.'

Caesar held the first man's gaze for a long moment.

'Peace,' he repeated, as if testing the word. 'I appreciate your commitment to peace and I share it. But peace requires honesty, and honesty requires that we acknowledge what is happening. Pompey and the Senate have declared me an enemy of the state. They have left Rome rather than face me. You know this, I know this, and everyone in this room knows this.'

The magistrates shifted uncomfortably. One of them started to speak but Caesar raised his hand slightly and the man fell silent.

'I did not cross the Rubicon to conquer Rome,' Caesar continued. 'I crossed it because I was given no choice. The Senate demanded I disband my legions and return as a private citizen to face prosecution for crimes I did not commit. They wanted to destroy me, and they were willing to destroy the law itself to do it.' He leaned forward slightly. 'So now we find ourselves here, and you must decide what loyalty means. Does it mean following men who have abandoned their posts? Or does it mean standing with someone who is trying to save the

Republic from itself?'

'We wish only to avoid bloodshed,' the chief magistrate said carefully. 'Ariminum has no quarrel with you, Imperator, nor with Pompey Magnus. We are a trading town and we want only peace.'

'Then you shall have it,' said Caesar. 'But on these terms. You will provide grain for my army at fair market price. You will provide lodging for any wounded who cannot travel and you will send riders to the towns south of here with letters bearing your seal, informing them that Caesar's army comes in peace and expects no resistance. In return, I will ensure that my men behave as Romans should behave. There will be no looting, no violence against civilians, and no forced requisitions. Your walls will not be breached, your temples will not be touched, and your daughters will sleep safely in their beds. Do we have an understanding?'

The magistrates looked at each other, a silent conversation passing between them. Finally, the chief magistrate bowed again.

'We have an understanding, Imperator.'

'Excellent,' said Caesar, 'then let us seal our agreement with wine and bread, as Romans have done since the founding of the city. In a few days I will move my army south, yet you will still be here, living your lives as you always have. And everyone will remember that Ariminum chose wisdom over stubbornness.'

That night, Marcus stood on the walls of Ariminum and looked north towards the Rubicon. The river was out of sight far to the north, but he knew it was there, a line they had crossed that could never be uncrossed. Below him, the camp sprawled across the fields outside the town, thousands of fires burning in neat rows like stars fallen to earth.

Balbus climbed up to join him, carrying two cups of wine. He handed one to Marcus and leaned against the parapet.

'They took it better than I expected,' said Balbus after a moment.

'They had no choice,' Marcus replied. 'What were they going to do? Fight five thousand veterans with a militia that has probably never seen real combat?'

'Some towns will fight anyway. Pride makes men stupid.'

Marcus took a sip of his wine. It was better than the usual military issue, probably from the magistrate's own cellar.

'Do you think we can really do this? Take all of Italia without a major battle?'

Balbus was quiet for a moment.

'I think Caesar believes we can, and Caesar is usually right about these things. But eventually we will have to fight. Pompey has too much pride to surrender without testing us, and the Senate has too much fear to negotiate. Blood will come, Marcus. Maybe not tomorrow or next week, but soon enough.'

'I know,' said Marcus. 'I just keep thinking about those men this morning. The ones we killed on the road. They were also Romans. They wore the same armour as we do, spoke the same language, and worshipped the same gods. Yet we still killed them.'

'They made their choice,' said Balbus. 'Just as we made ours. That is all any of us can do for now. Make our choices and live with the consequences.'

They stood in silence, drinking their wine and watching the fires burn in the darkness. Somewhere in the camp below, men were singing a marching song from the Gallic campaigns, the words drifting up through the cold night air. It was a song about going home, realised Marcus, though none of them knew what home would look like by the time they finally reached it.

Back in Rome, Aurelia stood in the atrium of Caesar's house on the Palatine and dismissed another servant. The girl was perhaps sixteen, her eyes red from crying, and she clutched a small bundle of possessions as if they were the only things keeping her anchored to the world.

'Go whilst you still can,' said Aurelia, not unkindly. 'I fear that if it comes to fighting, you are too pretty a girl to be ignored by men of violence starved of female attention for so many years. Take the servants' gate and do not look back. Find your family if you have one, or find work in the countryside if you do not. But leave the city now, before it is too late.'

The girl tried to speak, her mouth opening and closing, but no words came out. Finally, she bobbed a quick bow and fled down the corridor towards the back of the house, her footsteps echoing on the marble floor before fading into silence.

Aurelia turned to the steward, an older man named Quintus who had served the household for many years.

'How many does that make?'

'Five today, Domina,' Quintus replied, 'and two yesterday. At this rate, we will have no one left but the family by the end of the week.'

'Then we will manage with just the family,' said Aurelia. 'Better a small household we can trust than a large one full of frightened people who might turn on us if the situation grows worse.'

Quintus bowed and withdrew, leaving Aurelia alone in the atrium. The space felt larger than it should have, the painted walls and expensive furniture somehow emphasising the emptiness rather than filling it. The pool in the centre reflected the ceiling beams in perfect still lines, undisturbed by the usual bustle of servants going about their work.

Calpurnia entered from the peristyle, her face pale and her movements careful, as if she were trying not to disturb something fragile. She had not slept well. Aurelia could see it in the shadows under her eyes and the way her hands trembled slightly when she set down the scroll she had been carrying.

'They are saying the consuls have fled,' Calpurnia said without preamble. 'Lentulus and Marcellus. They left last night with their families and their household goods loaded onto carts. Someone saw them on the Via Appia, heading south towards Capua.'

Aurelia nodded slowly. She had expected this, had known it was coming, but hearing it confirmed still sent a chill through her.

'And Pompey?'

'No one knows for certain. Some say he is still in the city, others that he has already gone to raise his legions in the south. The Forum is full of rumours and no one seems to know which ones to believe.'

'They will believe whatever makes them feel safer,' said Aurelia. 'That is what people do in times like these. They tell themselves comforting lies and hope that reality will be kind enough to match them.'

Calpurnia sat down on one of the marble benches that lined the atrium, her legs seeming to give out beneath her.

'What do we do, Mother? Should we leave as well? I have family in Tibur so we could go there and wait until this is resolved.'

'And for how long?' Aurelia turned to face her daughter-in-law directly. 'A month? A year? This will not be resolved quickly, Calpurnia. This is not a political disagreement that can be settled with speeches and voting. This is war, and wars take time.'

'But if we stay here…'

'If we stay here, we show that Caesar's family does not run,' interrupted Aurelia. 'We show that we believe in his cause, or at least that we are not afraid of his enemies. If we flee, every magistrate and merchant in Rome will see it as a sign that even his own mother and wife do not trust him to protect them. Do you understand what that would mean?'

Calpurnia was quiet for a long moment, her hands twisting in her lap. Finally, she nodded.

'I understand. But I am still frightened.'

'Good,' said Aurelia. 'Fear will keep you careful. Just do not let it make you foolish.'

A door opened at the far end of the corridor and Quintus appeared again, his expression apologetic.

'Domina, forgive the interruption, but some of the remaining household wish to know if they should prepare the evening meal as usual, or if we should conserve our stores.'

'Prepare the meal as usual,' said Aurelia without hesitation. 'We will not live like refugees in our own home. If the stores run low, we will deal with that when it happens. For now, we maintain our routine.'

'Yes, Domina,' said Quintus, and disappeared again.

Calpurnia stood and moved to the window that looked out over the city. From here, she could see the Forum in the distance, its temples and basilicas rising above the surrounding buildings. Smoke drifted across the view, thicker than it should have been at this time of day.

'When he returns,' Calpurnia said quietly, 'what will he return to? Will there even be a city left, or just ruins and memories?'

'There will be a city,' said Aurelia. 'Rome has survived worse than this. It has burned and been rebuilt, been conquered and risen again, lost wars and found new enemies to defeat. The stones will remain, and the people will remain, and my son will walk through those gates whether they are opened for him or broken down before him.'

They stood together in silence as the light shifted across the mosaic floor, creating patterns that changed and dissolved and reformed with the movement of the sun. Outside, the city continued its uncertain existence, waiting for whatever came next whilst trying to pretend that everything was normal, that life could continue as it always had, even as the foundations crumbled beneath their feet.

Aurelia closed her eyes for a moment, letting herself feel the weight of it all, then opened them again and straightened her shoulders.

'Come,' she said. 'We will light the household altar. He should not return to find it cold.'

They went together into the small shrine beside the peristyle, where the Lares of the household watched over the family with painted eyes that saw everything and nothing. Aurelia poured a measure of wine onto the altar, the liquid dark and fragrant in the lamplight. Calpurnia placed a pinch of incense on the glowing coals, and for a moment the smoke rose clean and white, carrying their prayers to gods who might or might not be listening anymore.

It was going to be a long night, and an even longer tomorrow, but they would face it as Caesar's family always had, with dignity, with courage, and with the absolute certainty that whatever came next, they would endure it.

Chapter Three

Rome

The Curia Hostilia was loud enough that guards stationed three streets away could hear the muffled shouting. Inside, senators stood packed shoulder to shoulder, their togas dishevelled and their faces red from hours of argument. The air was thick with the smell of sweat and lamp smoke, and the marble floor was slick where someone had spilled wine and no slave had been allowed in to clean it.

The guards at the doors kept their expressions neutral. They had seen the Senate argue before, had watched tempers flare and heard voices rise, but not like this.

Cicero sat near the front of the chamber with his fingers pressed to his temples, trying to ward off the headache that had been building for hours. Around him, voices collided and overlapped, fear of Caesar mixing with fear of Pompey mixing with fear of the mob outside. Reason had fled the building sometime around the third hour, leaving only men grasping for safety in words.

At the centre of the chamber stood Cato, his voice cutting through the noise like a blade through cloth.

'There can be no compromise with tyranny,' he shouted, his thin frame rigid with conviction, 'and no negotiation with a man who has already betrayed his oath. Caesar's legions have crossed the Rubicon. Even now they march south, and he has declared war on the Republic.'

'He claims to defend it,' someone shouted from the back benches.

'Then he lies,' Cato shot back. 'He has always lied. Every victory he has won has been for himself, every law he has passed is another chain around Rome's neck. If we treat with him now, we are not saving the Republic, we are signing its death warrant.'

A few senators cheered. Others pounded their benches in anger, though whether they were angry at Cato or at Caesar was unclear. The noise built until Cicero finally rose, raising one hand for calm.

'Cato speaks for his conscience, as he always does,' said Cicero, his voice weary but steady. 'But I remind you all that there is more at stake here than pride or principle. I know Caesar. I also know Pompey. Both are men of ambition, yes, but both are also men of Rome. Is there not still a path between surrender and slaughter?'

'Peace?' Cato turned on him, making the word sound like an accusation. 'You would negotiate with a traitor who leads armed men against his own country?'

Cicero sighed, and the sound carried more exhaustion than any words could have.

'I would negotiate with any man who might prevent Romans from killing Romans.'

His appeal lasted perhaps three heartbeats before being drowned by a fresh surge of shouting. The words *'coward'* and *'appeaser'* rose from the benches, and Cicero sank back down, his plea smothered beneath the noise like a candle in a storm.

At the far end of the chamber, Pompey stood apart from the chaos. He had said nothing since the session began, had simply stood and watched whilst men half his ability shouted about what should be done.

Finally, when the noise fell enough for him to be heard, he spoke.

'If Caesar comes south,' he said, his voice carrying the authority of decades of command, 'he comes not as a friend of

Rome but as an enemy of order. You all demand action and call for defence. But I tell you this: there is no wall strong enough, no legion large enough, to hold him at the gates forever.'

A murmur ran through the assembled senators. Some leaned forward, others exchanged glances. Pompey had their attention now.

'Then what do you propose, Imperator?' demanded Cato.

Pompey looked at him directly.

'That the Senate invest me with full command of the Republic's forces. Temporarily, of course. Until the threat is contained.'

The chamber erupted. Men leapt to their feet, some shouting approval, others protest. A few cried out that such powers belonged to the consuls, not to any general, no matter how distinguished. Others countered that the consuls had already proven themselves useless, that Caesar's name carried more weight amongst the legions than any magistrate's title.

Cicero felt a chill run through him. He had known this was coming, had seen it building for days, but hearing it spoken aloud was like watching a friend draw a knife on another friend. The Republic was eating itself.

'You cannot fight Caesar with decrees and votes,' said Pompey, raising his voice above the chaos. 'Only with soldiers. If you would have the Republic survive, then let me lead its defence. Give me the authority I need, or admit that you would rather argue than act.'

Cato stepped forward, his face dark with anger but also with calculation.

'If we grant you this power, we will hold you to account. This is not monarchy you seek, but guardianship. Is that understood?'

Pompey inclined his head.

'So let it be written.'

The debate raged for another two hours. Senators who had shouted themselves hoarse earlier now found new reserves of energy for fresh arguments.

When the vote was finally called, Cicero watched hands rise around the chamber. Not many, but enough and Pompey was given supreme command of the Republic's military forces, answerable only to the Senate as a body, until such time as the emergency had passed.

Outside, the crowd in the Forum had been growing all morning. Their voices echoed off the colonnades and temple steps, a constant background roar that rose and fell like the sea. Some shouted for Caesar, calling him a hero who would save Rome from corruption. Others shouted for Pompey, proclaiming him the Republic's last defender. Most just shouted for bread and security, caring less about who provided it, only that someone did. When word reached them of the Senate's vote, the noise became a storm.

'Pompey saves Rome!' cried voices on one side.

'Pompey fears Caesar!' answered voices on the other.

Within minutes, the shouting turned to pushing, the pushing turned to fists and blood was spilled. Men grappled near the Rostra, tearing at each other's tunics, and someone ripped down a civic standard and trampled it underfoot whilst the crowd surged around him.

From a balcony overlooking the square, Cicero watched the chaos unfold with something close to horror. He had seen mobs before, had witnessed violence in the streets during the Catiline conspiracy and other crises, but never a mob that seemed to hate itself as much as this one. The Republic was tearing its own flesh, and there was no one left who could stop it.

Pompey joined him a moment later, his face pale in the fading afternoon light. He looked down at the fighting below, his lips pressed into a tight line.

'You have your powers now,' said Cicero quietly. 'All of Rome looks to you for resolution.'

Pompey gave a hollow laugh that held no humour.

'Do they? Or do they simply look to see who survives? I did not want this, Cicero, but I was the only name left that still frightens Caesar. They give me the power but it is also a curse, and now I must use it or watch everything burn.'

Below them, the mob roared again, a mixture of confusion and fear that rolled through the city like thunder. Torches swayed in the growing darkness, and somewhere near the Temple of Saturn, a statue toppled with a crash that sent pigeons scattering into the sky.

Cicero looked northward, towards the hills and the unseen road that led to Ariminum, where Caesar's army was gathering strength with every passing day.

'What will you do?' he asked.

Pompey's eyes remained fixed on the flames below.

'What I must. Gather what remains of our forces and pray that the Republic remembers how to fight.'

Another messenger arrived in the early hours of the following morning, his horse lathered with sweat and foam, its eyes rolling white with exhaustion. The man himself was in scarcely better condition. His tunic was torn, his helmet was gone, and the left side of his face bore the raw scrape of a bad fall. He had ridden from Ariminum without stopping, changing horses three times but never pausing to eat or sleep.

He reported to the Praetorian officer on duty at the Esquiline Gate, who immediately sent word to the consuls and by the time the sun rose, every senator still in the city knew the news. Ariminum had surrendered without battle.

The Senate met again that same morning, though fewer members attended than the day before. The Curia's marble steps were slick with mud from the boots of guards and servants, and the interior felt colder somehow, as if the building itself knew what was coming.

Cicero arrived to find the chamber half empty, the remaining senators divided into desperate clusters of conversation. Men paced and gestured wildly, speaking over one another, and the words *'Ariminum'* and *'Caesar'* rose again and again, each repetition carrying more alarm than the last.

Cato stood at the centre of the floor, trying to be heard over the chaos.

'We are betrayed,' he called out, his voice cutting through the noise. 'He moves faster than any of you dreamed possible. His scouts will be in the hills by week's end, and still you stand here debating letters and decrees as if words could stop legions.'

'Where is Pompey?' someone asked.

'At the Praenestine Gate,' another senator answered. 'He has ordered the treasury packed and the magistrates assembled. He says we march south before sunset.'

Cicero's heart sank. He had hoped for another day, another chance to find some path between Caesar and catastrophe, but it was too late. The Republic had already chosen flight.

'He means to abandon the city,' said Cato bitterly. 'The

great Magnus, protector of Rome, running from his own shadow less than a day after he was appointed special powers.'

'He means to fight another day,' Cicero replied, though his voice carried little conviction. 'You know as well as I do that the legions stationed here cannot face Caesar's veterans. Better to retreat and regroup than to be slaughtered in the Forum.'

Cato turned on him, his eyes burning.

'Then let us die like Romans, not scatter like leaves before a storm. If we run now, we teach the people that authority means nothing, that power belongs to whoever can frighten us most.'

'The people are already running,' said Cicero quietly. 'Look outside if you do not believe me.'

Cato hesitated, then strode to the doorway. Beyond the steps, the Forum boiled with confusion and fear. Merchants were closing their stalls early, women hurried children indoors, and wagons loaded with household goods clogged the narrow streets. Somewhere, a rumour had started that Caesar's cavalry was already approaching the city gates, and though it was certainly false, people believed it anyway because belief was easier than uncertainty.

Cato turned back, his face showing defeat for perhaps the first time Cicero had ever seen.

'I will not leave,' he said, though his voice had lost some of its edge. 'Not whilst one free voice remains in Rome.'

Cicero stepped forward and placed a hand on Cato's arm. The gesture was not friendship exactly, but recognition, one man acknowledging another who understood the depth of what was being lost.

'You cannot hold Rome alone,' said Cicero quietly. 'It will not make you a martyr, it will only make you a corpse, and Rome needs living men, not dead heroes.'

Cato met his eyes, and for a heartbeat the fury faded, replaced by something older and sadder. Then he nodded once and walked out of the chamber.

By midday, the evacuation was in full motion. The great doors of the Temple of Saturn, which housed the Republic's treasury, were thrown open for the first time in years and chests of gold and silver dragged out by teams of slaves and loaded onto heavy carts. Records, scrolls, account books, and legal documents followed, each one carefully wrapped and packed as if the clerks truly believed they would be needed again someday.

The sound of iron-shod wheels echoed through the Forum as the carts began to move, and everywhere Cicero looked he saw the machinery of government being dismantled and carted away like furniture from a house whose owners had died.

Pompey oversaw the operation from horseback, surrounded by aides and military officers. His expression was hard to read. Some who watched him thought he looked resolute, ready for whatever came next. Others saw only weariness and doubt. Cicero, approaching on foot, saw resignation.

'You move quickly,' said Cicero. 'Faster than the Senate ever has.'

Pompey nodded without taking his eyes off the loading operation.

'Caesar moves faster still. We must stay ahead of him, or everything we take with us will end up in his hands anyway.'

'And if he does not pursue? If he is content to simply take Rome and declare victory?'

'He will pursue,' said Pompey with certainty. 'He cannot

afford not to. Every step he takes now defines how history will remember him. He will follow us until one of us is dead, because anything less would be weakness, and Caesar cannot afford to look weak.'

Cicero looked towards the temple steps, where more chests were being carried out by sweating slaves under the watchful eyes of armed guards.

'You are taking the Republic's wealth.'

'I am merely protecting it,' Pompey corrected. 'It is not mine to take, only to keep safe until this is over. When we have won, I will return every coin to where it belongs.'

'If you win,' Cicero murmured.

Pompey turned sharply in his saddle.

'I will live long enough to save Rome, or I will die trying. There is no middle path left for any of us.'

He spurred his horse forward, shouting orders to the column. The line of wagons stretched down the hill, flanked by soldiers and behind them, the rest of the Senate's retinue, magistrates with their families, scribes clutching document cases, and servants carrying whatever they could manage.

Cicero lingered beneath the bronze she-wolf statue on the Capitoline, watching the column wind its way through the narrow streets towards the southern gate. He could hear distant sobs from the watching crowd, the clatter of wheels on stone, and the bark of orders shouted through the growing fog that had rolled in from the Tiber.

The Senate of Rome was leaving its own city, retreating from itself and Pompey, riding just ahead of the treasury carts, carried the burden of command like a man walking beneath an invisible yoke that grew heavier with each step his horse took.

As the torches began to fade into the distance, Cicero turned back towards the Forum. The streets were almost empty now. A few beggars huddled beneath the colonnades, watching in disbelief as their rulers fled. A dog nosed through discarded refuse from the market and the last light of day caught the bronze of various statues, making them glow briefly before darkness claimed them.

    Cicero whispered to himself, knowing no one would hear,

    'They flee from a man who has not yet drawn his sword.'

The wind carried the sound of hooves and wheels one last time before silence settled over the city like a shroud. There was nothing left now but the slow burn of torches and the faint, eerie sound of ravens settling onto the temple roofs for the night. The Republic still stood, but it no longer had a heartbeat.

Chapter Four

Rome

The house on the Palatine stood above the city like a silent sentinel, its terrace overlooking Rome's scattered lamplight. Most of the neighbouring villas were dark now, their occupants having fled south with the Senate, but Caesar's house remained lit, a statement of defiance or perhaps simply stubbornness. Inside, the atrium smelled of lamp oil and old stone, of incense from the household shrine and the faint mustiness that came from rooms where too few people moved through too much space.

Most of the household had gone. Servants had been dismissed with small purses of coin and advice to find new masters, and clerks had been sent home to their families.

Guards had been pulled away to join the exodus south, either by Pompey's orders or by their own fear and only a handful of servants remained, those too old or too loyal or too poor to have anywhere else to go.

Aurelia sat in the atrium with a scroll open on her lap, though she had not turned a page in over an hour. She was perhaps seventy years old now, her hair more white than grey, her face creased with the deep lines that came from bearing children and burying husbands and watching a son become something she had never quite expected.

Calpurnia entered from the corridor carrying a small oil lamp, and the light caught her face as she crossed to the older woman. She was younger by decades, Caesar's wife by arrangement and then by genuine affection, and her face showed the strain of the past days in ways that Aurelia's did not.

'The senate has fled the city,' she said quietly, setting the lamp on the table.

Aurelia looked up from her unread scroll.

'That does not surprise me.'

'Then we simply wait?'

'We wait,' said Aurelia. 'As Roman women have always waited, for news brought by men who think themselves braver for having carried it.'

They sat in silence whilst the lamp flame wavered in a draft that came from somewhere in the house. From the courtyard came the faint creak of the gate hinge, then the soft tread of sandals on stone. A servant appeared and he knelt before Aurelia with a sealed letter in his hands.

'From Ariminum, Domina,' said the servant. 'The rider said it was urgent.'

Aurelia broke the seal and read by the lamplight. Her lips tightened into a thin line but she did not speak until she had reached the end. Then she passed the letter to Calpurnia without comment.

The writing was Caesar's, unmistakable in its economy.

My mother, my wife.

I march south so let no one in our house show fear. Rome will not fall to those who run from it.

I will come soon.

Gaius.

Calpurnia's eyes lingered on the last line. The words were measured, as always, but she could hear the restraint in them, the same restraint she had heard in his voice the night before he left for Gaul all those years ago.

'He writes as if this were just another campaign,' she

said, folding the letter carefully.

'It is,' said Aurelia. 'Only this time the enemy speaks Latin and prays to the same gods.'

'I cannot tell if that comforts me or frightens me more.'

From somewhere in the city came the distant roll of cart wheels and the hollow echo of hooves on stone. Calpurnia flinched before she could stop herself, and Aurelia's hand rested briefly on hers, the touch dry and steady.

'If it were an army, we would hear the horns,' she said.

The steward appeared at the far end of the corridor, his head bowed.

'Domina,' he said, 'some of the remaining household wish to leave before dawn. They fear what will happen in the streets when word spreads that the Senate has gone.'

'Let them go if they wish,' said Aurelia without hesitation. 'I will not hold anyone here against their will, but neither will I beg them to remain.'

The steward bowed and withdrew.

Calpurnia rose and walked to the window that looked out over the Forum. From this height, she could see the temples, dark and shuttered, the usual bustle of the market reduced to a few lonely figures moving between shadows. Smoke hung above the lower districts like a veil, thicker than it should have been, as if people were burning things they did not want found.

Outside, the city murmured with the sound of thousands of families contemplating what came next, whether to stay or flee, whether to hide their valuables or their children, whether Caesar would be merciful or whether the stories they had heard from Gaul were true.

The following morning arrived without fanfare. For the

first time in years, no messenger waited at the gate with dispatches from the Senate, no clerk arrived with scrolls for dictation and no clients came seeking favour or justice or simply the reflected glory of being seen entering Caesar's house.

The servants who remained moved softly, their voices kept low, as if a sick man slept somewhere nearby and they feared to wake him. In truth, they feared something else entirely, though none of them would say it aloud. They feared that the world they knew was ending, and they did not know what would replace it.

Aurelia was already up. She had taken her breakfast alone, as she often did, and now sat at the table in the tablinum with the household steward, checking the inventories by lamplight even though dawn was breaking outside. Nothing in her posture showed uncertainty. She treated the task as if it were any other morning, as though Rome were not emptying itself beyond the gates, as though the Republic itself were not bleeding to death in the streets.

'We will close the outer storerooms,' she said, running her finger down a column of numbers on the wax tablet before her. 'There is no sense leaving them accessible to thieves. Move the grain and oil to the inner courtyard and post two men there. Honest men, not the young ones who look over their shoulders when they think no one is watching.'

'Yes, Domina,' said the steward, making a note on his own tablet.

'And the guards on the main gate?'

'They remain, Domina. Two during the day, four at night.'

'Keep them,' said Aurelia, 'and increase their pay. They will not stop soldiers if soldiers come, but they will discourage common thieves. And if soldiers do come, I want those men to open the gates immediately. No heroics, no resistance. Gates are nothing but decoration when facing a legion, and dead servants are of no use to anyone.'

The steward bowed and withdrew.

Calpurnia entered soon after, her cloak drawn loosely over her shoulders. She had not slept much. The noise from the lower districts had risen and fallen through the night, shouts and crashes and once what might have been screaming, though it was hard to tell at this distance. She looked pale and drawn, shadows under her eyes that had not been there a week ago.

'Do we have word?' she asked. 'Any new messages?'

'No courier today,' said Aurelia.

Calpurnia crossed to the table and her eyes fell on the letter from Ariminum, still neatly folded beside the household accounts. She touched it with one finger, not to read it again but simply to confirm it was still there, still real.

'I keep thinking of him on the march,' she said. 'Every mile brings him closer to Rome, yet somehow it feels as though he is moving further away from us. Do you think he has changed? Do you think crossing that river changed him?'

'He would be foolish not to change,' said Aurelia. 'You cannot lead an army against your own country and remain the same person. The question is not whether he has changed, but what he has changed into.'

Before Calpurnia could respond to that, a servant appeared in the doorway. It was a young woman, one of the kitchen slaves, and she looked nervous about interrupting.

'Domina,' said the girl, 'there is a visitor at the gate. He says he comes from the house of Cicero.'

Aurelia set down her stylus and straightened in her chair.

'Show him in. Immediately.'

The man who entered was one of Cicero's freedmen, a thin Greek with intelligent eyes and grey hair. He bowed deeply to both women and produced a sealed tablet from inside his tunic.

'My master leaves the city today, Domina,' said the freedman. 'He asked that this message reach you before he departs. He said it was important that you know his mind.'

Aurelia took the tablet and broke the seal. She read quickly, her face showing nothing, then passed it to Calpurnia without comment. The wax bore Cicero's familiar hand, elegant even in haste.

My dearest ladies,

Rome empties faster than reason allows. Pompey and the consuls are already on the road south and the Forum stands almost empty. Those who remain, do so either from courage or from having nowhere else to go.

I cannot remain without purpose, and so I follow the Senate to Capua, though not without regret.

If Caesar's men reach the city before I return, let them see that Rome still holds decency in some corner of it.

Do not leave unless you are forced to, for the times may yet turn, and someone must remain to remember what Rome was before this madness began.

Your friend in eternal hope

Marcus Tullius Cicero.

Calpurnia folded the tablet closed and set it on the table beside Caesar's letter. Two messages, two men, two very different tones, yet both speaking of the same inevitable thing.

'So even Cicero runs,' she said.

'Cicero does not run,' said Aurelia. 'He retreats with

eloquence and carefully worded justifications. But yes, he leaves. As they all do.'

Calpurnia almost laughed at that, a sound that was more despair than humour, then stopped herself.

'What happens now?' she asked, 'what do we do if Caesar's army arrives sooner than we expect? Tomorrow, or the day after?'

'Then the city will open its gates as it always does,' said Aurelia, rising from her chair and moving to the open doorway that led to the courtyard. 'To whoever gives the loudest orders and makes the most convincing threats. That is how Rome has always worked, despite what the poets say about honour and virtue.'

She looked out across the roofs of the city. Dawn light was spreading across the hills now, pale grey and cold, revealing how still everything was. Only the smoke rising from the poorer districts showed any sign of life, and even that seemed muted, as if the city itself were holding its breath.

'When I was a girl,' said Aurelia, still looking out at Rome, 'my father would take us to climb the Janiculum on festival days. We would stand there at sunrise and watch the light touch every temple and dome and column. You could see the whole city turn gold. That Rome is gone now, or at least sleeping. But it will return. It always does. Too many men need Rome for it to die, no matter how hard they try to kill it.'

Calpurnia watched the older woman in silence. Aurelia's composure both steadied her and made her feel more uncertain. There was no visible fear in Aurelia, no panic, just a calm that had been shaped by years of disappointment and loss and watching powerful men make terrible decisions.

'Do you think he will keep the Senate?' asked Calpurnia. 'Or will he dismiss them entirely and rule alone?'

'He will keep what he can use and discard the rest,' said Aurelia. 'My son does not break things for the pleasure of breaking them, he is practical, not vindictive. But the Senate that returns will not be the Senate that fled. That much is certain.'

She turned as a faint knock at the outer door drew their attention. Through the corridor they could see one of the gate guards speaking with someone, and then a boy appeared, perhaps twelve years old, breathless and wide-eyed. His tunic was dusty and his feet were bare despite the cold.

'I come from the Forum, Domina,' said the boy, the words tumbling out between gasps. 'They are saying the Senate is truly gone. Pompey Magnus was seen crossing the river before dawn with a column of wagons and the treasury has been emptied. The consuls have fled south.'

Aurelia nodded once, her face showing no surprise.

'Go home, boy. Go home before someone decides you know too much or before you see something that will give you nightmares.'

The boy bowed awkwardly and ran back through the gate.

When he was gone, Calpurnia sank into the nearest chair.

'It has begun, then,' she said, 'it has truly begun.'

'It began the day they sent him to Gaul,' said Aurelia, turning from the doorway. 'Everything since then has been inevitable, just men pretending they could still choose a different path when the path was already chosen for them. This is only the part that the poets will write down, the part with battles and speeches and dramatic gestures. The real decisions were made years ago.'

Calpurnia looked towards the window, where the first

47

true sunlight was touching the edge of the courtyard wall. For the briefest moment it made the painted plaster glow with warmth and colour. Then the angle of light shifted, and the glow faded, and everything looked grey and cold again.

Aurelia turned back to the table and closed the ledger she had been working on, setting it aside with the other household accounts.

'We will prepare the house for his return,' she said. 'Even if he never reaches the gate, even if something goes terribly wrong, we will be ready. The house of Caesar must look as though it expected victory, as though there was never any doubt. That is what he will require, and that is what we will provide.'

'He would like that,' said Calpurnia quietly.

'He would not merely like it,' said Aurelia. 'He would require it. And so we will do it, whether we feel brave or not, whether we believe in victory or not, we will do it because it is what must be done.'

Her tone left no room for discussion or doubt and she moved towards the inner corridor, pausing only once to glance at the small shrine where they had burned incense the night before. The ashes still lay on the bronze dish, grey and fine as dust, evidence of prayers offered to gods whose attention might be elsewhere.

'See that the altar is lit again before nightfall,' said Aurelia. 'and every night after that. Fresh incense, fresh wine. He should not walk into darkness when he returns, whenever that may be.'

She left the room, her steps firm echoing on the marble floor. Calpurnia remained at the table, staring at the two folded letters before her, one from her husband and one from Cicero, both speaking of the same inexorable future in their different ways.

Outside, the noise of the waking city swelled faintly, but it was not the proud murmur of Rome going about its confident business. It was the uncertain stir of something waiting to be claimed, waiting to see what sort of man would eventually walk through the city gates, and what he would do when he arrived.

Chapter Five

Italia

The Via Flaminia stretched ahead of the column like a white ribbon laid across sleeping land. Winter had left its mark on the ancient stones, frost whitening the paving slabs and ice pooling in the drainage channels. The sun gave little warmth despite the clear sky, and the air carried the smell of smoke from distant hearths mingled with the sharp bite of frost that promised colder days ahead.

Marcus rode near the front of the column, his cloak pulled tight around his shoulders and his breath visible in the cold. He watched the farms slide past on either side of the road, with shuttered windows and barred doors. Italia was afraid of her own sons, and he could not blame the people for their fear. The stories from Gaul had not painted Caesar's legions as liberators.

Behind him, the long line of soldiers moved steadily. Their shields were wrapped in leather to protect the paint and bronze, their spears bundled and bound for the march, and their breath rose in white clouds that hung briefly in the still air before dissolving. The eagle of the Thirteenth Legion caught the weak sunlight, its bronze wings gleaming dully, its shadow stretching across the frost like a promise or a threat depending on who watched it pass.

Balbus came riding up from the rear of the column, his horse's flanks steaming despite the cold.

'There's another village boarded up ahead,' he said, nodding towards the next rise in the road. 'Smoke from the chimneys but not a soul visible. They must think we have come to burn their fields and carry off their daughters.'

'Fear travels faster than any army,' said Marcus. 'If you had heard what the Senate has been saying about us, you would be hiding too. They paint us as monsters worse than the Germans.'

Balbus laughed quietly.

'I have heard it,' he said, 'merchants carry the news faster than we march and if I believed half of what they say about us, I would hide from myself.'

They rode on in silence for a time and the road dipped into a shallow valley where frost had turned the marsh reeds to glass and the stream that ran beside the road was edged with ice. A crow lifted from a fence post as they approached, cawing once before flying off across the empty fields. The only other sound was the dull, patient tramp of thousands of hobnailed caligae on frozen earth.

Marcus looked towards the hills to the west, where a thin thread of smoke rose into the pale blue sky. Someone was there, watching, waiting to see what would happen when Caesar's army passed through their valley.

'There are still people living here,' said Marcus quietly.

'Hiding, not living,' said Balbus. 'They will come back when they see that no one is dying, that the fields are not burning.

Marcus nodded but said nothing more. In Gaul, he had learned what a dying country sounded like, the particular silence that came when hope had fled and only survival remained. This was not that, but Italia was holding her breath, waiting to see which god would claim her, which man would prove stronger, and which side would write the history that everyone else would have to live with.

A scout came galloping down the road from the south, his horse dark with sweat despite the cold morning. He wore the light armour of the auxiliary cavalry and carried a dispatch case strapped across his chest. He saluted as he drew near, bringing his mount to a sliding stop that scattered frozen mud across the road.

'Praefect,' said the scout, his voice quick with the excitement of someone bearing important news. 'Mevania has closed its gates, but the magistrates sent word that they wish to negotiate surrender. There is no garrison or armed resistance as such but they ask for assurances of safety.'

'Tell them they have nothing to fear,' said Marcus. 'The general forbids plunder or harm to civilians. If they open their gates, and provide whatever supplies we require at a fair price, they will be protected in Caesar's name and their town will not be touched.'

'Understood, Praefect,' said the scout, and wheeled his horse about, spurring it back up the road.

'This is a strange war,' said Balbus, as the scout rode away. 'No enemy to fight, no battles to win, no glory to be had. Just roads and negotiations and trying to convince people that we are not what the Senate says we are.'

'That is precisely what makes it dangerous,' said Marcus. 'Soldiers without glory grow restless and soldiers without an enemy to hate grow confused. We must keep them disciplined and moving, or they will find their own entertainment, and that would destroy everything Caesar is trying to build.'

They continued south as the day lengthened towards a pale afternoon. The frost began to melt on the road where the sun touched it, and mud clung to the men's caligae, making the march harder. When they finally halted to rest and eat, Marcus watched his soldiers build fires with the quiet efficiency of veterans who had done this a thousand times before. They spoke in low voices whilst sharing bread and dried meat, their laughter muted, as if the empty fields themselves might be listening and reporting back to someone.

Marcus stood for a long time on a slight rise, looking down at the line of orange fires that stretched along the road for over a mile. Each one marked eight men huddled together against the cold, sharing food and warmth and the unspoken bond that came from marching into uncertainty together. From this distance, the fires looked like a wound across the heart of Italia, a scar of flame and smoke marking where Caesar's army had passed.

By noon the following day, they reached the town of Mevania. The gate stood half open, one wooden door sagging on its hinges where the iron had rusted through, the other pulled back against the wall as if someone had started to open it and then fled before finishing the task. There were no guards visible, no sign of soldiers or militia, only the whisper of wind moving through the narrow streets beyond the entrance.

Marcus dismounted and gestured to Balbus.

'Take two files of men and go ahead. Move carefully. If anyone means trouble, they will show themselves soon enough. Check the main square and the temples and make sure there are no weapons stored where they should not be.'

'Understood,' said Balbus, and rode forward with sixteen soldiers behind him, their shields now unwrapped and held ready, their pilums gripped loosely but prepared for use.

The advance party moved cautiously into the town, and the echo of their footsteps bounced from the plastered walls, too loud in the emptiness. Marcus followed more slowly with the rest of his staff officers and a full century of legionaries. The square was deserted except for perhaps two dozen townsfolk who had gathered near the steps of an old temple dedicated to Jupiter. Their faces were thin with what might have been fear or hunger or both.

An elderly priest stepped forward from the group, his white robe showing patches where it had been mended, his hands raised in the traditional gesture of supplication. His voice trembled when he spoke.

'Noble Praefect,' said the priest, 'we are loyal Romans. We wish only for peace. Spare our homes and our people, and you will find no resistance here. We have no soldiers, no weapons, and no will to oppose you.'

Marcus reined in his horse and studied the man for a moment. The priest was perhaps seventy years old, his face deeply lined, his hands shaking slightly though whether from age or fear was impossible to tell.

'Peace is already yours,' said Marcus. 'Caesar asks for obedience and respect, not tribute or blood. No harm will come to those who remain calm and cooperative. We are not barbarians, whatever the Senate may have told you.'

The priest lowered his hands, and relief softened his weathered face.

'They sent word that you would come as enemies of Rome, that you would burn our fields and take our children as slaves. Were they lying?'

'The Senate has abandoned Rome,' said Marcus. 'They fled south rather than face Caesar. You will find no senators here to threaten you or to give you orders, there are only Romans now, and Caesar offers you the same protection he offers to any Roman who does not stand against him.'

The priest bowed deeply, his old knees cracking audibly.

'Then perhaps Rome may yet be saved from itself.'

Marcus dismounted and motioned to Balbus, who had

returned from his inspection of the town.

'See that the townspeople receive bread from our supply wagons. Distribute it fairly, one measure per family. Make it known that Caesar's mercy feeds them before it would ever need to punish them. I want these people to remember us as bringers of order, not chaos.'

'Understood, Praefect,' said Balbus, and rode off to organise the distribution.

Marcus watched as the people gathered near the supply carts, each family waiting their turn in quiet disbelief. Children clutched at their mothers' cloaks, staring at the soldiers with wide eyes that showed the pure and ancient fear of those who had never seen an army before. An old woman wept when she received her portion of bread, pressing it to her chest as if it were gold rather than grain.

'They will remember this,' said Balbus when he returned, brushing flour dust from his cloak. 'Not the Senate's warnings and speeches, but the bread in their hands and the fact that we did not burn their homes.'

'That is the hope,' said Marcus. 'Mercy travels faster than fear when it is honest, and people believe what they see more readily than what they are told.'

As the column prepared to leave Mevania an hour later, the bells of the temple began to toll, slow and uncertain at first, then gaining confidence. Marcus turned in his saddle and saw smoke rising from the townspeople's hearths for what he suspected was the first time in days. They had been too frightened to light their fires, afraid the smoke would draw attention, but now they were cooking again, living again. It was a small thing, yet it felt like victory.

Two days of steady marching brought them to the great

crossroads south of Narnia, where the Via Flaminia met two other major roads and merchants had built a small market town that served travellers. The landscape opened into wide, rolling fields dotted with olive groves and vineyards, though the vines were bare now and the olive trees stood stark against the winter sky. Frost still clung to the grass in the shadows where the sun had not reached, but the air had softened somewhat, carrying a promise of eventual thaw even if that thaw was still weeks away.

Caesar's army made camp, a sprawling city of leather tents and cooking fires stretching across the plain for what looked like a mile in every direction. Standards marked each legion's position, and Marcus could see the organised chaos of an army at rest: men washing clothes in a stream, blacksmiths working at their portable forges, and officers drilling new recruits in a field cleared of stones.

Marcus found Caesar standing near the main road, his horse tethered to a post beside him, reading a dispatch in the pale light of late afternoon. He wore his red general's cloak and his travelling armour, and he looked up as Marcus approached.

'Praefect,' said Caesar, folding the parchment. 'Report.'

'Mevania surrendered without incident, Dominus,' said Marcus. 'The people were frightened but obedient once they understood we meant them no harm. The soldiers remain disciplined and understand what you are trying to accomplish here, even if they do not entirely agree with the method.'

Caesar smiled faintly, tucking the dispatch into his belt.

'Do they truly understand? I doubt most of them know what I am trying to do. They follow orders because that is what soldiers do, not because they have grasped the strategy.'

'They know you mean to avoid bloodshed where possible,' said Marcus, 'and they know you want Italia intact, not destroyed. That is enough for now. The rest they will understand when it is over and they are still alive.'

Caesar regarded him thoughtfully for a moment, his sharp eyes assessing.

'Fear wins obedience, Marcus, but mercy wins history. Remember that when you speak to the men. Every door they do not break, every coin they do not steal, every woman they do not touch, is worth more than a victory won in blood. Those are the things that will be remembered when we are all dust.'

Marcus inclined his head in acknowledgment.

'They follow your example, Dominus. If you show restraint, they will show restraint. If you show mercy, they will be merciful. They trust you that much.'

'Then I must be very careful what example I give,' said Caesar, glancing towards the southern horizon where the road dipped away towards Rome. 'We march in three days. I want the roads clear and the supply wagons doubled. Remind every cohort commander, every centurion, every optio, that any soldier who steals from an Italian civilian will answer to me directly, and my justice will not be gentle.'

'It shall be done,' said Marcus.

Caesar placed a hand on his shoulder, a rare gesture of familiarity between them.

'You have served me long enough to know that I have no wish to be king and I do not want to rule Rome as a tyrant. But if we act like conquerors, the Senate will make me a tyrant by accusation alone, and then I will have no choice but to become what they claim I am. Let us take Italia with calm hearts and clean hands, and let history judge us by what we preserve rather than what we destroy.'

'It will be done, Dominus,' said Marcus again.

Caesar nodded once, mounted his horse with the ease of

a man half his age, and rode away across the plain towards the main camp.

Marcus watched him go, the figure growing smaller against the white haze of approaching dusk. There was something unsettling in the ease with which Caesar carried his destiny, as though it weighed less for him than it would have for other men, as though he knew with absolute certainty that he was on the right path even when that path led into darkness.

Balbus joined him, stamping his feet against the cold that was settling in again as the sun dropped.

'He makes it all sound so simple when he talks like that. As if we are just going for a walk through Italia rather than marching an army against our own capital.'

'He always does,' said Marcus. 'That is why we believe him. If he showed doubt, we would all start to doubt. So he shows us certainty instead, whether he feels it or not.'

Balbus looked towards the southern horizon where the mist was beginning to lift. 'Do you think Pompey will stand and fight? When it comes to it, I mean. Will he actually give battle, or will he just keep running until he runs out of land?'

'Not yet,' said Marcus. 'He still believes this is politics, that he can outmanoeuvre Caesar with alliances and speeches and the weight of the Senate's authority. When he realises this is war and finally understands that words will not stop Caesar, it will already be too late. By then we will be at the gates of Rome and he will be isolated in the south with no way back.'

Chapter Six

Italia

Caesar's command tent stood at the centre of the camp, its entrance facing east to catch the first light of dawn. Inside, oil lamps burned despite the growing daylight outside, their flames casting steady shadows across the canvas walls. The tent smelled of lamp oil and damp leather, of ink and wax and the particular staleness that came from too many men spending too many hours in too small a space.

Caesar stood over his campaign table, the same scarred wooden surface that had travelled with him from Gaul. Wax tablets lay scattered across it alongside scrolls weighted with stones, and a small wooden map showed the towns of Italia marked with different coloured pebbles. Each pebble represented a decision made or yet to be made, a town that would open its gates or close them, a magistrate who would cooperate or resist.

The tent flap opened and Antonius ducked inside, his broad frame filling the entrance. Curio followed him, then Balbus carrying another roll of maps under his arm. They saluted briefly, the gesture perfunctory amongst men who had campaigned together for years, and stood waiting whilst Caesar moved around the table.

'I received some interesting information last night,' said Caesar, straightening from the map. 'Pompey has gone to Capua.'

Antonius raised an eyebrow.

'Capua? I would have thought Brundisium, where he could control the ports and bring reinforcements from Greece.'

'Not yet,' said Caesar. 'He apparently thinks the south

will rally to him, that Campania will provide him with men and money. But Campania is a land of merchants and vineyards, not soldiers. He will raise voices, not legions.'

'He will raise excuses, Dominus,' said Antonius with a snort. 'He talks of defending liberty, yet he runs from its defence. If he truly believed in the Republic, he would have stayed in Rome and faced you.'

'Possibly,' said Caesar, picking up one of the scrolls and unrolling it partway. 'But we will not underestimate him simply because he has made poor decisions so far. He has men, money, and the Senate's support, and no matter what we think of the Senate, they still hold legitimacy in the eyes of many Romans.' He looked up at Balbus. 'What do you have for me?'

Balbus moved to the table and unrolled one of his maps, smoothing it with his palms. It was newer than Caesar's wooden model, drawn on good parchment with careful attention to roads, rivers, and the distances between towns. He pointed to a cluster of settlements marked in ink.

'These towns ahead are small, Imperator,' said Balbus. 'Hispellum, Narnia, then Ocriculum. Now that Mevania has yielded without resistance, I do not believe the others will fight. The people are watching the road, trying to judge which way history walks. They want to be on the winning side, but they are not yet certain which side that is.'

'Then let them see us pass as liberators,' said Caesar, 'not as conquerors. I will not have Italia burned to warm my ambition. The Senate paints me as a monster, so let us answer with mercy. Blood makes rebels, but pardon makes citizens. That is what history will remember.'

The tent was quiet for a moment. Marcus had learned to recognise that tone in Caesar's voice. It was not the beginning of a debate. It was the end of one. The decision had been made, and now it was simply being explained to those who would carry it out.

'Instruct the scribes to prepare a letter to the Senate,' continued Caesar, moving to another part of the table where clean wax tablets waited. 'The text should be thus: I come not in arms against the Republic but to restore it. Let the magistrates return to their posts and let the laws be kept as they always have been. I seek peace, though I march prepared for war should peace be refused.'

Curio exchanged a glance with Antonius, but neither man spoke. Caesar was still talking, his voice measured and deliberate, each word chosen with care.

'Add this as well,' said Caesar. 'That Pompey Magnus has abandoned Italia without cause. He feared my presence, not my legions. If he truly calls himself the defender of Rome, let him first defend her soil rather than flee from it. Seal the letter under my name and send it south to Capua with fast riders. Also send copies to every town between here and Brundisium. The Senate will not believe a word of it, but the people will hear the message, and the people are Rome.'

'As you command, Imperator,' said Antonius, bowing his head slightly.

Caesar turned to Marcus.

'Praefect, you will keep the vanguard moving steadily. No campfires near villages unless absolutely necessary, and no foraging without explicit permission from the local magistrates. Let the farmers see that Caesar's men protect their crops and their families, not plunder them. Every act of restraint now is worth ten victories later.'

'It shall be done, Dominus,' said Marcus.

'Good,' said Caesar, picking up his red general's cloak from where it lay folded on a camp stool. He shook it out and fastened it at his shoulder. 'I will not win this war by killing Romans. Not yet, at least and not unless they force me to.'

Outside, the horns sounded for the day's march, their brass voices carrying across the camp and echoing off the hills beyond. The tent flap lifted and cold morning light poured in, turning the lamp flames pale and weak. Caesar stepped out into the dawn and the others followed, blinking against the sudden brightness.

By midday, the sun had burned through the morning mist and the road stretched ahead of them, the stone paving showing the wear of centuries of traffic. The sky above was pale blue and empty of clouds, promising no rain but also no warmth.

The army halted at a crossroads where an old shrine to Mercury stood half buried in weeds, its painted plaster cracked and faded by weather and neglect. Villagers watched from a safe distance, their faces showing curiosity now rather than pure fear, and mothers held their children's hands whilst pointing at the eagle standards that marked each legion.

Caesar dismounted near the shrine, handing his reins to an orderly, and watched as the men broke ranks to drink from a nearby stream. They moved with easy efficiency, dropping their packs in neat rows and checking their sandals for stones whilst the centurions walked amongst them, offering corrections and praise in voices that carried across the cold air.

Caesar moved among the soldiers without ceremony, stopping to speak with one group and then another. His voice was quiet but it carried, and wherever he went, the legionaries straightened their backs and stood a little taller, as if his presence alone was enough to remind them of their pride.

'You have marched like true Romans,' said Caesar,

standing in the centre of a loose circle of soldiers who had gathered to listen. 'Not one house burned, not one theft reported. The world will remember this as the march of order, not the march of ruin. You have taken Italia without striking a blow, and that is the truest victory any army can achieve. Remember this when you grow old and tell your grandchildren about the war.'

The men cheered, though it was a subdued sound, more acknowledgment than celebration. They were weary from days of marching, but they were proud of what they had accomplished, and Marcus, watching from nearby, could see it in their faces and in the way they held themselves.

Balbus approached with another dispatch, this one sealed with wax that bore the mark of a town Marcus did not recognise. Marcus himself had just returned from riding ahead with a small cavalry detachment, and his cloak was dusty and his face streaked with sweat despite the cool air.

Caesar turned towards him.

'Praefect, you have been farther south than the rest of us. What news do you bring?'

'The people yield, Dominus,' said Marcus. 'Some towns close their gates when they see us approaching, but they open them once we actually appear at their walls with the legions in formation. I think they no longer know who Rome belongs to, or which master they should serve.'

Caesar was quiet for a moment, looking past Marcus towards the distant mountains that marked the approach to central Italia.

'Then we will remind them. Rome belongs to whoever protects her without tearing her down, whoever preserves rather than destroys. That is the lesson we are teaching with every step we take.'

He remounted his horse and gazed down the long road that cut through the valley, the mountains ahead showing as faint blue shadows against the pale sky. Beyond them lay the Tiber, and beyond the Tiber lay Rome herself, waiting.

'We move again within the hour,' said Caesar. 'By nightfall I want to reach the Anio crossing. Rome waits, even if she pretends not to notice our approach.'

As the army began to form ranks once more, the centurions calling out orders and the men shouldering their packs with groans and good-natured complaints, a small boy from the nearby village approached. He was perhaps seven or eight years old, barefoot despite the cold, and he carried a wicker basket of dried figs that looked far too heavy for his thin arms. He stopped a few paces from Caesar's horse and held the basket out, his eyes wide with a mixture of fear and excitement.

'For you, Dominus,' whispered the boy.

Caesar leaned down from the saddle and took a single fig from the basket. He examined it for a moment, then smiled at the boy with genuine warmth.

'Keep the rest and feed your family. They are more important than generals, more important than senators, and more important than anyone who wears the purple or carries standards. Always remember that.'

The boy stared at him, his mouth slightly open in amazement, then turned and ran back towards the cluster of huts where his mother stood watching with her hand pressed to her mouth. Caesar watched him go, still holding the fig in his hand.

'That,' murmured Caesar to Marcus, 'is why we march carefully. Loyalty takes years to build and only a moment to destroy. That boy will remember this day for the rest of his life, and he will tell his children about the day Caesar took one fig and told him his family was more important than any general.'

They rode on together, the army falling in behind them in perfect formation. The sound of hobnailed caligae on stone slabs and the jingle of equipment merged into one continuous rhythm that echoed down the valley and sent birds scattering from the trees in alarm.

That night the camp lay quiet under a brittle sky scattered with stars. The fires burned low, just enough to cook the evening meal and provide minimal warmth, and the men wrapped themselves in their cloaks and lay down to sleep on ground they had stamped flat. The watch changed with quiet efficiency, soldiers moving to their posts without needing orders, and somewhere in the darkness beyond the perimeter a dog barked once before falling silent.

Caesar sat alone in his command tent with a single lamp burning on the table. The flame cast long shadows across the canvas walls and made the scattered tablets and scrolls look like small mountains in a landscape of parchment and wax. He had sent everyone away, even his personal secretary, and now he sat with a blank sheet of good parchment before him.

The scratching of the stylus on parchment was the only sound as he wrote. He paused occasionally, reading back what he had written, testing how the words sounded, then continued.

'Marcus Tullius Cicero, orator of the Republic and guardian of its words,' wrote Caesar, forming each letter with care. *'I write not as conqueror but as citizen. The Senate has fled, yet Rome remains. Let it be known that I will protect her laws, her temples, and her people. Let those who doubt me look upon my march and judge by deeds, not by accusations spread by frightened men.'*

He paused and read the lines aloud in a low voice, testing how they would sound to Cicero's ear. The words seemed right, balanced between strength and conciliation.

'If Pompey Magnus believes himself the saviour of liberty,' continued Caesar, his stylus moving steadily across the parchment, 'let him prove it by returning to the city whose liberty he claims to defend. I am here, unarmed against her citizens, armed only against those who make war upon peace itself.'

He set down the stylus and leaned back in his chair, which creaked under the shift of his weight. The letter looked good. It struck the right tone, he thought, neither too aggressive nor too weak. Whether Cicero would believe any of it was another matter, but that was not really the point. The point was that the letter would be copied and read and discussed throughout Italia, and people would remember that Caesar had offered peace.

He rose and moved to the tent's entrance, pushing aside the flap. The cold night air hit him like a blade, sharp and clean after the stuffiness of the tent. In the distance he could see the faint glow of campfires stretching across the plain, hundreds of them, each one marking a group of soldiers who had followed him across the Rubicon and into history. Each flame represented lives given over to his cause, though most of those men could probably not explain exactly what that cause was beyond following Caesar.

He thought of Rome, of the marble temples gleaming in the sunlight, of the constant clatter of the markets, of the voices echoing beneath the dome of the Curia where the Senate met. He imagined those same voices now raised in fear, calling him traitor, tyrant, king, monster. Perhaps they were right. Perhaps he had become what they accused him of being, or perhaps he was simply doing what necessity demanded. History would judge, and history was written by the victors.

He drew his cloak tighter around his shoulders and

looked south towards where Rome lay in the darkness. The wind carried the scent of rain and woodsmoke, the breath of his homeland preparing for the storm that was coming.

'Mercy,' said Caesar softly to the empty night, testing the word as though it were a weapon he was learning to wield. 'Mercy will frighten them more than legions ever could. They expect violence, so we will give them restraint. They expect plunder, so we will give them protection. They expect a monster, so we will give them a saviour. And then they will not know what to do.'

He returned to his table and stared at the map once more, tracing the road south with his finger. The path to Rome was nearly clear now. Beyond the city lay Capua, where Pompey was gathering what forces he could. Beyond Capua lay Brundisium and the sea and beyond the sea lay Greece and the east, where Pompey had made his fortune and his reputation. This was going to be a long war, Caesar realised, longer than anyone in Rome expected. But it was a war he intended to win, whatever the cost.

He smiled faintly.

'If the gods truly guide me,' murmured Caesar to the shadows, 'then may they forgive what must be done in their name. And if they do not guide me, then may history be kind enough to lie about my intentions.'

The lamp flickered as a draft found its way through the tent seams, and outside the first drops of rain began to fall upon the silent camp, pattering on canvas and hissing in the dying fires. Somewhere in the darkness, a sentry called the hour, marking the passage of time in a night that felt like it might never end.

Chapter Seven

Rome

The house on the Palatine had grown quieter with each passing day. Most of the servants had already gone, dismissed or fled, and those who remained moved through the rooms like ghosts uncertain of their purpose. Aurelia stood in the atrium watching the morning light stretch across the mosaic floor, and she made a decision.

'I am going out,' she said.

Calpurnia looked up from the scroll she had been pretending to read, her face showing alarm.

'Into the city? Now? With everything that is happening?'

'Especially now,' said Aurelia. 'Rumour is a coward's map. I prefer streets and facts to whispers and speculation.'

'Then take guards. Take armed men.'

'I will take what is mine to command. Four guards, the litter, and the household's name. Nothing more is needed, and anything more would look like fear.'

She dressed without haste, selecting a plain cloak without ornament and fastening it with an old bronze pin. She ordered the litter brought to the inner gate and stood in the vestibule whilst a slave lifted the heavy bar and swung the wooden leaves back. Dust lifted from the threshold as the bearers shouldered the litter and moved out into the street.

Two household guards walked at either side, hands resting on sword hilts, and a pair of slaves went ahead to call out a path as the Palatine slope fell away in a crooked line of fine houses and oaken doors.

'Keep to the wider streets,' said Aurelia from inside the litter.

'As you command, Domina,' said the forward guard.

The street below the Palatine smelled of old wine and ashes. The shutters on the shops were barred, though several showed marks where hands had tried to prise them open with knives. A cart stood abandoned with one wheel broken and no owner in sight and a dog sleeping in the shade of a public fountain, did not stir as they passed.

A fishmonger's stall lay overturned, a smear of silver scales bright against the dark stones and a boy with a shaved head knelt beside the smear, rubbing the scales on his wrists as if they were perfume or some kind of charm. He did not meet Aurelia's eyes when the litter passed.

A young man called something from a doorway, his voice brittle with drink.

'Look at the mother of the city's butcher, riding out to see her son's work. How many throats will he cut today, Domina?'

A woman beside him slapped his sleeve hard and told him to be silent. He laughed and looked away, but the words hung in the air like smoke. Words had become weapons that cost nothing to throw.

They turned towards the Forum, passing walls covered in fresh graffiti. One message read Pompey saves Rome in confident letters. Beneath it, written more carefully, someone had added Bread saves Rome. Another hand had scratched a simple line deep into the plaster: Who saves me? The question looked like it had been carved by someone with nothing left to lose.

Aurelia lifted the litter's curtain and breathed through her mouth. The Forum was not empty, but it felt unfinished, like a theatre after the play's last act when the lamps gutter and nobody has come to strike the scenery. A hawker had laid out two chipped bowls and a knife on a stained cloth and sat waiting for buyers who would never appear and three dogs quarrelled near the Rostra over something that might once have been meat.

'Stop here,' said Aurelia.

She stepped down from the litter before the guard could assist her and walked towards the great statue of Concordia. A crowd had gathered in a loose ring at the statue's base, perhaps twenty or thirty people, and they stood in complete silence. The body of a young man was swaying from the statue's outstretched arm, hung with his own belt.

'Who was he?' asked Aurelia.

An older woman answered without turning her head.

'Livius. He made speeches yesterday in the Forum. He said the city should close its gates to both armies, that Rome should starve herself before she fed either wolf. Someone heard him and he paid the price for independent thought.'

'Which side killed him?'

'Does it matter?' said the woman. 'He is dead either way.'

Aurelia looked up at the statue's arm until her eyes began to water. The marble did not tremble with the weight. Stone cared for nothing except being stone.

'Cut him down and cover him,' said Aurelia.

One of her guards shrugged off his cloak and handed it to the man nearest him before climbing up and cutting the belt. The body fell to the ground with a thud and lay there, the focus of attention for the last time.

'Can you arrange a burial?' asked Aurelia to the woman, offering her some coins.

The woman looked down at the offered money before looking back up at Aurelia.

'The man will be buried in a descent fashion.' she said. 'But we do not need your soiled coins to do so.' She turned away as some of the men picked up the body and headed down an alley.

Aurelia watched them go before moving on, away from Concordia. She rounded a corner where a nobleman lay beside a fountain as if he had decided to rest and had fallen asleep. His rings had left pale grooves where they had been torn from his fingers and the cut at his throat had been competent rather than angry. His tunic was torn where hands had searched for coin, and the blood had made an intricate pattern on the stones.

A priest in torn robes stood on basilica steps, preaching to no one about how the gods were punishing Rome. He had no audience, yet he kept speaking because words were the only hope he had left.

Aurelia walked past him without offering alms until she stood at last before the Curia. The great bronze doors were shut and sealed, the wax still bearing the Senate's crest and cobwebs already blurred the corners of the lintel.

Aurelia placed her palm flat against the cold metal.

'I once thought these doors were Rome itself,' she said quietly. 'I thought they swung on principles, not hinges.

The guard beside her studied the street rather than her face. It was respect for something he could not mend.

'We will return home,' said Aurelia finally and she climbed back inside the litter before heading back toward the Palatine.

As they retraced their path, man darted from an alley and caught the litter's curtain with grubby fingers.

'Protect me, Domina. Your son will have pity if his mother tells him to show it.'

Aurelia parted the curtain and met his eyes.

'I do not command my son in matters of war. Find work, or shelter or simply wait. Those are the only prayers Rome hears now.'

The man's hand fell away and a stone bounced near the litter, thrown by someone too young to understand consequences. The guard raised his arm but Aurelia shook her head.

'There has been enough striking for one day. Let it pass.'

They began the climb back up the Palatine and when the house swallowed her again, Calpurnia came rushing from the inner rooms.

'Is it as bad as they say?' she asked.

'It is not,' replied Aurelia. There is death and destitution, but Rome knows how to fall. She learned it over many years from those who promised to hold her up.'

Calpurnia's hands trembled.

'Will he hurt the city when he comes?'

'I do not believe he will,' said Aurelia. 'My son understands the craft of mercy for it is the only craft left to great men if they intend to live among their neighbours afterwards.'

Aurelia ate a mouthful of bread from a plate waiting on the table then went to the peristyle, looking across the still water, trying to remember her son's footsteps as a boy. The memory was bright for a moment and then gone.

She crossed to the balcony that overlooked the street. Somewhere in the distance a jar fell and broke and no one cursed.

'They say he is close,' said Calpurnia from behind her.

'He is close,' said Aurelia.

She remained at the balcony until her shoulders ached,

then placed both hands on the stone balustrade to steady them.

'Come like rain on fields after harvest,' whispered Aurelia. 'Do not come like fire.'

A few miles away, Caesar walked the front line of the finished palisade whilst his men set the last stakes. He stopped where a ditch bit into hard ground and rested his hand on a post that had not existed the day before. Work had turned chaos into geometry, and geometry could be read from the city walls.

'Double the pickets on this side,' said Caesar. 'Rome must look at us and see what obedience builds.'

'It is done, Dominus,' said Marcus. 'The scouts report that the guards on the Aurelian Gate are few and mostly old men. We have been told that they have not slept in days and there is no command binding them. They just wait the way cattle wait for a new owner.'

Caesar spent the rest of the morning among the tents without escort. He spoke to men oiling their shields and paused with a standard bearer telling a story about his son's first tooth.

He stood with the baker and watched loaves emerge from the oven's black mouth. He accepted one, broke it, and ate it slowly before sharing it with those men standing nearby who had never dreamt they would one day share bread with Caesar.

In the second hour he called a small council where Curio delivered a report from his observations of the walls surrounding the city.

'The gates open and close like mouths that cannot choose a sentence,' said Curio. 'but they remain unbarred because no one wants to order it. The people watch us and whisper that you will enter as Sulla did.'

'The men say it is a bad omen to stop at the sacred stones,' said Antonius.

'Let them have their omens,' said Caesar. 'I have mine. Rome will surrender to a hunger for calm, and we will provide it.'

He dismissed them and wrote the latest in a long line of communications, to Pompey, to Cicero, to the Senate. He knew it was a futile action and yet he persisted. It was important that everyone knew that he offered a peaceful hand to all that would listen before any blood needed to be spilled.

In the afternoon he walked to the boundary stones and placed his hand on one. He said nothing for he did not believe the gods were in the stone. He believed men had made the stone sacred with fear and bravery, and both those things were in him in sufficient measure to merit a pause.

Marcus came and waited until the pause ended.

'The walls are quieter,' said Marcus, 'but they are lined with many people, watching and listening.'

'Then let's give them something to see,' said Caesar. 'Form a line of standards on the ridge at the seventh hour and keep it until the eighth. No drums or horns, then break the line without command. Let the city wonder how an army operates without sound.'

'As you command, Dominus.'

That night Caesar walked with the pickets and listened to their soft talk. He heard a man whisper about his wife keeping a lamp burning because their child could not sleep. He heard another man hum a tune from a village beyond the mountains and a third mutter the names of his long dead comrades, as if naming them would keep their memories alive. He was not comforted, but he was steadied.

When the second day lifted, a deputation came from the city, sent by some magistrate who still had the courage to stay. They spoke of limits and asked for time. Caesar gave them water and food but returned without a promise and without an enemy to point at.

On the morning of the third day, Marcus came from his latest circumnavigation of the city.

'There are no more guards on the walls,' he said, 'only a levy of old men too stubborn to run. Just citizens with spears. Shall we form up and prepare to enter the city?'

'Not yet,' said Caesar. 'We will let them absorb what is about to happen.'

'There is talk you hesitate because the stones are holy,' said Marcus, repeating the rumour he had heard from several men.

'I have no time for rumours,' said Caesar. 'Only facts.'

'Then what do we tell them?'

Caesar thought for a few moments before replying.

'We will give them the facts they crave,' he said, 'and let them learn something along the way. Come with me.' He remounted and took the road with Marcus and Balbus at his side.

When the boundary stones came into view, Caesar kept riding and let his horse walk between them, passing both stones at the exact midpoint, before stopping and looking back at Marcus.

'Nothing happened,' said Caesar, 'and if those on the wall or in the legion at my back wait to see if I burst into flames, they'll be disappointed.'

He turned back and stared towards the city. The two

gates stood open, pushed inward to a courteous angle by men who had then retreated, or fled.

'These gates want to let us in,' he said, 'but let's see if they hold their nerve.'

He urged his horse forward and the gates stayed open. A knot of old men with spears stood pressed against the wall, watching but not moving and eventually a messenger appeared from inside the city.

'Greetings, Imperator,' he said nervously. 'The magistrates are asking if you intend to enter the city.'

'Not until Rome decides she wants me,' said Caesar. 'I've just crossed the sacred boundary so tell them I'll wait at the fountain near the old market, neutral ground for all parties. They can send someone official if they want to talk.'

The messenger nodded and hurried back toward the city gates as Marcus moved his horse closer.

'That was easier than expected,' he said.

'They're frightened,' said Caesar, 'and frightened men don't fight. They negotiate.'

'And if they decide not to negotiate?'

'Then we wait longer,' said Caesar, gathering his reins. 'Come. Let's see what the legion think of their first view of Rome in eight years.'

Chapter Eight

Rome

    A few days later, the boundary stones lay behind them and Caesar had passed through the gates at the invitation of the remaining city magistrates.

    Marcus rode two lengths behind Caesar, close enough to reach him in three heartbeats if needed, far enough to give the moment its proper weight. Behind them, three cohorts of the Thirteenth Legion moved in perfect formation, shields held high, pilums angled precisely, every step measured to the same rhythm they had marched across Gaul. But this was not Gaul. These were Roman streets beneath their caligae, Roman walls on either side, and Roman faces watching from shuttered windows.

    Caesar sat astride a white stallion, the animal's coat catching the morning light like polished marble. He wore his full regalia today, the scarlet paludamentum of a commanding general flowing from his shoulders, his cuirass polished to a mirror shine, and the ceremonial greaves on his legs worked with images of victory and conquest. The purple-edged cloak had been brushed clean of road dust and his helmet, crested with red horsehair, sat firmly on his head. He looked every inch the triumphant general, except there had been no enemy defeated in glorious combat. Only this strange, silent entry into a city that did not know whether to cheer or weep.

    The silence was unnatural for Rome was never silent. Marcus had been born here, had grown up with the constant noise of the city as his lullaby: merchants shouting their wares, women arguing over prices at market stalls, and children playing in the streets, the thousand voices of Rome mixing into one continuous roar.

Now there was nothing but the rhythmic tramp of hobnailed caligae and the jingle of military equipment.

People watched from doorways and windows. Marcus could see them, shadows behind the shutters, and faces appearing briefly before pulling back. A woman held a child against her chest on a second-floor balcony, her hand over the boy's mouth as if his breathing might draw attention, while an old man stood in a shop entrance with his arms crossed, his face unreadable.

A priest in faded robes stood on temple steps and did not move, did not bless, and did not curse, he simply stood and watched with the fixed stare of someone witnessing something they had prayed would never come.

No one spoke, no one threw flowers or stones and no one cheered or jeered. They just watched and waited to see what kind of conqueror had come to claim it.

Caesar did not acknowledge the watchers, he sat straight in his saddle, his eyes fixed ahead on the road that led to the Forum, his face composed into an expression that gave nothing away. There was no triumph in his bearing, no anger, no satisfaction, just the calm certainty of a man who had made his decision and would now see it through to whatever end awaited.

Behind them, the column stretched back through the gate, eighteen hundred men moving in perfect order through streets designed for crowds and markets, not for legions. At each intersection, a century peeled away and took position, fanning out to cover the side streets and alleyway. Marcus watched them deploy with practised efficiency, checking corners and rooftops, establishing sight lines, and creating a network of control that spread through the northern district like roots through soil.

'No resistance yet,' said Balbus quietly, riding up on Marcus's left. His hand rested on his gladius hilt, not gripping it, but ready.

'They are too frightened to resist,' said Marcus. 'Look at them. They expect us to start killing.'

A door slammed somewhere to their right and both men's heads snapped towards the sound. A century broke formation slightly, shields coming up, but it was only a shutter blown closed by the wind. The soldiers settled back into position, but Marcus could see the tension in their shoulders, the way their eyes moved constantly, searching for threats that might or might not exist.

They turned onto the Via Sacra and the Forum opened before them. The great open space lay empty except for a few pigeons pecking at the stones and a dog that ran away when it saw the column approaching.

The temples rose on either side, their painted columns bright in the morning sun, but their doors were closed and barred. The Rostra stood silent, its bronze speakers' platform gleaming dully. The Senate House loomed at the far end, its bronze doors sealed with wax and ribbon, the official marks of closure pressed into the soft material.

Marcus had seen the Forum filled with thousands of people, so crowded you could barely move, voices rising in a constant din of argument and commerce and life. He had seen it during festivals when the whole city gathered to watch processions and sacrifices, and he had seen it during elections when candidates shouted themselves hoarse trying to win votes. He had never seen it empty like this, hollow and echoing like a tomb.

Caesar reined in his horse at the centre of the Forum and sat for a long moment, looking around at the emptiness. Then he dismounted with a fluid motion, handing his reins to an orderly who appeared at his side. His boots struck the stone with a sharp crack that echoed off the surrounding buildings and he walked forward a few paces, his red cloak sweeping behind him, before stopping in the exact centre of the space where speakers traditionally stood to address the people.

'Secure the perimeter,' said Marcus quietly to the nearest centurion. 'Full watch on all approaches. No one enters or leaves without my permission.'

'Yes, Praefect,' said the centurion, and began issuing orders to his men.

Marcus dismounted and joined Caesar at the centre of the Forum. Around them, legionaries took up positions but Marcus could see the strangeness of it in their faces.

'It is quieter than I expected,' said Caesar, his voice carrying in the empty space despite speaking barely above normal volume.

'They are waiting to see what you will do,' said Marcus.

'Then let us show them.'

Caesar turned and walked towards the Senate House. His boots echoed with each step, the sound bouncing off marble and bronze and painted plaster. Marcus followed, and behind them came two centuries in close formation, their shields forming a wall of red and bronze.

The bronze doors of the Curia stood twice the height of a man, decorated with reliefs showing the founding of Rome and the great victories of the Republic. The official seals hung from the handles, wax impressed with the consular insignia, the ribbons that marked them as legally closed fluttering slightly in the morning breeze.

Caesar stopped before the doors and placed his palm flat against the cold metal. He stood like that for a long moment, his hand on the door, his head slightly bowed. Then he stepped back.

'Break the seals,' he said.

A legionary came forward with a knife and cut through the ribbons. The wax seals fell to the ground and the soldier put his shoulder to one of the doors and pushed.

Darkness lay beyond, broken only by thin shafts of light from high windows and the smell of old incense and lamp oil.

Caesar entered the Curia with slow, deliberate steps, his boots echoing off the marble floor with a hollow sound that spoke of emptiness and absence. Marcus followed him inside and felt the weight of the space press down on him like a physical thing.

The Senate House was empty except for the tiers of benches, rising in semicircles on either side, carved from good marble and polished by the touch of countless robes over many centuries. But no senators sat there now. No voices filled the air with argument and oratory and no scribes sat ready with their tablets to record the words of great men. There was nothing but silence and shadows and the faint smell of wax from the lamps that had burned here days ago before the Senate fled.

Caesar walked down the central aisle between the benches, his footsteps marking time like a drum beat. He climbed the steps to the tribunal platform where the consuls sat, where he himself had sat years ago during his own consulship. He turned and looked out at the empty benches, at the space where the heart of the Republic should have been beating but now lay still and cold.

'The Senate and People of Rome,' said Caesar quietly, his voice carrying in the emptiness despite its softness. 'One half has fled and the other holds its breath. This emptiness is what they have made of the Republic.'

Marcus said nothing. There was nothing to say. The emptiness spoke for itself more eloquently than any words could have.

Caesar descended from the platform and walked back down the aisle. When he reached the doors, he paused and looked back one more time at the empty chamber.

'Find whoever remains,' said Caesar. 'Magistrates, priests, anyone with any authority who has not fled. Tell them I wish to address them at noon tomorrow, here, in this place. Let us see if we can make Rome speak again.'

He stepped out into the sunlight and Marcus followed, blinking against the brightness after the dimness inside. The Forum still lay empty except for the soldiers standing guard. But Marcus could sense the city around them, watching and waiting, holding its breath to see what came next.

'They will not come willingly,' said Marcus. 'The ones who remain are either too old or too frightened to face you.'

'Then we will be gentle with them,' said Caesar. 'We will show them that I am not the monster the Senate claimed. We will show them that Rome can continue, that the sun still rises, that bread will still be baked and distributed, and that laws will still be kept. We will show them order, not chaos. Peace, not slaughter.'

He looked around at the empty Forum, at the closed shops and barred temples, at the faces watching from windows.

'We will show them a Rome that still stands,' said Caesar. 'And we will make them choose whether to be part of it.'

The house on the Palatine had its own silence, different

from the Forum's emptiness but no less profound, the silence of people trying not to draw attention to themselves, trying to become invisible in their own home. The remaining servants moved through the corridors like ghosts, their sandals barely whispering on the stone floors, their voices reduced to mouths forming words without sound.

Aurelia stood in the atrium with her hands folded before her, listening. The house had good walls, thick and well-built, but sounds still carried up from the city below. Distant shouts, the tramp of many feet on stone and the crash of something heavy falling or being thrown. A woman's scream was cut short, then silence again, which was somehow worse than the noise.

Calpurnia paced near the window, pulling the curtain aside every few moments to look out at the street below, then letting it fall back as if what she saw frightened her too much to watch for long.

'They are everywhere,' said Calpurnia. 'Soldiers in the streets, people running. I saw a man fall and no one stopped to help him.'

'Come away from the window,' said Aurelia.

'But...'

'Come away.'

Calpurnia obeyed, though her hands twisted together and would not be still.

'Should we not bar the outer gate?'

'It is already barred.'

'But if they come here, if soldiers come looking...'

'Then we will deal with it when it happens,' said Aurelia. 'Until then, we wait.'

The household steward appeared in the doorway, his face pale and his hands shaking slightly.

'Domina, the slaves are asking if they should hide the

silver. They fear looting.'

'Tell them to leave it where it is,' said Aurelia. 'If soldiers come to loot, hidden silver will only make them angry when they find it. Better to let them take what they want and leave quickly.'

'Yes, Domina,' said the steward, and withdrew.

The sound of many running feet came from outside, the slap of sandals on stone and the harsh breathing of people running in panic. Voices shouted words that could not be distinguished and something crashed against a wall somewhere close by. Calpurnia flinched at each sound, her eyes wide with fear.

'Breathe,' said Aurelia. 'You are safe here.'

'How can you be sure?'

'I cannot. But fear will not make us safer, and panic will not protect us. So we breathe, and we wait, and we prepare to face whatever comes.'

The running feet passed the house and faded into the distance. Then came more, from a different direction, and the sound of someone sobbing as they ran. The city was tearing itself apart, not with violence, but with fear, fleeing from shadows and rumours, not knowing where safety lay or even if safety existed anymore.

A pounding came at the outer gate, sudden and violent. Fists hammering on wood, voices shouting to be let in.

'Sanctuary! Please! They are coming!'

The steward appeared again, his face now grey with fear.

'Domina, there are people at the gate. They beg to be let in.'

Aurelia moved to the vestibule where she could see through the narrow window that looked out onto the entrance courtyard. Perhaps a dozen people stood pressed against the gate, men and women both, some with children. They looked back over their shoulders constantly, expecting pursuit.

'How many?' asked Aurelia.

'Twelve, perhaps fifteen.'

'Let them in. Give them water and put them in the servants' courtyard. Tell them to be silent.'

'Yes, Domina.'

The gate was unbarred and the people tumbled through, gasping their thanks, clutching children and each other. They were herded quickly to the back of the house whilst the gate was closed again. But before it could be barred, more people appeared, running up the hill, and they too hammered on the gate, shouting to be admitted.

'Please! The soldiers! They are killing anyone in the streets!'

This was a lie, Aurelia knew. The soldiers were not killing anyone, or she would have heard the screams, but fear made people believe lies, and belief made lies true enough to run from.

'Let them in as well,' said Aurelia. 'But bar the gate after them.'

More refugees crowded through, perhaps twenty this time, and they brought the smell of the city with them, sweat and dust and panic. They babbled their thanks and their terror in equal measure, and they were directed to the courtyard where they huddled together like sheep who had escaped wolves.

The gate was being pushed closed when even more people appeared, but these were different. Men, this time, perhaps a dozen of them, and they moved with purpose rather than panic. They saw the gate closing and rushed forward, throwing their weight against it, trying to force it open.

'Hold it!' shouted the steward. 'Hold the gate!'

The household slaves threw their weight against the wood, pushing back, their sandals slipping on the stone as they strained. The men outside shouted and cursed, their hands reaching through the gap, trying to grab the edges, trying to prise it open.

'Push!' shouted one of the slaves. 'All together!'

They pushed as one and the gap narrowed. Fingers scrabbled at the edge, withdrawing just before they would have been crushed and the gate slammed closed with a boom that echoed through the courtyard. Immediately the bar was dropped into place, thick oak reinforced with iron, settling into its brackets with a solid thud.

The men outside hammered on the gate for a few moments longer, shouting threats, but then footsteps approached from down the hill, the measured tramp of soldiers in formation, and suddenly the men were gone, fleeing as quickly as they had appeared.

The household slaves leaned against the gate, breathing hard, some of them bleeding where fingernails had scratched their arms. The steward looked at Aurelia with wide eyes.

'Bar all the doors,' said Aurelia. 'No one else enters. We cannot protect the whole city, only those already inside these walls.'

'Yes, Domina.'

The house settled into uneasy quietness. The refugees in the courtyard whispered among themselves but did not dare speak loudly. The slaves returned to their posts, though their hands still shook and Calpurnia sat on a bench in the atrium with her face in her hands.

Aurelia stood alone in the vestibule, listening to the city. The sounds of panic had faded and now there was only the distant tramp of soldiers, regular and measured, moving through the streets in a pattern that spoke of control rather than chaos. Caesar's men were establishing order, whether the city wanted it or not.

Time passed. Aurelia did not know how much, but she did not move from her position near the entrance. She listened and waited, preparing herself for whatever would come next.

When the tenth hour had surely passed and the city had fallen into an unnatural stillness, there came a single knock at the gate. Not pounding, not desperate hammering, just one knock, measured and deliberate, the sound of knuckles on wood in a pattern that was almost casual.

The household froze. The slaves in the courtyard stopped whispering and the steward emerged from the inner rooms, his face questioning.

Another knock, identical to the first... patient... waiting.

Aurelia walked slowly towards the vestibule window and looked through the narrow opening. She could see the gate but not who stood beyond it. The street outside appeared empty except for one figure standing directly before the entrance, but the angle was wrong to see clearly.

'Domina?' whispered the steward. 'Should we answer?'

Aurelia stared at the gate. The knock came again, the same rhythm, the same patience. Three knocks now, each one separated by enough time to let silence settle between them.

She knew that knock, she had heard it a thousand times over the years when he came home late from the Senate and did not want to wake the household. And when he returned from campaigns and stood at the gate in the dark hours before dawn, not announcing himself with trumpets but simply knocking, waiting to be recognised.

'Open it,' said Aurelia.

The steward stared at her.

'Domina, we cannot know who...'

'I know that knock,' said Aurelia. 'Open the gate. *Now.*'

The steward looked at the slaves who had held the gate against the mob. They were exhausted, frightened, uncertain. He looked back at Aurelia, saw something in her face that left no room for argument, and nodded.

'Unbar the gate,' he said quietly.

The slaves lifted the heavy bar and set it aside. They took hold of the gate's edge and pulled. The hinges creaked and the gate swung slowly inward.

Outside, standing alone in the empty street, stood Caesar.

He wore his full regalia still, the scarlet paludamentum hanging from his shoulders, and his cuirass catching the afternoon light. His right hand rested on his sword hilt, not gripping it but ready. Behind him, the street stretched empty in both directions. No soldiers, no guards and no escort. Just one man standing at his mother's gate.

Aurelia stood in the vestibule, looking at her son. He looked back at her, and for a long moment neither of them moved.

Slowly, deliberately, Caesar brought his right hand up and removed his helmet, holding it loose at his side. The red horsehair crest swayed slightly in the breeze. Without the helmet, his face was clearly visible, and the household slaves gasped. Some dropped to their knees and one began to weep.

Caesar did not look at them. His eyes remained fixed on

his mother.

Footsteps came running from inside the house, sandals slapping on marble, and Calpurnia appeared in the doorway. She stopped when she saw her husband, her hand going to her mouth. Then she was moving again, running across the courtyard, her cloak flying behind her, and she threw herself into his arms.

Caesar caught her, his left arm wrapping around her automatically, but his eyes never left his mother's face. Calpurnia buried her face against his cuirass and held him so tightly her knuckles went white. She was making sounds that might have been words or might have been sobs or might have been both as her whole body shook with relief.

Aurelia walked forward slowly, her steps measured and deliberate. She came down into the courtyard and stopped an arm's length from her son. She studied his face, noting the new lines around his eyes, the grey that had appeared in his hair at the temples, the weariness that showed despite his straight posture.

'You came alone,' said Aurelia.

'I came home,' said Caesar.

Calpurnia was still clinging to him, her face pressed against his armour, her breath coming in ragged gasps. Caesar's arm remained around her, but his eyes stayed on his mother.

'The city is quiet now,' said Aurelia. 'Your men have established order.'

'For now.'

'And tomorrow?'

'Tomorrow we begin the work of keeping it.'

Aurelia nodded slowly. She reached out and placed her hand on her son's cheek, the gesture so simple and so intimate that several of the watching slaves looked away, feeling they witnessed something too private for their eyes.

Calpurnia finally lifted her face from his chest, her cheeks wet with tears, and looked up at him.

'I thought you would never come,' she said, her voice breaking. 'I thought you would stay with your army, that you would send others.'

'There are many things that I have to do,' said Caesar, 'but I came home first.' He kissed her forehead gently, then looked back at his mother. 'We should go inside. The streets are not yet safe, even if they appear empty.'

Caesar allowed himself to be led inside, his wife still clinging to his arm, his mother walking beside him. The household slaves bowed as he passed, some of them weeping, all of them uncertain whether to feel relief or fear or both. The steward closed the gate behind them and dropped the bar back into place, and the house of Caesar sealed itself once more against the outside world.

In the atrium, Caesar stood in the centre of the room where he had played as a child, where he had studied under tutors, where he had first put on the toga virilis and become a man, and he looked around at the painted walls and expensive furniture as if seeing them for the first time.

'It is smaller than I remembered,' he said quietly.

'Or you have become larger,' said Aurelia. 'Sit, eat, rest. Tomorrow you can conquer the rest of Rome. Tonight, you are simply home.'

Caesar sat, and for the first time in three days, perhaps for the first time in months, he allowed the weight to leave his shoulders. His wife sat pressed against his side, his mother sat across from him and the household moved quietly around them, bringing food and drink, and lighting lamps against the gathering dusk.

Outside, Rome held its breath and waited to see what the morning would bring, but inside this house, for a few hours at least, there was only a family reunited, and the war could wait.

Chapter Nine

The Road to Capua

The column stretched for two miles along the ancient road, a serpent of wagons and horses and walking men that moved south through the winter landscape like a wound across the face of Italia. Pompey rode at its head, his broad shoulders hunched against the cold wind that came down from the mountains, his face set in an expression that gave nothing away to those who watched him pass.

Behind him came the senators, some mounted, others in litters, all maintaining the dignity of their office even as they fled from the city they claimed to govern. Then the wagons carrying the treasury, guarded by soldiers who looked more like mercenaries than legionaries and finally, the household slaves and servants, the camp followers and the opportunists, all the human debris that attached itself to any great movement of powerful men.

They had been five days on the road since leaving Rome, and the initial panic had settled into something harder and more dangerous. Fear had given way to anger, and anger to the cold calculation of men who saw their world collapsing and were beginning to look for someone to blame.

Pompey sent riders ahead at every town they approached, and to settlements visible from the road. The message was always the same: Caesar had broken the sacred law, crossed the Rubicon with his legions, and now marched on Rome itself like some barbarian king. Every man of military age, every veteran who remembered his oath, and every citizen who valued the Republic must take up arms and join the lawful government in its righteous defence of liberty.

The rhetoric was Cato's work, polished and passionate, speaking of freedom and tradition and the glory of Rome. It worked better than Pompey had expected and at every town, men came forward, drawn by the words and by the promise of the land and coin that Pompey's agents offered.

Old soldiers who had served in his eastern campaigns, young men seeking glory, and farmers' sons who saw a chance to escape their fields, all followed in the column's wake like iron filings drawn to a lodestone.

By the time they reached the hill country south of Rome, Pompey commanded perhaps three thousand men, and more were arriving every day. It was not an army, not yet, but it was the beginning of one, and that gave him something he had not felt since leaving the city. Hope.

The road descended from the hills towards Campania, and the landscape changed as they travelled south. The harsh winter cold of Latium gave way to milder air, and the fields became richer, dotted with prosperous villas and well-maintained farms. This was wealthy country, and Pompey sent more riders ahead with carefully worded messages to the great landowners whose estates dominated the region. He needed their support, their money, and their influence with the local magistrates.

Some responded favourably. Others sent polite refusals or did not respond at all. Caesar's shadow reached even here, it seemed, and men were beginning to wonder which side would prove victorious when all the rhetoric faded and real blood was spilled.

On the ninth day, they saw Capua. The city rose before them like a vision from better times, its walls catching the afternoon sun and its temples gleaming white against the blue sky. It was the second city of Italia, wealthy beyond measure from its position on the great road and from the rich farmland that surrounded it. The Capuans had grown fat on trade and luxury, and their city showed it. Broad streets, fine houses, and public buildings that would not have shamed Rome itself. This was a place that valued pleasure and profit above all else, and Pompey hoped that pragmatism would make them allies.

The city gates stood open, but there were armed men on the walls. Not many, and they looked more ceremonial than martial, but their presence was noted. Capua was taking no chances.

Pompey rode through the gates with Lentulus and Marcellus, the two consuls who had fled with him. Behind them came enough senators to make an impressive showing, all mounted, all wearing their best togas despite the dust of the road. They were making an entrance, proclaiming to Capua and to themselves that the legitimate government of Rome had arrived.

The streets were crowded with people who had come to watch the spectacle. Merchants and shopkeepers, slaves running errands, children darting between the legs of adults, all drawn by the news that had swept ahead of the column. Pompey Magnus himself, three times consul, conqueror of the East, had come to their city. Some cheered, but many simply stared, trying to understand what this meant for them and their families.

The column made its way through the streets towards the Forum, where the local magistrates waited with carefully neutral expressions. There were pleasantries, formal welcomes and an offer of the city's resources that was polite but not enthusiastic. Capua would help, but Capua would also watch closely to see which way the wind blew.

The senators scattered almost immediately, claiming the

best houses in the city with a high-handedness that made the Capuans bristle. Lentulus requisitioned a merchant's villa overlooking the Forum, evicting the owner with barely a word of explanation while Cato took over a philosopher's school, turning its rooms into offices for the bureaucracy of a government-in-exile. Others followed their example, and within hours half the wealthy quarter had been occupied by Romans who acted as though conquest rather than flight had brought them south.

Pompey watched this pillaging with distaste but said nothing. They needed Capua's cooperation, but they also needed to maintain the fiction that they remained Rome's rightful rulers.

He took quarters in a smaller house near the theatre, a comfortable place that had belonged to a local magistrate who was wise enough to offer it before it could be seized. The man's slaves unpacked Pompey's belongings with nervous efficiency whilst his officers established a command post in the building's courtyard.

By evening, the transformation was complete. A basilica near the Forum had been commandeered, and the senators gathered there in what they insisted on calling the Curia, though it was barely half the size of Rome's Senate house. They arranged themselves on benches borrowed from the law courts, maintaining the traditional divisions and procedures as though nothing had changed. Pompey stood at the back and watched them pretend.

Heralds had been sent through Capua's streets at sunset, making proclamations in the Forum and at major crossroads. Their message was clear and carefully crafted: Caesar was a criminal who had betrayed his oath and marched on Rome with hostile intent. The Senate, fleeing before his tyranny, had established itself in Capua to continue the lawful government of the Republic and all loyal citizens must rally to the defence of liberty. Those who supported the traitor Caesar would be marked as enemies of Rome itself.

The heralds spoke well, their voices carrying across the evening crowds. Some listeners nodded while others frowned. Most simply absorbed the information and reserved judgement. Capua had survived for centuries by being clever about politics, and cleverness meant waiting to see who would actually win before committing too firmly to either side.

The Senate met again after dark, the basilica lit by dozens of oil lamps that cast dancing shadows on the walls. Perhaps two hundred senators had made the journey south, less than half the full membership, but enough to maintain the forms. Lentulus, as senior consul, presided from a raised platform at the front of the chamber.

The debates were familiar, the same arguments that had been made in Rome repeated here with growing desperation. Cato spoke of principle and honour, his voice ringing with righteous fury as he painted Caesar as everything evil that could threaten the Republic. Marcellus detailed the military situation with grim precision, listing the towns that had surrendered and the legions that Caesar still commanded in Gaul, and Cicero, looking older and more tired than Pompey remembered, still spoke of moderation and the possibility of negotiation.

As expected, he was shouted down by Cato's faction, who saw any compromise as betrayal and the chamber grew heated, voices rising as old grievances surfacing alongside new fears.

Halfway through the meeting, another messenger arrived, dusty from hard riding, carrying news from Rome and the chamber fell silent as the man delivered his report. Caesar had entered the city three days ago. He had brought his army but there had been no violence, no looting, and no bloodshed of any kind. He had gone to the Forum, made a brief speech about reconciliation and unity, then retired to his own house. The city was calm, the people were calm, and the markets were operating normally. Life was continuing as though nothing had changed.

The silence stretched as the senators absorbed this information. It was the worst news imaginable.

'The monster shows his true face,' said Lentulus, but his voice lacked conviction. 'He lulls them with false mercy before the real tyranny begins.'

'He gave them bread,' said the messenger quietly. 'Opened the granaries and distributed grain to any household that needed it. He said it was a gift to the people of Rome.'

There was more silence and Pompey saw the calculation happening behind every set of eyes in the chamber. Caesar was making them look like fools. They had fled in panic, abandoning the people to a tyrant who turned out to offer bread instead of swords. The contrast could not have been more damaging if Caesar had planned it deliberately, which Pompey suspected he had.

'This changes nothing,' said Lentulus, though his voice lacked conviction. 'Rome is stones and temples. The Senate is what gives it meaning, and the Senate sits here, in this chamber. We remain the lawful government. We will raise our legions, and we will take back what Caesar has stolen.'

But Pompey, watching from the side of the chamber, knew that everything had changed. Caesar had won the first battle without violence, and that victory would echo through every town in Italia. The people would remember that Caesar brought order whilst the Senate brought only flight and fear.

They would remember that Caesar shared his bread whilst the Senate seized houses and made demands.

The meeting dissolved into smaller arguments and anxious conversations. Senators clustered in groups, speaking in low voices, making calculations about what this meant for their estates, their families, their futures, and some looked towards Pompey, hoping for reassurance from the general who was supposed to save them.

But Pompey offered none. He walked out of the basilica into the cool night air and stood in Capua's Forum, looking up at the stars that cared nothing for the struggles of men and their fragile republics.

'It would have been better if Caesar had burned Rome,' he thought. 'It would have been better if he had shown himself a tyrant from the start. Now we must fight not just his legions but his clemency, and I do not know which is more dangerous.'

He stood there for a long time, alone in the darkness, whilst behind him the Senate argued about principles and procedures and all the forms that meant nothing without the power to enforce them.

When he finally returned to his quarters, he called for his secretary.

'I need you to take a letter,' said Pompey.

The secretary, a Greek named Theophanes who had served him for twenty years, prepared his writing materials without comment. He had learned long ago when to remain silent.

'*To Publius Attius Varus,*' he said, '*propraetor and commander of Brundisium.*' Pompey paced the small room as he spoke. '*From Gnaeus Pompeius Magnus, in the name of the Senate and People of Rome.*'

He paused, choosing his words carefully. This letter would determine whether they could continue the fight or whether Caesar had already won.

'Greetings my friend. You will have heard by now of the criminal actions of Gaius Julius Caesar, who has violated his oath, crossed the Rubicon with armed force, and marched on Rome in open rebellion against the lawful government of the Republic. The situation in Italia deteriorates daily. Caesar advances south with multiple legions whilst we struggle to raise adequate forces to oppose him. The towns surrender without resistance, seduced by his promises of clemency, and our recruiting efforts, though successful, cannot match the speed of his advance.'

He stopped pacing and faced Theophanes directly, speaking more slowly now, emphasizing every word.

'I have therefore determined that we cannot hold Italia against Caesar's forces. The only viable strategy is to evacuate to Greece, where we can combine with the legions stationed in the East and return with overwhelming force to reclaim what has been stolen.'

It was the admission he had avoided making in the Senate, the acknowledgement that they had already lost the first campaign. But Varus needed to know the truth if he was to prepare properly.

'Your role in this evacuation is critical. Brundisium is our only viable port for crossing to Greece. You must prepare to receive the entire Senate, treasury, and such forces as we can gather. I estimate we will arrive within two weeks, possibly sooner if Caesar presses his advance.'

Pompey outlined the logistical requirements: ships,

supplies, security arrangements for the treasury, and provisions for several thousand men. He knew he was asking Varus to accomplish what would normally take months of preparation in a matter of days, but there was no alternative.

'Caesar will certainly attempt to prevent our departure,' he continued, *'and will know that if we reach Greece successfully, the war becomes vastly more difficult for him. Therefore, you must prepare Brundisium's defences. Strengthen the walls, gather supplies for a siege, ensure that the harbour remains under our control at all costs.'*

He dictated details about which approaches to fortify, where to position artillery, how to organise the civilian population to assist in the defence. Varus had been a competent officer under Pompey's command in the East, capable and reliable if not brilliant, but he would need to be better than competent in the coming weeks.

'Regarding the fleet: secure every vessel in Brundisium and the surrounding ports. Merchant ships, fishing boats, anything that can carry men across the Adriatic. Pay fair prices if possible, but commandeer what you must. We will need capacity for at least ten thousand men, possibly more. The treasury will reimburse all legitimate expenses once we are established in Greece.'

Pompey paused again, considering what else needed to be said. The letter was already longer than he had intended, but the stakes demanded thoroughness.

'Be aware that Caesar will likely send agents to Brundisium ahead of his army. Trust no one who arrives claiming to represent him. His greatest weapon is not his legions but his ability to divide and seduce those

who should oppose him. *Maintain strict security, screen all arrivals carefully, and remember that the fate of the Republic may depend on your vigilance.'*

The concluding section required careful phrasing. Pompey needed to convey urgency without seeming desperate, authority without arrogance.

'I place the defence of Brundisium and the success of our evacuation entirely in your capable hands. You have my complete confidence, as you had in Pontus and Armenia when we faced enemies who thought us beaten. We overcame them then through discipline and courage, and we will overcome Caesar now through the same virtues.'

He added final instructions about maintaining communication, establishing signal stations along the coast, preparing evacuation procedures for civilians who wished to leave. Then he gave the closing:

'The Senate and People of Rome depend upon you. Do not fail them. Written at Capua, in the third year of my third consulship, by my own hand.'

The last phrase was traditional but important. It confirmed that the message came directly from Pompey himself, not filtered through subordinates or faction.

'Add my personal seal,' said Pompey. 'And find your fastest rider. I want this in Varus's hands within two days.'

Theophanes wrote quickly, his practised hand transforming speech into the formal Latin of military correspondence. When he finished, he read the letter back to Pompey, who listened carefully and made only minor

101

corrections. Then the secretary heated wax and affixed Pompey's seal, the lion that had been his personal symbol since the eastern campaigns.

'There is one more thing,' said Pompey as Theophanes prepared to leave. 'Write to my wife. Tell her I am well, that she should prepare the household for a journey, and that I will send for her when arrangements are complete. Tell her...'

He stopped, uncertain what he wanted to say. That he was sorry for bringing her into this disaster? That he feared what was coming? That he sometimes wondered if Caesar had been right all along, and they were simply old men clinging to power they no longer deserved?

'Tell her I love her,' he said finally. 'And that everything will be well.'

It was a lie, but a kind one, and Theophanes wrote it down without comment.

When the secretary left, Pompey stood alone in the small room and allowed himself a moment of doubt. He was almost sixty years old, his body aching from the hard ride south, his mind exhausted from days of crisis and decision.

He had conquered half the known world, earned three triumphs, and served three consulships. He had thought himself retired, his glory secured, his position unassailable, but instead, he found himself fleeing from a man he had once called friend, preparing to abandon Italia itself to save what remained of his cause. The Republic he claimed to defend was dying, and he was not certain it could be saved even if they won the war.

But these doubts could not be spoken aloud, not to his officers, not to the Senate, not even to himself most of the time. So he buried them deep and went to the window, looking out at Capua sleeping under the stars.

Somewhere to the north, Caesar was eating a civilised meal in a peaceful Rome, while somewhere to the south, Varus was would soon receive orders that would shape the course of the war. And here, in this comfortable house in this wealthy city, Pompey Magnus stood alone with his thoughts and wondered how it had all gone so wrong.

Tomorrow he would be the confident general again, the saviour of the Republic, the man who never doubted or feared. But tonight, just for the briefest of moments, he experienced the slightest flutter of an emotion he had buried on eastern battle fields many years earlier… *fear.*

Chapter Ten

Rome

The days following Caesar's entry into Rome settled into a pattern of careful diplomacy and quiet preparation. He moved through the city like a physician tending a sick patient, speaking soft words whilst administering bitter medicine, always careful to maintain the fiction that everything remained normal even as the Republic fractured around them.

Marcus watched him work with a soldier's admiration for efficient command. Caesar understood that battles could be won without swords, that sometimes the appearance of legitimacy mattered more than its substance, and that frightened men needed reassurance more than they needed truth.

The morning visits began early, Caesar rising before dawn to make his rounds of the magistrates and senators who had remained in the city. There were perhaps fifty of them, men too old or too cautious or too poor to flee south with Pompey, and Caesar treated each one as though his opinion carried the weight of the full Senate.

Marcus accompanied him on these visits, along with a small escort that was more ceremonial than protective. They would arrive at a magistrate's house, be received with nervous courtesy, and then Caesar would spend an hour discussing grain supplies or aqueduct maintenance or some other mundane detail of civic administration as though civil war was not consuming Italia.

'The Aqua Marcia needs attention,' said Decimus Flavius, a minor aedile whose family had served Rome for generations. 'The eastern section shows signs of deterioration.'

'Then it shall have attention,' said Caesar, making a note on the wax tablet he carried. 'Marcus Antonius will arrange for engineers to inspect it tomorrow. We cannot allow Rome's water supply to fail simply because ambitious men have forgotten their duty to the people.'

The careful phrasing was typical. Caesar always spoke of others' failures, never his own actions. He was the restorer, the protector, the man who remained loyal to Rome whilst others betrayed it. The magistrates wanted desperately to believe him, because the alternative was to acknowledge that they served a conqueror.

They visited the grain commissioners next, elderly men who managed Rome's food supply with the careful precision of accountants. Caesar assured them that his own stores remained available, that ships from Sicily and Africa would continue arriving, and that no citizen would starve whilst he held authority in the city.

'But Magnus controls the treasury,' said one commissioner quietly. 'Without funds, we cannot purchase grain at the usual rates.'

'Then we shall find other arrangements,' said Caesar. 'I have resources of my own, earned through years of service in Gaul. Those resources belong to Rome, and Rome shall have them. Let no man say that Caesar allowed the people to suffer for lack of bread.'

The commissioners nodded, needing to believe, because their world had narrowed to the simple question of whether the city would eat.

The pattern continued through the day. Visits to priests who worried about the sacred chickens and the proper observance of festivals, meetings with the praetors who still administered justice in the law courts, and consultations with the urban cohorts' commander about security and the prevention of looting.

Caesar listened more than he spoke, asked questions that showed respect for expertise, and made promises that sounded reasonable rather than grandiose. He was building something, Marcus realised, a network of small loyalties and practical dependencies that would bind Rome to him more surely than any garrison.

They returned to Caesar's house in the late afternoon, both men exhausted from hours of political performance. Balbus waited with dispatches from the south, his face grave as he handed them to Caesar.

'Capua,' said Balbus simply.

Caesar read in silence, his expression revealing nothing, then passed the tablets to Marcus. The news was not good. Pompey had established himself firmly in Capua, the city's wealth and position making it an ideal base. More importantly, his recruitment efforts were succeeding beyond what anyone had expected. Veterans from his eastern campaigns, young men seeking glory, even some serving soldiers from the scattered garrison posts of Italia. They were gathering in Capua by the hundreds, and Pompey's officers were training them into something that might become an army.

'He moves faster than I anticipated,' said Caesar quietly. 'I had hoped the shock of flight would slow his preparations, but Magnus remembers his craft.'

'Will he stand at Capua?' asked Marcus.

'No. He cannot hold Italia against us with just the one city, and he knows it. But he needs time to organise his evacuation, and every week we give him means more troops aboard his ships when he crosses to Greece.'

'Then we march south immediately.'

'Soon,' said Caesar. 'But first, Rome must be secured. I will not leave an unstable city at my back whilst pursuing Magnus across the sea.'

The evening brought more meetings, this time with businessmen and moneylenders whose support would be needed if Rome was to function without its traditional government. Caesar received them in his home's atrium, standing amongst the ancestral masks of his family, presenting himself as a patrician among equals rather than a conqueror receiving suppliants.

He made no threats, offered no bribes, simply explained the situation with the calm logic of a man discussing business. Pompey had fled, taking the treasury and the traditional magistrates. Someone needed to maintain order to ensure the food supply and keep the courts functioning. Caesar was willing to do this, but he needed their cooperation. Would they help, or would they allow the city to collapse into chaos?

They agreed, of course. What choice did they have? But Caesar made them feel as though the decision was theirs, as though they were partners in governance rather than subjects of conquest. It was masterful, and Marcus filed away the lessons for future use.

Three days passed and Marcus walked besides Caesar as he returned to his home after a long days coercion carefully disguised as negotiation. Marcus saw the discomfort in his posture as they walked through the familiar streets, the tension in his shoulders that spoke of a man who felt he should be elsewhere.

Aurelia waited in the atrium, standing in exactly the same place where she had stood the first night. She wore a simple stola, her white hair braided in the old style, and her face showed nothing of what she felt.

'Dominus,' she said formally.

'Mother,' said Caesar, and for just a moment the mask slipped and Marcus saw exhaustion in his eyes.

They ate in the triclinium, a simple meal of bread and cheese and cold meat that Aurelia served herself rather than calling slaves. Calpurnia joined them, taking her place beside Caesar with the quiet dignity she had shown throughout the crisis. Marcus sat across from them, feeling oddly intrusive in this family moment.

'The city speaks highly of you,' said Aurelia, breaking bread with steady hands. 'They say you move through Rome like Aeneas returned from Troy, bringing order from chaos.'

'They flatter,' said Caesar. 'I do only what must be done.'

'And yet you barely sleep here, in your own house, your own bed. You choose your officers' camp instead.'

It was not quite a criticism, but Caesar heard the weight behind the words. He set down his cup and looked at his mother directly.

'There is work to be done and until it is finished, I cannot rest easy in comfort whilst my men sleep on campaign cots.'

'Your men sleep in barracks with heated floors and regular meals,' said Aurelia. 'Do not pretend hardship where none exists. You avoid this house because you are uncomfortable here whilst Italia burns.'

The bluntness caught Marcus by surprise, but Caesar merely nodded slowly.

'You are not wrong. I crossed the Rubicon to save the Republic from men who would strangle it in the Senate house. But doing so made me an outlaw in the eyes of those same men, and everything I touch now carries the stain of rebellion. Even returning to my own home feels like claiming a prize I have not yet earned.'

'Then earn it,' said Aurelia simply. 'Win your war, settle your accounts with Magnus, and come home with clean hands. But do not pretend that sleeping in military quarters makes you more virtuous. It only makes you tired.'

Calpurnia reached across and took Caesar's hand, a small gesture of support that needed no words. He smiled at her, some of the tension leaving his face, then turned back to his mother.

'I will try to visit more frequently. But I make no promises. Events move quickly, and I must move with them.'

'I ask nothing more,' said Aurelia. 'Only that you remember this house still stands, and your family waits here when you have time to be something other than Imperator.'

They finished the meal in a more comfortable silence, and afterwards Caesar spent an hour in his study attending to correspondence whilst Marcus waited in the atrium. When they finally left to return to the camp, Caesar paused at the threshold and looked back at the house that had been his home for decades.

'She is right, you know,' he said quietly. 'About the discomfort. I built this life, this family, this place in Rome. And now I risk destroying it all to save a Republic that may not survive regardless of who wins.'

'Then why continue?' asked Marcus.

'Because the alternative is to let men like Cato and Bibulus tear it apart through their own rigidity and hatred.' Caesar stepped out into the street. 'At least if I destroy the Republic, it will be in the process of building something better.

If they destroy it, nothing will remain but ashes and regret.'

The main camp had been established in the Campus Martius, the broad field outside the city walls where Rome's armies traditionally gathered before campaigns. Marcus had spent the past three days transforming a parade ground into something resembling a proper military installation, and the results showed in the neat rows of tents and the ordered bustle of soldiers going about their duties.

The Thirteenth Legion had accompanied Caesar from Gaul, veteran soldiers who had served through eight years of brutal campaigning and learned their craft in forests and sieges from the Rhine to the Atlantic. But one legion was not enough to hold Italia, much less pursue Pompey across the sea, and so Marcus had begun the careful work of expansion.

He walked the camp perimeter at dawn, inspecting the watch posts and the equipment storage, making mental notes about what needed adjustment. The sentries saluted as he passed, their discipline showing the Thirteenth's quality. These were men who understood that military routine mattered, that small details prevented large disasters, that an army was only as strong as its least prepared soldier.

The recruitment centre occupied a corner of the camp where the Via Flaminia entered the field. A wooden platform had been erected, and behind it stood a series of tables where scribes recorded names and assessed fitness. Marcus had stationed his most impressive-looking soldiers nearby, veterans whose bearing and equipment would inspire young men considering military service.

The response had been modest but steady. Rome's urban population was not particularly martial, and most citizens viewed military service as something best left to the poor and desperate. But enough had come forward to begin filling out a cohort, and more arrived each day as word spread that Caesar paid well and treated his soldiers fairly.

Marcus stood on the platform and watched them come. Farmers' sons seeking escape from failing land, craftsmen whose businesses had collapsed in the economic chaos and young men looking for glory or simply for regular meals and military pay. He evaluated each one with the practised eye of a career soldier, separating those who might become legionaries from those who would never survive the training.

'You there,' he called to a broad-shouldered youth who moved with an athlete's grace. 'Ever used a sword?'

'In the ludus, Praefect. Training only.'

'Good enough. Report to the third table. You,' he gestured to another candidate, this one older and scarred, 'where did you serve?'

'Eighth Legion, Praefect. Seven years in Hispania under the elder Magnus. Discharged three years past.'

'Why enlist again?'

The veteran shrugged.

'Farming didn't suit me. And I heard Caesar pays in actual coin rather than promises.'

Marcus grinned.

'That he does. Second table, ask for Centurion Vorenus. Tell him I sent you, and that you have experience. We need men who can train recruits.'

The work continued through the morning, a steady stream of Rome's cast-offs and surplus sons transforming into the raw material of military power. It was slow, inefficient work compared to simply requisitioning trained soldiers from existing units, but those units were scattered across the Republic and many of uncertain loyalty. Better to build from scratch than to rely on men whose hearts might still belong to Pompey.

By midday, Marcus had processed perhaps fifty new recruits and identified three veterans suitable for immediate promotion to junior ranks. He turned the operation over to Vorenus and made his way to the principia, the command tent where Caesar conducted the legion's business.

He found the Imperator surrounded by maps and correspondence, tracing routes with one finger whilst dictating orders to a scribe. Labienus stood nearby, Caesar's most trusted legate and the man who had commanded the cavalry in Gaul. They looked up as Marcus entered.

'How many today?' asked Caesar without preamble.

'Fifty-two enrolled, forty-three accepted. Nine failed the physical standards. We also gained three experienced men suitable for training duties.'

'Good,' said Caesar, though his attention remained on the maps. 'Continue the effort, but prepare the Thirteenth for immediate march. We move south within three days.'

Marcus stepped closer to examine the maps spread across the table. They showed Italia's southern regions, the Via Appia traced in red ink, and various markers indicating reported positions of forces.

'Magnus gathers his strength at Capua,' said Caesar, pointing to the city's position on the map. 'My scouts report at least three thousand men under arms there now, with more arriving daily. But he does not fortify, he moves supplies towards Brundisium.'

'Evacuation,' said Labienus immediately. 'He prepares to cross to Greece.'

'Undoubtedly.' Caesar's finger traced the route from

Capua to the port city on Italia's southeastern coast. 'Brundisium is the only viable harbour for moving an army across the Adriatic. If Magnus reaches it with his forces intact, he escapes to Greece, gathers the eastern legions, and returns with overwhelming strength.'

'Then we must march now,' said Marcus. 'Catch him before he reaches the port.'

'We march, yes. But catching him?' Caesar's expression was thoughtful. 'Magnus has almost a month's head start and moves with purpose. We pursue with a single legion and even if we match his pace, we will arrive at Brundisium to find him already fortifying the harbour approaches.'

'A siege, then,' said Labienus. 'Block the harbour, and prevent the evacuation.'

'Perhaps.' Caesar rolled up one map and selected another, this one showing Brundisium's harbour and the surrounding coastline. 'But Magnus has the advantage of time. Every day we besiege Brundisium is another day his eastern forces gather strength. Every week gives him more ships and more opportunity to slip away.'

Marcus studied the map, seeing the problem. Brundisium sat on a narrow peninsula, easily defended, with access to the sea on multiple sides. Blocking such a port completely would require forces Caesar did not possess.

'What are your orders, Dominus?' he asked.

'We march south and pursue Magnus to Brundisium. We will make the attempt to prevent his escape, because we must be seen to try, but we also prepare for what comes after, when Magnus crosses to Greece and we face a longer war than anyone anticipated.'

'The recruitment,' said Marcus, understanding now why Caesar had delayed their departure from Rome.

'The recruitment, yes. Every man we enlist now is one fewer for Magnus's agents to recruit later. Every day we hold Rome, we strengthen our position in Italia whilst Magnus weakens his and when he finally crosses to Greece, he leaves behind a peninsula that remembers we brought order whilst he brought flight.'

It was political calculation dressed in military necessity, and Marcus recognised Caesar's genius in seeing both dimensions simultaneously. The war would not be won only on battlefields but in the perceptions of towns and cities, and in the loyalty of soldiers and citizens.

That evening, Caesar invited Marcus to dine in his command tent, a simple meal served on campaign ware that made no pretensions to luxury. They ate in comfortable silence, both men tired from the day's work, until Caesar set down his cup and fixed Marcus with an appraising look.

'You questioned the recruitment earlier?' said Caesar. It was not an accusation, merely an observation.

'I wonder at its necessity,' admitted Marcus. 'You have five legions in Gaul, Dominus. Veteran troops who know you and have fought under your command. Why recruit inexperienced men in Rome when you could simply summon them south and march on Capua with overwhelming force?'

'Because moving five legions from Gaul takes time,' said Caesar. 'Months, possibly, to gather them, march them over the Alps, and position them where they are needed. Magnus moves now, and we must move with him or lose the chance to prevent his escape.'

'But we cannot prevent it with the Thirteenth alone.'

'We can't. But we must make the attempt anyway, because to do nothing is to sow the seeds of doubt amongst those who watch. In the meantime, my legates in Gaul will begin moving reinforcements south. Some will reach us before Brundisium, others will secure northern Italia, but all will be in position when we need them for whatever comes next.'

Marcus considered the strategy, seeing the layers of planning that extended beyond the immediate crisis. Caesar was not simply reacting to Pompey's movements but positioning forces for a campaign that might last months or years.

'The men sense something larger is at play,' said Marcus carefully. 'They know we march south, but they wonder why the urgency if Magnus simply flees to Greece.'

'The men need not know everything,' said Caesar mildly. 'They need only to trust that I do. When the time comes to explain strategy, I will reveal it. Until then, they march where I command and fight when I order, and that discipline is what separates legionaries from armed mobs.'

It was a gentle rebuke, and Marcus accepted it with a nod. Caesar's methods had won Gaul and brought him from the Rhine to Rome. Questioning those methods served no purpose beyond satisfying curiosity.

They finished the meal in silence, and Marcus left with more questions than answers, but also with a soldier's faith in his commander. Caesar had brought them this far. He would bring them the rest of the way, wherever that led.

Outside the tent, soldiers prepared for the night, checking equipment and sharing meals, talking in the low voices of military men relaxing between duties. They did not know where they would march or what battles waited ahead. They knew only that Caesar commanded them, and for soldiers of the Thirteenth Legion, that knowledge was enough.

Chapter Eleven

Corfinium

The town sat in the valley like a clenched fist, its walls ancient but well-maintained, its gates barred against the world. Corfinium had been a Roman settlement for generations, a prosperous market town where the roads from the interior met the route to the Adriatic coast. Now it had become something else, a fortress held by Lucius Domitius Ahenobarbus in Pompey's name, representing the first real obstacle to Caesar's advance south.

The Thirteenth Legion had marched south from Rome in forced stages, covering the distance in less time than Marcus had thought possible. Caesar drove them hard, understanding that speed mattered more than comfort, and that every day delayed gave Pompey more time to strengthen his position or complete his escape.

Behind them, in northern Italia, the Twelfth Legion followed at a steady pace, and further north, the Eighth was marching down from Gaul with supplies and reinforcements.

Marcus stood on a low hill overlooking Corfinium and assessed its defences with a professional eye. The walls were perhaps twenty feet high, built of good stone, with towers at intervals that would allow defenders to enfilade any assault. A small river provided water, and the gates were reinforced with timber and iron. Nothing spectacular, but solid work that would cost lives to overcome.

'Domitius chose well,' said Balbus, standing beside Marcus. 'The town can be supplied from the east, the walls are sound, and he has sufficient men to man them properly.'

'How many do you reckon?' asked Marcus.

'Intelligence suggests thirty cohorts, but our spies report perhaps no more than ten thousand under arms, a mix of veterans and recruits. Domitius commands personally, with several senators who fled Rome with Magnus. They believe Corfinium can hold until Magnus brings relief from Capua.'

Marcus looked south towards where Pompey's main force reportedly gathered.

'Do you think he will come?'

'That depends on what Magnus values more, Domitius and his senators, or his own escape route to Brundisium. Were I Magnus, I would already be planning evacuation rather than relief.'

The war council met that evening in a requisitioned farmhouse a mile from the town. Caesar sat at the head of a rough table, surrounded by his senior officers and the maps that had guided their march. Torches provided light, and the smell of the evening meal still lingered in the air.

'Corfinium blocks our advance,' said Caesar without preamble, 'and we cannot leave ten thousand enemy soldiers at our backs whilst we pursue Magnus to Brundisium. Therefore, we must reduce the town.'

Labienus leaned over the map, tracing the approaches with one finger.

'A direct assault would be costly. The walls are defensible, and Domitius has sufficient men to contest every section. We could lose hundreds taking it by storm.'

'Then we do not assault,' said Caesar. 'We besiege. We cut the town off completely, prevent resupply, and wait for our reinforcements to arrive.

'That could take weeks,' objected one of the tribunes, a

young man whose family connections had earned him his rank. 'Magnus approaches Brundisium with every day we delay.'

'Let him reach it,' said Caesar calmly. 'I would rather have Magnus flee to Greece than fight a major battle on Italian soil. Civil war between Romans is tragedy enough without adding wholesale slaughter to the account. And every day that Domitius watches more men arrive while Magnus sends nothing, our position strengthens and his weakens.'

The tent fell silent and Marcus watched faces around the table, seeing the calculations behind every expression. Some officers wanted glory, the kind that came from storming walls and winning heroic victories, while others understood Caesar's deeper strategy, that this war would be won through clemency and political positioning as much as through military force.

'Marcus,' said Caesar, turning to face him directly. 'You will command the siege works. Construct towers if needed, but do not assault unless I give explicit orders. I want Domitius to understand he faces professional siege craft from multiple legions, not impulsive attack from a single force. Fear makes better weapons than battering rams against men who doubt their cause.'

But our support is still weeks away,' said Marcus.

'We know that,' said Caesar, 'but Domitius does not. We will also spread the rumours that the other two legions are only days away.'

The meeting continued with logistics and assignments, the routine details that transformed strategic decisions into practical action. Marcus listened with half his attention, already planning the siege works in his mind, calculating strengths, weaknesses, distances and the placement of artillery.

When the council ended and officers dispersed to their duties, Caesar called Marcus back.

'I will be writing letters,' said Caesar quietly. 'To Magnus, to Domitius, and to the Senate in Capua. I will again offer terms explaining my position, making the case for negotiation rather than continued conflict. I expect no response, but the letters must be sent. History should record that Caesar sought peace whilst others chose war.'

'You believe they will refuse?'

'I am certain of it. Cato and his faction control the Senate's mood, and they would rather die than compromise with what they consider tyranny. But the letters serve their purpose regardless of response. Every man in Corfinium will know I offered clemency and every soldier in Magnus's army will hear that Caesar prefers reconciliation to revenge. When the war ends, and men ask who was reasonable and who was rigid, the letters will provide the answers.'

The siege began the next morning and Marcus divided the Thirteenth into work parties, each assigned a section of the circumvallation that would eventually surround Corfinium. The work progressed rapidly despite the cold weather, but the single legion was stretched dangerously thin across a perimeter meant for three times their number. By evening, the positioning was complete, though gaps remained that a determined sortie could exploit.

Domitius responded by lining his walls with soldiers, a show of strength meant to intimidate the besiegers. Marcus watched from his command post and counted standards, estimating numbers and assessing morale. The defenders looked well-equipped and reasonably disciplined, but there was something uncertain in their posture, a quality that suggested they were not entirely committed to their situation.

'They expected Magnus to relieve them,' observed

Balbus, standing beside Marcus as they watched the walls. 'Now they see legionaries surrounding them and no doubt will have heard rumours of more forces marching south. I suspect they begin to doubt their ability to defend the city.'

'Let them believe reinforcements are close behind us,' said Marcus. 'The Twelfth is still weeks away, but Domitius does not know that. Doubt spreads faster than confidence in a besieged garrison. Give them a few more days of watching our works grow and they will question why they fight at all.'

Caesar's letters went out daily, carried by heralds under flags of truce to Corfinium's gates. Each time, the response was the same, Domitius refused to receive them. But Marcus noticed that the refusals took longer each day, as though discussion occurred before rejection, as though some within the walls questioned their commander's stubbornness.

Some of the senators who had fled Rome with Pompey had established themselves in the town's better houses, maintaining the privileges of rank even in their reduced circumstances. They held councils in a basilica near the forum, debated strategy and made plans for the triumphant return to Rome they believed was imminent.

'Magnus gathers his forces at Capua,' declared Quintus Caecilius, a senator whose family had opposed Caesar for generations. 'Any day now, we will see his standards on the horizon, and this pretender Caesar will flee back to his Gallic forests.'

Only Domitius seemed to grasp the reality of their situation and he stood at the basilica's edge, watching the debates with an expression that revealed nothing of his thoughts. He was a capable soldier, experienced in warfare, and he understood what professional siege craft meant for a garrison of uncertain quality.

That evening, he climbed to the walls and looked out at the Roman lines. Torches marked the siege works, revealing the systematic construction that continued even after dark. Caesar worked his men in shifts, maintaining continuous pressure, demonstrating that time favoured the besiegers rather than the besieged.

Behind Domitius, his officers waited for orders that did not come. They asked about sorties, about attempts to break through the lines, about sending messengers to Pompey requesting urgent assistance. Domitius answered each question with patience he did not feel, explaining that there was a second experienced legion only hours away and if they marched into battle, Pompey might not be able to spare forces for relief.

What he did not say was that he suspected Pompey had already abandoned them, that the great Magnus was preparing his own escape and had written off Corfinium as an acceptable loss. That admission would destroy what remained of his garrison's morale, so Domitius kept silent and watched the siege works grow.

Over the next week, Marcus established a routine of patrols and inspections, maintaining pressure without exhausting his men. Towers grew taller, approaches crept closer to Corfinium's walls, and artillery positions took shape that would allow bombardment when Caesar gave the order.

The eventual arrival of the Twelfth Legion brought the siege to full strength, and Caesar deployed them to secure supply lines and provide fresh troops for the encirclement.

But the order for assault did not come. Instead, Caesar wrote more letters, sent more heralds, and made more offers of clemency to anyone who surrendered. The psychological pressure mounted steadily, undermined by the visible presence of two full legions surrounding the town, a force that made resistance seem futile rather than heroic.

On the twentieth day, the first deserters appeared. They came at night, three soldiers who lowered themselves from the walls on ropes and ran towards the Roman lines with hands raised. The sentries brought them to Marcus, who questioned them briefly before sending them to Caesar.

'The garrison argues amongst itself,' reported the senior deserter, an older man who had served under Pompey in previous campaigns. 'Domitius wants to fight, but the senators are afraid of defeat and insist relief is coming. The soldiers watch your legions dig and build and wait, but we realise the truth, that Magnus is not coming and every day, more men speak of opening the gates and accepting Caesar's terms.'

'What stopped you until now?' asked Marcus.

'Fear of Domitius. But tonight we decided fear of dying in a hopeless siege outweighed fear of punishment. Better to take our chances with Caesar's offered mercy than wait for Magnus's relief that will never arrive.'

More deserters followed over the subsequent nights. Never in large groups, and always cautiously, but the trickle was constant and demoralising for those who remained. Marcus recorded each desertion, noting details about garrison strength and morale, building a picture of an increasingly desperate situation within Corfinium's walls.

Caesar received many of the deserters personally, questioned them about conditions inside the town, then sent them to the rear with instructions to join the recruitment camps. His clemency was genuine, witnessed by the entire army, and the message spread, surrender to Caesar meant life, not death.

On the twenty-fifth day, Corfinium's gates finally opened. It happened without warning, the great timber doors swinging wide in the early morning to reveal a delegation of officers and senators standing in the gateway with hands raised in submission. Marcus, alerted by sentries, rode forward with a century of soldiers, approaching cautiously in case this was some stratagem.

'We seek Caesar,' called the lead officer, a grey-haired man whose uniform marked him as one of Domitius's senior subordinates. 'We wish to discuss terms of surrender.'

Marcus sent riders to fetch Caesar whilst maintaining watch on the open gates. Behind the delegation, he could see Corfinium's streets, soldiers standing in uncertain groups, townspeople watching from windows and doorways, the whole settlement holding its breath whilst it waited to learn its fate.

Caesar arrived within the hour, riding unhurried to the gates as though this was expected rather than surprising. He dismounted before the delegation and stood facing them with an expression of courteous attention.

'You wish to discuss surrender?' he asked.

'We wish to surrender,' corrected the grey-haired officer. 'Domitius commanded resistance, but the senators voted to end the siege. We have placed Domitius under arrest and offer him to you for judgement. The town submits to your authority and we ask only that you honour your promises of clemency.'

Caesar glanced at Marcus, who nodded fractionally. This was legitimate, not a trap. The delegation represented real authority, and behind them stood an exhausted garrison that had lost faith in its cause.

'Your surrender is accepted,' said Caesar formally. 'The garrison will stack arms in the forum and march out in good order. They will be split into smaller units and guarded until I decide what to do with them. Officers will report to my headquarters for individual assessment and Domitius will be held pending trial. The townspeople will not be harmed, and no looting will be permitted. Are these terms acceptable?'

'They are, Dominus.'

'Then see them implemented. Marcus, establish patrols throughout the town. I want discipline maintained at all times. Any soldier caught stealing or threatening civilians will be crucified. Make that very clear to the men.'

The surrender unfolded with surprising order. Corfinium's garrison marched out through the gates in formation, maintaining military bearing even in defeat then stood in ranks whilst Caesar addressed them.

Marcus watched from the side as Caesar delivered a speech that was partly military, partly political, and entirely calculated to win hearts rather than simply accept submission.

'You surrendered because you were abandoned,' Caesar began, his voice carrying across the field. 'Domitius told you Pompey would bring relief, but Pompey chose his own escape over your survival. You held these walls courageously for twenty-five days against two legions, but courage without support becomes mere stubbornness, and I do not punish men for their commanders' failures.'

He paced before the assembled soldiers, making eye contact with individuals, personalising the message.

'I offer you a choice. Return to your homes if you wish. I will provide travel permits and a small sum to ease your journey, or you can join my legions and serve under commanders who do not abandon their soldiers. Either choice is honourable and either choice is yours to make freely.'

The speech continued, but Marcus already knew its effect. These men would remember that Caesar offered mercy whilst Pompey offered abandonment. Some would go home, certainly, but many would stay, and those who stayed would carry the message of Caesar's clemency to every town they passed.

The following day, Domitius was brought forward under guard, his face set in an expression of grim resignation. He had commanded well, maintained discipline, and done everything a competent officer should do, his only failure had been trusting that Pompey would support him. Caesar spoke with him privately, and afterwards Domitius was escorted to the rear under light guard rather than chains. The message was clear, even enemy commanders received honourable treatment under Caesar's command.

The senators who had fled to Corfinium received similar treatment, though their expressions suggested they had expected harsher terms. Caesar met with each one individually, listened to their justifications and excuses, then granted them safe passage to wherever they wished to go. Some chose to remain with Caesar's forces while others requested permission to join Pompey in Capua. Caesar granted both requests with equal grace.

'They will tell Magnus what happened here,' observed Balbus as they watched the senators depart under escort. 'They will describe your clemency, your strength, and the efficiency with which two legions conducted this siege. That intelligence costs you nothing but gains everything.'

'Information travels in all directions,' agreed Caesar. 'Let Magnus hear that I conquered Corfinium without losing a single man. Let him wonder how many of his garrisons will resist when surrender brings life rather than death.'

The legions rested in Corfinium for two days, absorbing supplies and integrating willing volunteers from the captured garrison. Marcus used the time to reorganise his forces, promoting capable men from the ranks and establishing the disciplined structure that would be needed for continued campaigning.

Meanwhile, scouts brought news from the south. Capua had emptied and Pompey's forces, rather than marching north to relieve Corfinium, had withdrawn towards Brundisium. The great evacuation had begun, and every day brought more senators and soldiers streaming towards the port city where ships waited to carry them across the Adriatic.

'He abandons Italia,' said Labienus when Caesar shared the intelligence with his senior officers. 'Magnus concedes the peninsula rather than fight for it.'

'He makes the practical choice,' said Caesar. 'He cannot match our pace or our clemency. Every day he remains in Italia, more towns surrender, more soldiers defect, and more of his support dissolves. Better to cross to Greece, gather the eastern legions, and return with overwhelming force than to die slowly of political attrition here.'

'Then I assume we march for Brundisium immediately,' said Marcus, 'and prevent the evacuation before it completes.'

'We march, yes, but prevent?' Caesar's expression suggested doubt. 'Magnus has too much advantage. He will probably complete his evacuation before we arrive but we must make the attempt, because to do nothing would suggest acceptance of his escape.'

The legions departed Corfinium on the third day, leaving a small garrison to maintain order and moved south with renewed urgency. They marched hard, covering twenty miles per day, pushing through towns that barely had time to register their passage before the standards disappeared towards the horizon.

Capua, when they reached it, stood empty of military forces. The city remained inhabited, its markets functioning, its citizens going about their business, but Pompey's army had departed days earlier and the treasury had gone with him.

Caesar paused only long enough to establish civil administration, appointing local magistrates and ensuring grain distribution continued, then pressed south towards Brundisium with both legions moving in coordinated columns.

The legions' mood had shifted subtly. Marcus noticed it in the way men talked around evening fires, in the questions centurions asked during morning briefings, and in the glances cast towards Caesar's tent where strategies were planned beyond the soldiers' knowledge.

They had their victories, Corfinium surrendered, Capua abandoned, and every town between Rome and the Adriatic secured for Caesar's control. But these were not the kind of victories that earned triumphs or inspired songs. Two legions had marched the length of Italia without fighting a single major engagement, and the soldiers were beginning to wonder when their service would earn the recognition they believed it deserved.

'They want blood,' observed Balbus one evening as he and Marcus inspected the camp. 'Not just surrenders and clemency, but actual combat. Something that feels like war rather than occupation.'

'They are soldiers,' said Marcus. 'They understand that battles won without fighting are still victories.'

'Do they?' Balbus gestured towards a group of men arguing by their tent, their voices raised in frustration. 'Listen to them. They speak of missing the glory, of watching enemies flee rather than stand, of wondering whether Caesar fears battle or simply refuses to give it to them.'

Marcus listened and heard the truth in Balbus's assessment. The grumbling was not yet serious, not yet threatening to discipline, but it existed and it would grow. Soldiers needed more than pay and good commanders, they needed purpose and recognition that their service mattered in ways that would be remembered.

'What would you recommend?' he asked.

'Give them what they want. A battle, a siege, something that requires real courage and produces real glory. Or failing that, make clear that the campaign's end approaches and their patience serves a purpose beyond Caesar's political calculations.'

It was good advice, and Marcus carried it to Caesar that night, explaining the mood in careful terms that balanced respect for the men with recognition of their growing frustration.

Caesar listened without interruption, then nodded slowly.

'They are right to feel cheated,' he said. 'I have asked three legions to march the length of Italia whilst our enemies flee before them. I have given them sieges that end in surrender and pursuits that end in empty cities. They deserve better, and they shall have it. But not here, not in Italia if I can prevent it. When we cross to Greece, when we face Magnus with his eastern legions, then they will have their battles. Then they will earn the glory they seek but until that day, they must trust that I preserve them for a greater purpose.'

'Should I tell them this?' asked Marcus.

'Not yet. Let them grumble. Let them complain about lack of glory and missed opportunities. Soldiers who are slightly dissatisfied march harder than soldiers who are content. But watch for signs of real discontent, and if it appears, come to me immediately. An army that doubts its commander is more dangerous than any enemy force.'

Chapter Twelve

Brundisium

Four days later, the harbour lay before them like a knife wound in Italia's coast, a deep natural inlet protected by headlands and perfectly positioned for controlling maritime traffic across the Adriatic. Brundisium had served Rome for centuries as the gateway to Greece, and now it would serve Pompey Magnus in his flight from Italia.

Marcus stood on the hillside as twilight faded to darkness and watched the harbour below. Ships crowded the anchorage, dozens of them, their masts creating a forest of timber that swayed with the evening tide and torches burned along the waterfront, revealing the organised chaos of an army preparing to evacuate. Wagons rolled towards the docks, soldiers marched in formation towards waiting vessels, and somewhere in that confusion Pompey Magnus directed the exodus that would carry the Senate and its remaining forces across the sea.

'We are too late,' said Balbus quietly, standing beside Marcus. 'The evacuation is too well advanced.'

'How many ships do you reckon?' asked Marcus.

'Difficult to count in this light, but at least sixty. Perhaps more anchored beyond the harbour entrance. Enough to carry ten thousand men with supplies and equipment. Magnus planned this carefully.'

Caesar rode up the hill to join them, his expression revealing nothing as he surveyed the scene below. He sat motionless on his horse for a long moment, studying the harbour's layout, the positions of ships, the activity on the docks.

'We cannot prevent the evacuation,' he said eventually, 'but we can make it difficult, and show them that even in retreat, they face an enemy who refuses to simply watch and accept.'

'What are your orders, Dominus?' asked Marcus.

'Surround the town and establish siege lines. Then we build moles.'

'Moles?' Balbus looked up, confusion evident in his voice.

'Moles,' confirmed Caesar. 'Barriers extending from both headlands into the harbour mouth. We narrow the entrance to restrict ship movements, and create obstacles that force Magnus to navigate carefully rather than sail freely. It will not stop him, but it will complicate his evacuation, perhaps even trap some vessels that move too slowly.'

Marcus studied the harbour's geography, seeing what Caesar described. The entrance was perhaps five hundred paces wide where it opened to the sea. Narrow enough that substantial barriers projecting from each headland would create a bottleneck, forcing ships to navigate a restricted channel whilst under observation and potentially under fire.

'That will require extensive construction,' said Marcus. 'Timber, stone, countless work hours. We are speaking of structures extending hundreds of feet into deep water.'

'Yes,' said Caesar simply. 'Which is why we begin immediately. Divide the legions into work parties. Half maintain the siege lines around Brundisium's landward walls. Half construct the moles. I reckon we have perhaps two weeks before Magnus completes his evacuation and I want those moles substantially complete before his last ship departs.'

The orders went out that night, and by dawn the work had begun. Marcus had engineered all sorts of fortifications across Gaul under Caesar's command, but the moles at Brundisium presented unique challenges. Standard siege works involved earth and timber on solid ground. Moles required building into water, creating stable structures that would withstand waves and current whilst extending far enough to meaningfully restrict the harbour entrance.

He divided the work into sections, each supervised by experienced engineers who had built bridges and towers and fortifications in every terrain Gaul offered. The principle was straightforward: drive timber pilings into the seabed, create a framework, then fill the gaps with stone and rubble to form a barrier that ships could not pass. But the execution proved more difficult than the principle suggested.

The work began on both headlands simultaneously, the crews attacking the task with the systematic efficiency that characterised Roman military engineering. They started where land met water, digging foundations and setting the first pilings in shallow depths. The timber came from forests inland, entire trees dragged to the coast by oxen and processed by work parties who stripped branches and shaped points.

The pilings were massive, each one requiring teams of men to manoeuvre into position. They were driven into the seabed using pile drivers, wooden frameworks that lifted heavy weights and dropped them repeatedly onto the piling tops until the timbers sank deep enough to hold firm. The work was exhausting, dangerous, and essential.

As the moles extended into deeper water, the challenges multiplied, and the frameworks became more complex, requiring platforms built over existing work to provide stable surfaces for the pile drivers. Waves complicated everything, turning routine tasks into struggles against water that refused to cooperate with Roman engineering.

Marcus supervised from a command post on the northern headland, watching both moles grow with agonising slowness. The soldiers worked in shifts, fresh crews replacing exhausted ones every four hours, maintaining continuous progress through days and nights. Torches burned after dark, revealing the skeletal structures extending into the harbour like fingers reaching towards each other across the gap.

From Brundisium's walls, Pompey's soldiers watched the construction with fascination and growing concern. Some shouted insults across the water, while others simply watched in silence, recognising professional engineering when they saw it.

Within Brundisium, the mood had shifted from confident evacuation to anxious urgency. The senators who, as usual, had established themselves in the city's better houses now spent their days watching the harbour waiting for the next empty ships to arrive, and wondering if the evacuation would be complete before Caesar's moles closed the entrance entirely. Their earlier confidence had evaporated, replaced by the bitter understanding that even Pompey's escape would be contested and reduced to a race against Caesar's engineering.

They gathered in groups along the waterfront, arguing about priorities and precedence, each one trying to ensure his household and possessions secured places aboard the departing vessels. Slaves loaded trunks onto wagons that would carry senators' wealth across the Adriatic and officers shouted orders that competed with other officers' contradictory commands. The evacuation, though organised at the strategic level, descended into chaos in its details.

Pompey stood apart from the confusion, watching the harbour entrance where Caesar's moles grew daily. He had expected pursuit and he had prepared for siege, but this patient, methodical construction demonstrated something more threatening than simple military pressure. It showed that Caesar would not simply accept Pompey's escape but would contest every advantage, create every difficulty, and pursue every opportunity to complicate his enemy's plans.

'They will not complete the moles in time,' said an officer standing beside Pompey on the harbour wall. 'We have perhaps sixty per cent of the forces already on their way to Greece and the final ships are due any day. Another week and we will be gone.'

'And if Caesar completes his moles first?' asked Pompey.

'Then some ships will be trapped, unable to navigate the restricted entrance. But most will have already sailed. Caesar gains a symbolic victory, perhaps, but we still accomplish the strategic objective of reaching Greece with our forces largely intact.'

Pompey nodded slowly, wanting to believe this assessment but troubled by what he knew of Caesar's capabilities.

'Increase the pace of embarkation,' he said. 'Double the shifts on loading, I want every man, every wagon, every piece of equipment aboard vessels within days. Let Caesar build his moles. We will be gone before they matter.'

The order went out, and Brundisium's harbour became even more chaotic as soldiers rushed to complete the evacuation. Ships departed as soon as they reached capacity, sailing through the harbour entrance whilst it remained fully navigable, carrying senators and soldiers and supplies towards Dyrrhachium where Pompey's forces would reconsolidate.

Marcus watched them go from his command post,

counting vessels, estimating capacity, and calculating how many remained. The evacuation was succeeding despite Caesar's moles, and that reality frustrated soldiers who had marched the length of Italia only to watch their enemy sail away unmolested.

'We should attack,' said one of the younger centurions, his voice carrying the frustration shared by many in the legion. 'Storm the walls and prevent the evacuation through direct action rather than building barriers that arrive too late to matter.'

'Caesar's orders are clear,' said Marcus firmly. 'We build the moles and we maintain the siege. What we don't do is attack.'

'Then we accomplish nothing whilst Magnus escapes.'

'We accomplish what the Imperator orders accomplished, that is what soldiers do. Question your orders again, and you will find yourself digging latrines until I decide otherwise.'

The rebuke was harsh but necessary. The men needed an outlet for their frustration, but it would not be found in questioning Caesar's strategy.

By the eighth day, the northern mole extended perhaps two hundred feet into the harbour, a substantial barrier built of timber and stone that narrowed the entrance significantly. The southern mole, working in more difficult conditions, had reached perhaps one hundred feet. The gap between them was still wide enough for ships to pass easily, but the psychological effect was undeniable: Caesar was closing the harbour, and every ship that delayed departure risked being trapped.

Pompey responded by accelerating the evacuation even further. Ships departed in the night as well as the day, navigating by torch light, risking groundings and collisions in their haste to clear the harbour before Caesar's moles rendered escape impossible. The chaos increased, but so did the effectiveness and by the tenth day, perhaps eighty per cent of Pompey's forces had fled the harbour.

Marcus supervised construction on the northern mole, walking its length to inspect progress and encourage the exhausted soldiers. The structure had taken on impressive dimensions, a long causeway of timber and stone that projected into the harbour like a Roman road built on water. The engineering required constant attention, supports needed reinforcement, gaps needed filling, and the whole structure required maintenance against waves and weather.

Near the mole's end, where the most recent construction continued, he found a work party struggling with a particularly difficult piling. The timber had hit rock beneath the seabed and refused to sink further despite repeated blows from the pile driver. The men worked with grim determination, but frustration showed in their movements.

'Rest,' Marcus ordered. 'A new crew will bring a fresh approach.'

As the original crew withdrew, another took their place, examining the problem with fresh eyes. Marcus stayed to watch, knowing his presence encouraged the men even when he could offer no technical solutions they had not already attempted. As he watched, something heavy splashed into the water just south of the workings and a voice rang out above the noise of the workings.

'Take cover. We are under attack!'

The stones came from ships in the harbour, light artillery mounted on vessels that Pompey had positioned to harass the mole construction. The first volley fell short, splashing into the water perhaps fifty feet from the mole's end. The second came closer, one stone striking the timber framework with force enough to crack the beams.

Most men were already scrambling for cover behind the mole's bulk, the structure itself providing some protection, but work parties on the exposed end faced direct fire from vessels they could not effectively engage.

The harassment continued throughout the afternoon, ships sailing close enough to launch missiles then withdrawing before Roman artillery on the headlands could respond effectively. They killed three men in the first hour, wounded a dozen more, and halted work completely on the exposed sections.

Marcus pulled the crews back to safer positions and reported the situation to Caesar, who rode out to inspect the damage personally. They stood on the headland watching ships manoeuvre in the harbour, maintaining enough distance to be safe from land-based artillery whilst remaining close enough to threaten the mole construction.

'Magnus demonstrates that he still has teeth,' observed Caesar. 'Even in retreat, he finds ways to complicate our work. I approve of the tactical thinking, even as I regret the effect.'

'We cannot continue construction under fire,' said Marcus. 'The men are willing, but asking them to work whilst under bombardment serves no purpose beyond wasting lives.'

'Agreed. Suspend work until Magnus completes his evacuation. We have made our point. The moles need not be complete to demonstrate our determination.'

Later that night, a sortie from the town attempted to probe Caesar's siege lines, testing their strength and looking for weaknesses. The Thirteenth's sentries detected the movement quickly, and what started as reconnaissance evolved into a sharp firefight in the darkness between the walls and Caesar's fortifications.

Marcus reached the fighting with a cohort of reserves, arriving to find his soldiers engaged in close-quarters combat with Pompey's men in the no-man's-land between the forces. The darkness made coordination difficult, turning the skirmish into dozens of individual duels fought by torch light and shouted commands.

'Form up!' Marcus roared, his voice cutting through the chaos. 'Shield wall, drive them back to the gates!'

The Thirteenth's discipline reasserted itself, soldiers disengaging from individual combats and reforming into organised ranks. The shield wall advanced steadily, pushing Pompey's sortie back towards Brundisium's gates with mechanical efficiency. Some of the attackers fell, cut down as they tried to break contact while others made it back to the walls, scrambling through gates that opened briefly then slammed shut behind them.

The skirmish ended as quickly as it began, leaving perhaps a dozen dead scattered in the darkness and twice that number wounded on both sides. Marcus organised recovery parties to collect the casualties, whilst sentries resumed their posts with heightened vigilance.

The casualties were carried to the rear for treatment or burial, and the siege lines settled back into watchful waiting. But the skirmish had served a purpose for the Thirteenth's soldiers: finally, after weeks of marching and building and accepting surrenders, they had been in a real fight. Brief, inconclusive, and ultimately meaningless to the campaign's outcome, but real, nonetheless. Marcus heard the difference in the men's voices as they discussed the action, the satisfaction of having drawn blood and faced danger.

By the thirteenth day, only a rear guard remained in Brundisium, perhaps a thousand men whose task was to cover the departure of the last ships. The harbour had emptied dramatically, with most vessels already carrying their cargo across the Adriatic. A few remained at the docks, waiting for final loads, but the end was clearly approaching.

Caesar rode the siege lines daily, speaking with soldiers, inspecting fortifications, and maintaining the pressure that kept Pompey's rear guard bottled up in the town. He never spoke of the evacuation's success, never acknowledged that his pursuit had failed to prevent Pompey's escape. Instead, he focused on what had been accomplished: Italia secured, Pompey's forces driven from the peninsula, and the Senate-in-exile reduced to refugees sailing towards uncertain future.

On the fifteenth day, as dawn broke over the Adriatic, the last ships prepared to depart. Marcus stood on the headland and watched through the grey morning light as vessels cast off from Brundisium's docks.

They moved carefully through the harbour entrance, navigating between Caesar's moles that, though incomplete, still narrowed the passage and created obstacles that required attention. One ship, overcrowded and poorly handled, struck the northern mole and had to be manoeuvred free by oars before continuing its escape.

Caesar stood beside Marcus, watching in silence as the last ships cleared the harbour and set course for Greece. The morning wind filled their sails, and they picked up speed as they left Italia's coast behind. On their decks stood the magistrates and senators who had fled Rome, men who had chosen

Pompey over Caesar, and somewhere among them, the great Magnus himself, watching his homeland disappear over the horizon.

'So he finally escapes,' said Marcus quietly.

'He flees,' corrected Caesar, 'there is a difference. He turned from watching the ships and looked instead at Marcus.

'Magnus crosses to Greece because he cannot hold Italia and gathers eastern legions because he cannot match our strength here. He prepares for future campaigns because he has lost the current one but let no man say we failed at Brundisium. We drove Pompey Magnus from Italia without major bloodshed, without destroying Roman forces in civil war, and that victory matters more than any battle. The war is not over, Marcus, it has barely begun.'

The last ship disappeared over the horizon, and Brundisium's harbour stood empty except for a few fishing boats and the remains of hasty departure.

'What next?' asked Marcus. 'Do we take the city?'

'There is no need,' said Caesar. 'We have achieved what we came to achieve and Brundisium is no threat. We march back to Rome to consolidate our position and ensure Italia remains secure. Then we turn west, to Hispania, to deal with Pompey's legions there before we face the man himself in Greece. We have won Italia, now we must win the war.'

They walked down from the headland towards the camp where the legions waited. Behind them, the moles stood as monuments to Roman engineering and determination, incomplete but impressive, structures that had complicated Pompey's evacuation even if they had not prevented it.

Chapter Thirteen

Rome

The Thirteenth Legion marched through Rome's gates on a grey morning that matched the mood of the men. They had driven Pompey from Italia, secured every town from the Rubicon to Brundisium, and forced the Senate-in-exile to flee across the Adriatic. By any measure, these were victories worthy of celebration but the soldiers who filed through the streets did not celebrate. They marched with their eyes fixed ahead, and the citizens who lined the roads watched them pass without a sound.

Marcus rode near the column's head, watching citizens gather to observe the army's return. Some cheered, others simply watched in silence, their faces showing exhaustion more than enthusiasm. Rome had endured weeks of uncertainty, seen its government collapse, and witnessed the flight of those who claimed to lead. That Caesar had brought order rather than destruction earned gratitude, but gratitude was not the same as joy.

The legion established itself once more in the Campus Martius, that familiar field where they had camped before the march south. The soldiers went about the routine tasks of making camp with practised efficiency, erecting tents and settling into the patterns that governed military life. But there was a flatness to their movements, a sense that victory should feel different from this anticlimax of returning to where they had started.

Caesar rode directly to his house, taking only a small escort and leaving Balbus to manage the camp's establishment.

Marcus accompanied him, curious about what came next.

The streets showed the effects of weeks without proper administration. The grain distributions had become irregular, the public markets operated on reduced schedules, and the poorest quarters displayed the gaunt faces of people who measured food in careful portions. Rome had not starved, not yet, but hunger had become a daily concern for thousands who depended on the grain dole for survival.

'How bad?' Caesar asked Oppius, one of his agents who had remained in Rome during the campaign to Brundisium.

'The granaries have perhaps three weeks' supply at current distribution rates, and the normal shipments from Sicily have been irregular. The people manage, but they worry, and worry can become unrest if we do not address it soon.'

Caesar nodded, his expression revealing calculation rather than concern.

'What remains in the treasury?'

'Very little. Magnus stripped it thoroughly. But there is some reserve coinage, enough for immediate purchases if we can find grain to buy.'

'Then find it. Sicily, Africa, wherever it can be sourced. Pay premium prices if necessary. I want distributions resumed at full rates within the week.

The next days passed in a blur of administrative activity that felt mundane after the intensity of campaign. Once again, Caesar met with the magistrates about aqueduct maintenance, with merchants about grain contracts, and with the urban cohorts' commander about security. He attended the theatre one evening, sitting in his usual seats, maintaining the fiction that everything remained normal even as the Republic fractured around them.

Marcus observed these performances with growing

understanding of how Caesar operated. The military campaigns were only one dimension of the war. The other dimension played out in forums and marketplaces, and in the slow accumulation of small actions that convinced citizens their lives were better under Caesar than under those who had abandoned them.

Seven days later, the war council convened in the principia at the Campus Martius camp. Caesar's senior officers gathered around the command table, examining maps that showed Italia, Gaul, and Hispania. Labienus stood nearest Caesar, as always, whilst other tribunes and legates arranged themselves by rank and seniority. Marcus occupied a position near the rear, present to observe rather than contribute unless called upon.

Caesar began without preamble, his voice carrying the certainty of decisions already made.

'We march in two days,' he said, 'north to Gaul, where we will combine with the rest of the legions, then west to Hispania, where Pompey has stationed seven legions under Afranius and Petreius. Our objective is the elimination of these forces, securing the western provinces, and removing any threat that might interfere with our eventual pursuit of Pompey himself to Greece.'

He paused, letting the information settle, watching faces for reactions.

'Hispania?' said one of the younger tribunes, confusion evident in his voice. 'Should we not pursue Magnus directly? He flees to Greece and even now he will be gathering his forces. Every day we delay allows him to strengthen his position.'

'Every day we delay also allows us to strengthen ours,' said Caesar. 'Pompey gathers the eastern legions, yes, but gathering requires time and he will need months to prepare an army capable of returning to Italia. I intend to use those months to secure our western flank.' Caesar moved to the map, his finger tracing the strategic situation. 'Consider the position if we pursue Magnus immediately. We cross to Greece with perhaps four legions, enough to contest his gathering forces, but behind us, in Hispania, sit seven veteran legions loyal to Magnus's memory and commanded by capable legates. What prevents them from marching on Italia in our absence? What stops them from threatening Gaul, disrupting our supply lines, and forcing us to fight on two fronts simultaneously?'

Understanding dawned on several faces. Others remained sceptical, but they listened as Caesar continued.

'We cannot fight Magnus properly whilst his Hispanían legions threaten our rear. Therefore, we eliminate that threat first. We march west with overwhelming force, defeat Afranius and Petreius, secure the provinces, and remove any possibility of western interference. Only then do we turn east, cross to Greece, and face Magnus with our full attention and resources.'

'How long will the Spanish campaign require?' asked Labienus.

'Three months, perhaps four. The Hispanian legions are well-trained but isolated. They cannot easily reinforce or resupply. We move quickly, force decisive engagement, and use clemency to undermine their will to resist. If we move efficiently, we are back in Italia by late summer, prepared to cross to Greece in autumn or early spring next year.'

'And if Magnus returns to Italia whilst we are in Hispania?' The question came from Marcus, speaking for the first time.

Caesar looked at him directly, acknowledging the concern.

'Then he finds Italia garrisoned, held by forces I will leave behind specifically for that purpose. He finds towns loyal to the administration that brought them order and a population that remembers his flight and my clemency. Could he retake Italia? Perhaps. But at what cost, and to what purpose? Every day he spends reconquering towns is a day he is not gathering forces in Greece. Either he waits for us there, or he wastes strength here. Both outcomes serve our interests.'

The logic was characteristically multilayered, and Marcus saw officers processing the implications. Caesar was not simply planning the next campaign but positioning pieces for campaigns beyond that, seeing several moves ahead whilst others focused on immediate threats.

'Four legions against seven is not overwhelming,' continued Caesar, 'but it is sufficient if we use advantages of speed and surprise. Magnus's legates expect us to pursue him to Greece, they do not expect an immediate campaign in Hispania. That misconception buys us time to position forces and seize initiative before they can properly prepare.'

More questions followed, officers seeking clarity about logistics and command structure and the detailed planning that would guide their movements. Caesar answered each one patiently, demonstrating that the strategy was not impulsive but carefully considered, backed by intelligence and calculation.

When the questions subsided, Caesar delivered his conclusion.

'We march in two days. Prepare your men for extended campaign in difficult terrain. Pay attention to morale and make clear that Hispania represents necessary work before the glorious confrontation with Magnus in Greece. The soldiers want their battle and they will have it, but not until we have secured every advantage and eliminated every threat that might complicate that confrontation.'

The council dispersed, the officers departing to organise their commands and prepare for departure. Marcus remained behind, watching Caesar study the maps with an expression that suggested he was already marching across Hispania in his mind, already calculating the moves and countermoves that would decide the campaign's outcome.

'You make it sound simple,' said Marcus. 'Four legions against seven, months of campaign in hostile territory, complex logistics across difficult terrain. Yet you speak as though victory is assured.'

'Victory is never assured,' said Caesar quietly. 'But defeat becomes more likely when commanders doubt their strategies or hesitate in execution. I show confidence because my officers need to see confidence. I speak of victory because speaking of potential defeat serves no purpose beyond undermining morale. Whether I truly believe we will succeed...' He paused, looking at Marcus directly. 'That is a question I ask myself in private moments, and the answer changes depending on how tired I am.'

It was the most honest statement Marcus had heard Caesar make about the war, and it revealed something of the man behind the commander's mask. Caesar was not superhuman, and not immune to doubt or fear or uncertainty. He simply refused to let those weaknesses show where others might see them.

'The men will follow you to Hispania,' said Marcus. 'They followed you through Gaul and through Italia to Brundisium even though they questioned the strategy. They will follow you west because following Caesar has become what defines them as soldiers.'

'I know,' replies Caesar. 'Which is why I cannot fail

them. They have given me their loyalty and I owe them victory in return. And if victory proves impossible, then I owe them death with honour rather than defeat through hesitation.'

That evening, Caesar returned home one final time before departure. He found Aurelia and Calpurnia waiting in the atrium, both women dressed formally as though receiving guests rather than saying farewell to family. They had prepared a meal, simple but carefully presented, a final shared moment before months of separation.

They ate in the triclinium, speaking of inconsequential matters, avoiding the obvious subjects that dominated all their thoughts. Caesar described administrative details about grain distribution, Calpurnia mentioned a neighbour's daughter getting married and Aurelia reported on household repairs that would occur during his absence. The conversation was deliberately mundane, a refuge from the weight of what everyone knew was coming.

Only after the meal, when slaves had cleared the dishes and the three of them sat alone in the lamplight, did Caesar finally speak what they had been waiting to hear.

'I leave Rome in two days,' he said quietly. 'We march north to Gaul, then west to Hispania. Magnus has seven legions there under his legates, and I cannot pursue him to Greece whilst those forces threaten from the west. The campaign may take months but I do not know when I will return.'

Calpurnia's face showed the distress she tried to control. She was younger than Aurelia, less practised in the stoic acceptance that governed the older woman's response. Her hands moved towards Caesar then stopped, uncertain whether comfort was wanted or appropriate.

'So soon?' she said quietly. 'You have barely rested since

Brundisium. And Hispania? I thought you would pursue Magnus to Greece.'

'I cannot pursue him with seven enemy legions at my back. We secure the west first, then turn east. It is the only viable strategy.'

'While we wait,' said Aurelia. It was not a question, merely an acknowledgement of reality. 'As we waited when you went to Gaul, as we waited when you marched south, as we will wait until you return or we hear that you will not.'

The bluntness was characteristic, and Caesar met his mother's gaze without flinching.

'I wish I could offer certainty. I wish I could promise quick victory and safe return, but this war will not be won in single campaigns or decided by individual battles. It will be won by the man who persists longest, who makes fewest mistakes, and who understands that every decision matters. I intend to be that man. Whether I succeed remains to be seen.'

Aurelia moved to stand beside him, taking his hand in both of hers.

'Then succeed quickly,' she said. 'Win your wars, defeat your enemies, and come home. We will manage in your absence and we will keep your household standing. But the Republic cannot wait forever.'

'I know,' said Caesar softly. 'Which is why I must go now rather than later. Every day of delay makes the eventual reckoning more difficult.'

'I wish you would not go,' said Calpurnia quietly. 'I wish you could remain here, govern Rome, and let others fight the wars that seem to multiply without end.'

'Others cannot fight these wars,' said Caesar. 'The legions follow me because I have led them for eight years through Gaul. The officers trust my judgement because I have demonstrated that judgement in countless campaigns. If I remain in Rome whilst sending others to Hispania, I risk defeat through inferior command. I cannot delegate this. Not yet.'

'Then when?' asked Calpurnia. 'When do you stop leading armies and start governing the Republic you claim to save?'

'When the wars are won, when Magnus is defeated and when I can lay down command without risking everything we have built. That day will come, but it is not today, and it will not be tomorrow. I am sorry.'

'You are building something, whether you acknowledge it or not,' said Aurelia. 'Not preserving the Republic but creating something new from its ruins. The question is whether that creation will be better than what it replaces, or merely different. We will not know until you stop fighting long enough to govern, and I am not certain you know how to stop.'

Caesar looked at his mother for a long moment, seeing perhaps the truth she offered without sentiment or decoration.

'You may be right,' he said, 'but I cannot stop now. The momentum carries me forward, and stopping means defeat for everything I have worked towards. So I go to Hispania, and from there to Greece, and from there to wherever Magnus flees next. And perhaps, when all the fleeing and pursuing ends, I will discover whether I have saved anything or merely conquered it.'

'Go, then,' said Aurelia, 'and win your wars. We will be here when you return, if you return. We have waited before, we can wait again.'

Calpurnia stepped forward and embraced him, holding tightly for a moment that stretched beyond comfort into something that approached desperation. Then she released him and stepped back, composing herself with visible effort.

'Come home soon,' she said simply.

'I will try,' said Caesar.

He left before dawn, departing whilst the household still slept, avoiding prolonged farewells that would serve no purpose beyond pain. Marcus met him in the street with horses and a small escort, and they rode through dark streets towards the camp where the legion waited.

Two days later, the Thirteenth Legion marched north from Rome.

Chapter Fourteen

Southern Gaul

The Alps rose before them like a wall built by gods to separate the civilised world from the lands beyond. Marcus had crossed these mountains before, marching north with Caesar eight years earlier when Gaul was unconquered and the legions were untested. Then, the peaks had seemed impossibly high, the passes treacherous, the whole range a barrier that tested courage as much as endurance. Now, the mountains felt merely difficult rather than impossible, a challenge to overcome rather than an obstacle to fear.

The Thirteenth Legion climbed through foothills that gave way to the proper mountains, the road narrowing as it gained elevation. This was the Via Julia, one of several routes Caesar had improved during his years governing Gaul, but even with improvements the march tested men and animals alike.

Marcus rode with the vanguard, watching the road ahead and the mountains that still climbed higher. Spring had come to the lowlands, but here winter lingered in patches of snow that clung to northern slopes and in the cold wind that came down from the peaks. The air thinned as they climbed, making breath come harder, making every step require more effort than the one before.

Caesar rode the length of the column daily, speaking with centurions, checking on the men's condition, and maintaining the presence that reminded soldiers their commander shared their hardships. He stopped beside Marcus on the third day of climbing, both men looking up at the pass that marked the mountains' highest point.

'Do you remember the first crossing?' asked Caesar. 'Eight years ago, marching to war in Gaul with legions that had never seen real combat?'

'I remember thinking the mountains would kill us before the Gauls had their chance,' said Marcus. 'I remember wondering why anyone would choose to cross the Alps when ships could carry armies around them.'

'Because ships require favourable winds and calm seas and the cooperation of elements beyond our control. Mountains are difficult, certainly, but they are predictable. Climb high enough, and you reach the other side.'

It was characteristically pragmatic, reducing geography to logistics and the assessment of risk. They rode in silence for a time, the only sounds the creak of leather and the steady rhythm of hooves on stone.

They reached the pass on the fourth day, that high point where the road crested the mountains and began its descent towards Gaul. Marcus stood at the summit and looked both ways: south towards Italia, north towards the lands Caesar had conquered. The legion passed through in good order, soldiers moving with disciplined efficiency despite exhaustion.

The descent went well for the first two days, and they were all quietly acknowledging they had been lucky with the weather, but that over-confidence came to a shattering end when storm came without warning, rolling down from the high peaks with an unexpected fury.

One moment the sky was clear, the next it was black with clouds that seemed to boil as they advanced and the wind hit the column like a physical blow, strong enough to stagger men and horses alike.

Torrential rain followed, falling in sheets, and turning

the mountain road to mud within minutes, reducing visibility to a few paces. Thunder crashed between the peaks, echoing and re-echoing until it seemed the mountains themselves were breaking apart and lightning split the darkness, revealing glimpses of the cliffs dropping away to one side.

Marcus shouted orders that were lost in the wind and the column bunched together as soldiers sought any shelter the terrain offered. Wagons slid sideways on the mud, requiring teams of men to manhandle them back to stable ground and a mule lost its footing, its scream cut short by distance as it tumbled over the cliff edge.

The deluge continued for three hours and when it finally passed, leaving only drizzle and the sound of water running everywhere down the mountainside, Marcus assessed the damage. Three mules dead, two supply carts destroyed after slipping over the edge, and several men injured by falls or falling rocks. In the circumstances, it wasn't too bad until a few hours later, a patrol of scouts returned with devastating news. The pass ahead was completely blocked.

The landslide had come down during the storm, triggered by the weight of water-saturated earth, a chaos of mud and rock and uprooted trees that extended perhaps two hundred paces along the route. Above it, the slope rose steep and unstable while below it, the cliff dropped away into a gorge where a stream that had been a trickle was now a raging torrent.

Caesar arrived to inspect the blockage personally, Balbus and Labienus accompanying him. They stood in the rain and studied the obstacle whilst engineers examined it from multiple angles, searching for a way through or around.

'How long to clear it?' asked Caesar.

The chief engineer, a weathered man named Vitruvius

who had built bridges across every river in Gaul, shook his head slowly.

'Many days, Dominus, perhaps weeks. The mud is still unstable, and we would need to shore up the slope above whilst clearing below. Any attempt to rush the work risks another slide that could bury the work parties.'

'Can we go around?'

'Above is impossible, the slope is too steep and unstable. Below...' Vitruvius walked to the cliff edge and looked down. 'Perhaps, if we had equipment to build a temporary bridge across the gorge. But we do not have such equipment, and bringing it up from the rear would take as long as clearing the road.'

Caesar stood silent, rain dripping from his cloak, studying the blockage with an expression that revealed nothing. Behind him the legions waited, stopped not by a greater army, but by a mountainside's whim.

'Make camp,' said Caesar finally. 'As best you can on this cursed slope. Set engineers to work on clearing the road, but carefully. I will not sacrifice men to gain a few day's progress. And Send scouts in all directions. There may be other routes that bypass this section.'

The orders went out, and the legion set about making camp in conditions that were far from ideal. The slope did not allow for proper fortifications, but they managed a defensible position using the terrain's natural features. Tents went up in clusters wherever flat ground could be found and although fires proved difficult in the continuing rain, the veterans knew how to coax flame from damp wood, and eventually smoke began to rise from dozens of small blazes.

Marcus supervised the establishment of watch posts, ensuring sentries were positioned to give warning of further landslides or other threats, before the scouts departed, searching for alternatives whilst the bulk of the legion settled into uncomfortable waiting.

The following night, Marcus was checking the northern perimeter when a boy emerged from the darkness beyond the firelight, so suddenly that the sentry's spear was at his throat before anyone could speak. The boy froze, hands raised, showing no weapon beyond a shepherd's crook that looked older than he was.

'Easy,' said Marcus, approaching the scene. 'He is a child, not a threat.'

The boy was perhaps twelve or thirteen, thin to the point of gauntness, and wearing rough wool clothing that was soaked through from the rain. His dark hair was plastered to his skull, and his eyes were huge in a face that showed both fear and something harder, a wariness that came from surviving.

'Who are you?' asked Marcus in the local dialect, a variation of Gaulish he had learned during the campaigns.

'Gavius,' said the boy. His voice was steady despite the spear still hovering near his throat. 'I tend sheep in these mountains, or I did, before the landslides took my flock.;.'

'Lower the spear,' said Marcus to the sentry and studied the boy more carefully. 'You speak Latin?'

'Some. Traders taught me. Words are useful.'

'What do you want, Gavius?'

'I heard your men talking. You need a way through the mountains and the road is blocked.'

'It is. Do you know another route?'

The boy's expression did not change, but something shifted in his eyes, a calculation that Marcus recognised from a thousand marketplace negotiations.

'Perhaps. But information has value.'

Marcus felt a smile tugging at his lips despite the rain and the cold and the frustration of the blocked pass. 'How much value?'

'One silver denarius.'

Marcus stared at the boy, surprised at the small amount. A denarius was a legionary's daily pay, a modest sum by Roman standards but Marcus saw the boy's tension, the way his hands gripped the shepherd's crook, and understood. For a shepherd boy in these mountains, a single denarius might represent months of earnings.

'Come with me,' said Marcus. 'I will take you to the Imperator, and you will make your proposal to him.'

They found Caesar with his senior officers, all of them studying maps by lamplight and discussing alternatives. The maps were useless, showing only the main road, but the discussion continued because action felt better than paralysed waiting.

'Dominus,' said Marcus, interrupting the council. 'This boy claims to know another route through the mountains.'

Caesar looked up from the maps, his gaze moving from Marcus to the soaked boy standing just inside the tent entrance. Gavius stood straighter under that scrutiny, water dripping from his clothes onto the carpeted floor, but he did not lower his eyes.

'You are a shepherd?' said Caesar.

'I was,' said Gavius. 'Before the storm killed half my flock and scattered the rest.'

'So you know these mountains?'

'Since before I could walk. My father's father herded sheep here, and his father before him. We know paths the

Romans never built, and ways through the high passes that avoid the main road.'

'Show us on the map.'

'I cannot read your map,' said Gavius simply. 'But I can guide you. There is a path, narrow but passable, that rejoins your road beyond the landslide. Half a day's march for men on foot. Longer for your wagons, if they are not too wide.'

Caesar leaned back, studying the boy with an expression that revealed calculation.

'And your price for this information?'

'One silver denarius.'

Someone in the tent laughed, quickly cut off when Caesar raised one hand. He looked at Gavius for a long moment, and Marcus saw the boy refusing to flinch despite facing the man whose name was known from Britannia to the Rhine.

'One denarius,' said Caesar slowly. 'A princely sum for a lowly shepherd's boy.'

Marcus recognised the tactic immediately. Caesar was testing the boy, despite the meagre demand, probing for weakness, testing the strength of the boy's personality.

Gavius did not move.

'One denarius is what I ask, nothing less. Take it or leave it.'

'Perhaps we will just take you, without payment. You are in a Roman camp, surrounded by soldiers. What stops us from compelling your service?'

'Nothing stops you,' said Gavius, and for the first time Marcus heard steel beneath the young voice. 'Except that I would guide you poorly, and men would die in the mountains, and you would gain nothing but my death and your own dishonour. Romans claim to value honour, yes? Or are the traders' tales lies?'

The tent had gone very quiet. Around the table, officers watched this negotiation between conqueror and shepherd boy, fascinated by the audacity.

Caesar smiled, a genuine expression that transformed his face.

'The traders' tales are not lies. We value honour, boy. We also value courage, and you show more of both than some men three times your age.' He paused, letting the moment extend. 'But one denarius for saving my army from a week's delay? That seems cheap. I will pay ten denarii.'

'I asked for one.'

'I heard what you asked for. I offer ten because a service worth buying is worth buying well. Will you refuse money freely offered?'

Gavius's expression remained carefully neutral, but Marcus saw the boy's hands tighten on his shepherd's crook. This was not the negotiation he had expected, and the unexpected could be dangerous.

'Why?' asked Gavius simply.

'Because I want you to remember that Caesar pays fairly for fair service. Because I want you to tell others in these mountains that Romans can be generous as well as powerful. Because a few denarius more means nothing to Rome's treasury, but to you it might mean the difference between surviving the winter and starving. Is that reason enough?'

'One denarius,' said Gavius firmly. 'That is my price. If you pay more, you insult my word, which was given before I knew you would negotiate. A man's word should not change because someone offers more coin.'

This time Caesar's laugh was genuine, and he looked around the tent at his officers.

'This boy has more honour than half the Senate. Very well, Gavius. One denarius, as agreed, paid when you have delivered us safely beyond the landslide. But I will add this: if your path is as good as you claim, there will be work for you with the army, if you wish it. A guide who knows these mountains could be useful in future campaigns.'

'I will guide you to the path,' said Gavius carefully. 'After that, we will talk again.'

Caesar turned to Labienus.

'Select a patrol of scouts, experienced men who know mountain travel. They will go with the boy to verify this path exists. If it does, we move the entire column at first light.'

The patrol was assembled quickly, eight men under a veteran Decanus named Rufus who had spent years hunting Germans through mountain forests.

Marcus watched them depart into the darkness, the boy leading soldiers who could have killed him without effort, trusting that Romans valued honour as much as they claimed. It was either remarkable courage or remarkable desperation. Marcus suspected it was both.

The camp settled into restless waiting as the rain continued, lighter now but persistent, making everything damp and miserable. Fires sputtered, soldiers huddled in inadequate tents, and the officers gathered in small groups to speculate about whether the boy's path would prove real or fantasy.

Three hours passed, then four and some began to mutter that the boy had led the patrol into a trap, that local tribes had ambushed them, and that they would find bodies in the morning rather than answers.

Then, near midnight, the sentries called a challenge, and Rufus's patrol emerged from the darkness.

They were exhausted, but their expressions carried relief rather than defeat and Rufus went directly to Caesar's tent whilst his men collapsed near the fires, accepting wine and food from their comrades.

Marcus followed Rufus into the command tent, where Caesar waited with Labienus and Balbus.

'Report,' said Caesar simply.

'The boy spoke truth, Dominus. There is a path, narrow and steep in places, but passable. We followed it for two hours through terrain I would not have believed could carry a goat, let alone an army. But the boy knows it perfectly, never hesitated, never took a wrong turn in darkness. The path rejoins the main road approximately three miles beyond the landslide, at a point where the slope levels and the road broadens again.'

'What about the carts?' asked Balbus.

'They will require care and probably some pushing in the steeper sections, but yes, they can pass. The boy is remarkably precise about what will and will not fit.'

'What about the heavy wagons?'

'We will have to leave them or take them apart and carry everything through to the other side.'

Caesar nodded slowly, satisfaction evident in his expression.

'Is the boy is still with you?'

'Outside the tent, Dominus. He said he would wait for payment where he could run if needed. I think he still does not quite trust us not to take what we want without paying.'

'Bring him in.'

Rufus retrieved Gavius, and the boy entered the tent looking even more exhausted than the soldiers. His young face was drawn with fatigue, his clothes now more mud than wool, but his expression remained guarded.

Caesar reached into the purse at his belt and drew out a silver denarius. He held it up in the lamplight, letting it catch and reflect the flames, then held it out towards Gavius.

'Your price, as agreed. One denarius for saving my men from a week's delay. Rome pays its debts.'

Gavius took the coin with hands that trembled slightly, whether from cold or emotion Marcus could not tell. He studied it briefly, tested it between his teeth in the manner of merchants checking for false silver, then tucked it somewhere inside his ragged tunic.

'The path is yours,' he said. 'I have fulfilled my word.'

'You have,' agreed Caesar. 'And now I make you an offer. Stay with the legion and guide us through these mountains, and the ones between Gaul and Hispania. I will pay you one denarius per month as a runner and guide, with food and shelter provided. When we reach Hispania, you may leave with your pay or continue further if you wish. The choice will be yours.'

It was generous. A legionary earned twenty-five denarii per month, but provided his own equipment and food. For a boy whose alternative was homeless wandering through mountains, the offer represented security and wealth.

But Gavius did not answer immediately. He stood in the tent surrounded by Rome's power, dripping water onto carpets that cost more than he had earned in his life, and considered with the careful deliberation of someone who understood that choices mattered.

'One denarius per month?' he asked finally.

'That was my offer.'

'I want two.'

The tent went silent and Marcus felt a laugh building in

his chest at the boy's audacity. Here was Caesar, ex-Consul of Rome, conqueror of Gaul, and invader of Britannia, offering employment, and this shepherd boy was negotiating for higher wages.

Caesar's expression did not change.

'You drove a hard bargain for your knowledge of the path, now you drive another for your service. Explain why you are worth twice my offer.'

'Because I know these mountains and you do not. Because I speak the local dialects and you do not. Because I am small and quick and can go places your big soldiers cannot. But also because you will need guides in Hispania too, where the mountains are fiercer than these and because you said yourself that buying well is better than buying cheap.'

The last statement hung in the air, challenge and dignity mixed together. Marcus watched Caesar, wondering how he would respond to this boy who refused to be cowed by power or generosity.

'One and a half denarii per month,' said Caesar. 'Food, shelter, and clothing provided. You serve as guide, runner, and camp servant as needed. You follow orders, maintain discipline, and do not steal from soldiers or citizens. If you serve well, the pay may increase. If you serve poorly, you leave with nothing. Do we have an agreement?'

Gavius considered for a moment that stretched, then nodded once, sharply.

'We have an agreement.'

'Then welcome to Caesar's service, Gavius the shepherd. Try not to lead us off any cliffs.'

The boy managed something that might have been a smile, though exhaustion made it difficult to tell. He was dismissed with instructions to find the quartermaster for dry clothes and food, and he left the tent moving like someone whose knees wanted to fold.

The following morning, Caesar's army backtracked the way they had come to a gap between some rocks that looked like nothing, but which opened into a narrow track that switch-backed up the mountainside. Even in daylight it looked barely passable, but Gavius moved along it with confidence, pointing out the spots where wagons would need to be manhandled or partially unloaded.

The column reformed into a thin line and began the climb. It was slow, exhausting work that required constant attention to prevent animals or wagons from slipping on the steep sections, but Gavius had spoken the truth: the path was passable, barely, and it bypassed the landslide completely.

The front elements of the legions emerged back onto the main road in early afternoon. The rest followed and continued arriving throughout the day and well into the night.

The following day, the column reformed, standards were positioned, and the march towards Gaul continued as though the mountains had been merely an inconvenience rather than a potential disaster.

Marcus found Gavius sitting on a rock beside the road, wrapped in a legionary's spare cloak that was far too large for him, watching the army pass with an expression that might have been awe or might have been calculation.

'You did well,' said Marcus, reining his horse beside the rock. 'Caesar will remember this service.'

'He paid me,' said Gavius simply. 'The debt is settled.'

'Even so. Are you ready to continue? We march another six miles before camp.'

'I am ready.' But the boy made no move to stand, just continued watching the soldiers march past, and Marcus realised he was studying them, learning, filing away details that might prove useful later.

'You have no fear of us,' observed Marcus. 'Most people show some nervousness around the legions of Rome yet you negotiate wages as though speaking with merchants in a market.'

'Fear is useless,' said Gavius. 'I was alone in the mountains before you came, and I will be alone after you leave. Fear does not change that, so I make agreements that benefit me, and I serve those agreements until they are complete. I survive and that is all anyone can do.'

There was something in the boy's voice, a flatness that spoke of losses Marcus did not know and would not ask about.

'The legion is not so bad,' said Marcus. 'Harsh discipline, certainly, but fair. Food every day, shelter every night, and pay that arrives on time. Better than shepherding alone in these mountains.'

'Perhaps,' said Gavius. 'I will see. If it is not better, I will leave when my contract allows. If it is better, I will stay. But I make no promises beyond what was agreed.'

Marcus laughed despite himself.

'You will fit right in with the soldiers, they think the same way. Come, climb up behind me. You can ride until we make camp, and I will introduce you to the quartermaster properly. You will need boots that fit and a tunic that does not drag on the ground.'

Gavius considered for a moment, then stood and approached the horse. Marcus reached down and hauled him up behind the saddle.

They rode in silence for a while, following the column

as it descended from the mountains towards the easier terrain of Gaul's interior. Marcus felt the boy's presence behind him, light and tense, ready to jump clear at any perceived threat.

'What happened to your family?' asked Marcus finally. 'You said you tended your father's sheep.'

'Dead,' said Gavius flatly. 'The winter fever took him and my brothers. Then the spring rains killed half the flock, and the other half scattered in the storm that blocked your road. So I had nothing and was nothing. Now I have employment with Romans. Perhaps it will be better, perhaps it will be worse. I will see.'

There was no emotion, no self-pity, just the facts stated as though describing the weather. Marcus understood then that this boy had already survived more hardship than many soldiers would face in a lifetime, and had survived it alone.

'It will be better,' said Marcus, more to himself than to the boy. 'Caesar values loyalty and service. Serve him well, and he will reward you fairly. You made that deal yourself, negotiating like a merchant. Now live up to your side of it, and he will live up to his.'

'We will see,' said Gavius again, and Marcus let the conversation die, recognising that the boy would believe what he saw rather than what he was told.

They rode on through the afternoon, leaving the peaks behind. The path ahead led to Vesontio, to the gathering of Caesar's forces, and beyond that to Hispania and war.

And now, riding behind Marcus's saddle in a cloak too large and boots that would need replacing, came Gavius, who had saved Caesar's legions from a week's delay for the price of one denarius, and who had negotiated employment with Caesar himself without showing fear or deference.

Marcus looked back as the last ridge faded behind them,

seeing the high peaks where winter still lingered, where a shepherd boy had lost everything and found opportunity in Rome's passage. The mountains were empty now, cleared by the legions' march, and somewhere on those slopes a scattered flock of sheep wandered without a shepherd.

But Gavius did not look back. He looked ahead, towards whatever came next, already adapting, already surviving.

It was, Marcus thought, the most Roman quality a person could have. To look forward, and to transform loss into an advantage.

They reached Vesontio ten days after leaving the Alps, and Marcus introduced Gavius to the quartermaster, a pragmatic man named Publius who had outfitted everyone from generals to mules during eight years in Gaul. He looked at the mud-covered boy with the expression of someone assessing livestock, then nodded once.

'Small, but sturdy enough. Are you a fast runner?'
'Fast enough to keep ahead of wolves,' said Gavius.
'Good. Can you read?'
'No.'
'Write?'
'No.'
'Too bad. Literate runners earn more. You will learn, or you will stay at your current wage. We will get you cleaned up, find you a proper tunic and boots that fit, and put you with the other camp staff. If you cause trouble, you will be dealt with the same as any other man in Caesar's army. Understood?'

'Understood,' said Gavius, and followed the quartermaster to the supply tents without looking back.

Marcus watched him go, this boy who had negotiated

with Caesar, and wondered what would become of him. The legions chewed up the weak and swallowed the unwary, but they also rewarded the clever and the loyal. Gavius seemed to be both. Time would tell which qualities mattered more.

Chapter Fifteen

The Pyrenees

The Pyrenees rose before them like a wall separating Gaul from Hispania, their peaks still white with winter snow though spring had arrived in the valleys below. Marcus stood at the base of the pass, watching the four legions prepare for the crossing, and tried not to compare these mountains to the Alps they'd crossed just a few weeks earlier.

'Easier than the Alps,' said Gavius, following his gaze. 'Lower passes, better roads, and spring weather instead of winter storms. We should be through in three days.'

"Should be,' Marcus agreed, but mountains were mountains, and armies crossing them faced predictable problems. The Pyrenees might be easier than the Alps, but easy was relative when moving twenty thousand soldiers through hostile terrain.

The legions began the ascent at dawn, spreading into a column that stretched for miles along the Roman road that climbed towards the pass. Marcus marched in the middle of the formation, watching the mountains grow larger with each hour, feeling the air thin and cool as they gained altitude.

The road was good and well maintained even this far from Italia. They passed through small settlements who'd seen armies come and go, and knew that survival meant not antagonising twenty thousand armed men regardless of which Roman faction they claimed to serve.

By midday they'd reached the higher elevations where vegetation thinned and rocky slopes dominated the landscape. The air was noticeably colder here, carrying the bite of altitude that made breathing harder and legs tire faster. But the men were veterans, and they maintained pace without significant complaints.

'How much further to the summit?' asked one of the younger soldiers during a rest halt.

'Another day's march,' Marcus said, checking their position against what the scouts had reported. 'We camp tonight in the high valley, cross the peak tomorrow, then descend into Hispania.

That evening they made camp in a sheltered valley perhaps two thousand feet below the pass itself. The temperature dropped sharply once the sun disappeared behind the peaks, and the men huddled around fires that struggled in the thin air. But the altitude also meant clear views, and Marcus stood on the valley's edge looking back toward Gaul and forward toward Hispania, seeing both sides of the mountain range spread below like maps made real.

'Different from the Alps,' said Balbus, joining him at the overlook. 'When we crossed into Gaul all those years ago, we were following Caesar into unknown territory. Now we're veterans crossing into a civil war. The mountains are easier but the destination is harder.'

'The destination is Romans killing Romans for political disputes we barely understand,' said Marcus. 'Whether that's harder than fighting Gauls depends on whether you think civil war is worse than foreign war.'

'It's worse. At least when fighting Gauls, we knew they were enemies. In Hispania, we'll be killing men who speak our language, worship our gods, served in legions just like ours. That's the part the younger soldiers don't understand yet, that civil war means recognising your enemy's face before you kill him.'

They returned to the fires and tried to sleep in the cold mountain air.

Dawn came early at this altitude, the sun striking the peaks while valleys remained in shadow. The legions broke camp and resumed climbing, following the road as it switch-backed up the final slopes toward the pass.

The summit itself was windswept and barren, marked by a boundary stone that separated Gaul from Hispania. Caesar halted there briefly, letting the legions file past the marker, transforming them from soldiers in friendly territory to invaders entering a hostile province. It was a legal distinction that mattered to Senate lawyers but meant little to the men who would do the actual fighting.

'Hispania,' said Caesar, addressing the officers who'd gathered at the summit. 'Pompey's legates control the province with seven legions and significant cavalry. They hold fortified positions and probably know we're coming. This won't be like Italia, with towns surrendering after token resistance. Afranius and Petreius are competent commanders with veteran troops and we'll earn this victory through manoeuvre and patience, not through intimidation.'

The descent into Hispania took another full day, the road dropping through a series of valleys that opened gradually into broader terrain. By the evening of the third day since leaving Gaul, the mountains were behind them and the Spanish plains spread ahead, rolling hills, cultivated valleys, and somewhere beyond sight, the rivers where Pompey's forces waited in prepared positions.

'There,' said Balbus, pointing to smoke rising in the distance. 'Ilerda. We'll reach the valley by tomorrow afternoon.'

Marcus looked toward the smoke, toward the town that represented their first real test against Roman opponents who wouldn't flee at Caesar's approach. The easy part, crossing the Pyrenees, was complete. What came next would test whether Caesar's genius extended to defeating enemies who knew his tactics because they'd learned the same ones.

That night they camped in enemy territory for the first time, establishing fortifications with the habitual thoroughness of soldiers who never assumed safety. Guards were posted, patrols sent out, and scouts dispatched toward Ilerda to assess enemy positions before the main force arrived.

Marcus walked the perimeter before sleeping, checking sentries and studying the terrain. The land here was different from Gaul, drier, more open, with vegetation that looked scrubby compared to Gallic forests. This was frontier country, fought over by Romans and locals for generations, marked by wars and conquests that had made the province wealthy but unstable.

'Strange to be here,' said Balbus, joining him at the camp's edge. 'All these years following Caesar through Gaul, and now we're in Hispania fighting other Romans. It feels wrong somehow.'

'War always feels wrong until the fighting starts,' replied Marcus. 'Then it feels necessary.'

The following day brought them to the hills overlooking the valley of the Sicoris River, and Marcus got his first view of the ground where the campaign would be fought. The valley opened before them like a wound in the Spanish landscape, broad and fertile but dominated by the town that crouched on the hill above its northern bank. Ilerda was old, its walls weathered by centuries of sun and siege, a fortress that had seen armies come and go whilst it endured.

Marcus stood on the rise south of the river and studied the terrain. The town occupied high ground that made direct assault costly, its walls extending down to protect the bridge that spanned the Sicoris. To the west, another river, the Cinga, joined the Sicoris in a confluence that created a natural barrier and between the rivers and the town, Afranius had positioned his forces in a series of strong fortresses, each supporting the next.

'They chose well,' said Balbus, standing beside Marcus with maps that were already proving inadequate to the reality of Spanish geography. 'The high ground, the rivers protecting their flanks, and supply lines running east to the coast. We will have difficulty bringing them to battle.'

'That is their intention,' said Marcus. 'Pompey's legates know Caesar prefers movement and aggression, so they offer him a fortress and rivers, and dares him to waste his strength against prepared positions.'

'Do we assault?' asked Balbus.

'I suspect not,' replied Marcus. 'If I know Caesar, he will want to amass all the intelligence available before he commits a single man to the fray. Come, we should be getting back.'

The four legions established their camps south of the Sicoris, their ditches and ramparts rising as though the landscape itself was being reorganised according to Roman preferences.

Marcus supervised the construction work, walking the lines and checking the progress whilst keeping one eye on Ilerda's walls where enemy soldiers watched their preparations.

Gavius appeared during the construction, moving with a leather bucket that was supposed to contain water for the soldiers but which Marcus suspected held less than it should. The boy had acquired proper boots and a tunic that almost fit.

'The Spanish cavalry rode close this morning,' said Gavius, setting down the bucket near where Marcus stood. 'I counted near fifty horses. They circled twice, watching the camp boundaries, then went back to the town.'

Marcus looked at the boy, noting how he reported the observation as simple fact, without emphasis or interpretation.

'You counted them?'

'I count everything because numbers matter. Fifty horses means they could raid our supply lines if we are not careful. Fifty horses also means they have fodder enough for cavalry, which means the town is well-stocked.'

'That is good thinking for a water carrier.'

'Water carrying is boring. Watching is interesting.' Gavius glanced towards Ilerda. 'The soldiers on the walls change every four hours, different formations each time with different standards. I think there is a strong army inside.'

Marcus studied the boy more carefully.

'And where did you learn to estimate garrison strength?'

'I watch and I count. The rest is guessing, but I guess carefully.' Gavius picked up his bucket. 'The shepherds at the river say there will be rain soon. They say Spanish spring rains are different from Gallic rains, heavier and more sudden. They also say the rivers will rise.'

Gavius walked away before Marcus could respond, moving between the working soldiers with the easy invisibility of someone who had learned to be overlooked.

The rains came three days later, not the brief showers common to the region but heavy, sustained downpours that turned the valley into a quagmire. The Sicoris swelled beyond its banks, then the Cinga followed, and within a week both rivers had merged into a single vast flood that stretched across the plain. The bridges Caesar's engineers had built were swept away in the first surge, along with the ford markers and the carefully constructed approach roads.

Marcus stood on the high ground watching the brown water rush past, carrying uprooted trees and the wreckage of abandoned farmsteads. The supply wagons from Italia that had been due to arrive within days, now sat stranded on the far side of an impassable torrent, visible in the distance but utterly beyond reach.

Chapter Sixteen

Hispania

Ten days later, the floodwaters finally receded, revealing a landscape transformed by their passage. What had been roads were now channels of churned mud and nearby fields lay buried under silt.

Marcus stood at the northern perimeter and watched the work parties wade into the subsiding waters to begin the bridge construction that would restore their supply lines. The engineers had planned well during the days of rain, and now they executed those plans with the methodical efficiency that characterised Roman military engineering. Pilings were driven into the riverbed where it was shallow enough to reach solid ground and frameworks rose above the water line. Planking followed, creating platforms that would bear the weight of wagons once the connections were complete.

But the work was slow, hampered by the current's strength and the continuing need to guard against raids from Ilerda. Afranius had recognised that the bridges represented Caesar's lifeline, and he sent patrols regularly to harass the construction sites, forcing the engineers to pause while Caesar's soldiers dealt with the constant attacks.

'How much longer?' asked Caesar, inspecting the northern bridge personally on the fifth day after the rains had stopped.

'Three days, perhaps four,' said Vitruvius, the chief engineer whose weathered face showed the strain of working under impossible conditions. 'The current remains strong, and we lose progress every time we must stop to repel raiders. If we had more protection, or if the enemy would allow us to work in peace, we could finish in two.'

'The enemy will not cooperate with our schedule,' said Caesar. 'But three days is acceptable.'

Marcus knew the calculation Caesar was making. The stockpiled food was running low, carefully rationed to extend its use but diminishing regardless. Another week without resupply would force decisions no commander wanted to make, reduce rations further, risk major foraging expeditions into hostile territory, or consider the unthinkable option of retreat.

The bridges grew, section by section, whilst the legions tightened their belts and made grim jokes about Spanish hospitality. The mood in camp remained disciplined but Marcus could feel the edge that came from soldiers who were hungry and frustrated, who had marched across mountains to fight an enemy that refused to offer battle, and who now found themselves trapped by weather rather than tactics.

It was during this period of strained waiting that Gavius proved his value in ways that had nothing to do with carrying water.

Marcus first noticed the boy's activity when he saw him near the supply tents speaking with one of the quartermasters, a conversation that seemed too intense for a simple servant asking about duties. When Marcus approached, the quartermaster was nodding and making marks on a wax tablet whilst Gavius gestured and spoke rapidly.

'Problem?' asked Marcus.

'Solution, actually,' said the quartermaster, a veteran named Publius whose responsibility was stretching the inadequate supplies across four legions. 'The boy has been watching the foraging parties return each day. He noticed patterns in what they find and where they find it. He says there are probably farms further south, hidden in valleys where our patrols have not looked, places where the locals hid supplies before we arrived.'

'And he knows this how?'

'I asked,' said Gavius simply. 'The ones who sell food to the army, and the ones who work as guides. They talk if you ask the right questions. They say the rich farmers moved their grain and livestock into the hills when they heard Romans were coming. The poor farmers who remained are the ones we have been trading with, but they have little to sell. The real supplies are hidden, waiting for us to leave so they can be brought back down.'

'You interrogate civilians without authorisation?' said Marcus, though he was more impressed than angry.

'I talk to people. Sometimes I buy them wine with coins I save from my wages and sometimes they tell me useful things. Is that wrong?'

Publius laughed, a sound rare in the hungry camp.

'Wrong or not, it may save us from short rations. I am sending a patrol south tomorrow with guides he has arranged. If they find what he claims, we will have food for another two weeks at least.'

The patrol departed at dawn, led by a Spanish farmer who accepted Caesar's silver and guided them to valleys where sheep and cattle had been hidden in rough pastures far from the main roads. The foragers returned with livestock and several wagonloads of grain, enough to ease the immediate crisis and extend the army's endurance until the bridges could be completed. Caesar was informed of the source of this intelligence and summoned Gavius to his tent.

Marcus accompanied the boy, partly from curiosity and partly from a growing sense of responsibility for this child who seemed determined to insert himself into matters beyond his station. They found Caesar with his maps, calculating distances and supply requirements with Balbus.

'You are the shepherd who saved us in the mountains,' said Caesar, looking at Gavius.

'I am, Dominus. I guided you through the pass.'

'And now you guide my foragers to hidden supplies. You speak Spanish, observe enemy positions, and apparently interrogate civilians as though you were an intelligence officer rather than a water carrier. Explain.'

Gavius stood straight, showing neither fear nor false bravado.

'I watch and I listen and I learn, because those are the things that keep me alive. In the mountains, knowledge of paths was valuable. Here, knowledge of where food is hidden is valuable. I provide what has value, and I am paid. It is simple.'

'He is a mercenary,' observed Balbus. 'A twelve-year-old, but a mercenary nonetheless.'

'I prefer to think of it as practical,' said Caesar. 'The boy offers useful service and expects fair compensation. That is more honest than many transactions in Rome.' He studied Gavius thoughtfully. 'Your wage is one and a half denarii per month. For locating supplies that may have prevented a crisis, I will add a bonus of five denarii. Use it wisely.'

'I will save it,' said Gavius immediately. 'Silver is security, and security is what I lacked when your army found me. I do not intend to lack it again.'

'A sound philosophy. Now tell me what else you have observed. You watch the enemy from what I understand. What have you seen?'

Gavius glanced at Marcus, perhaps seeking permission or perhaps simply acknowledging his presence, then spoke with the confidence of someone reporting facts rather than opinions. 'Afranius sends patrols four times daily. Morning, midday, afternoon, evening. Always the same routes, always the same strength: fifty cavalry, one hundred infantry. He is predictable. His men are disciplined but not aggressive. They probe but do not press. I think he is content to wait and let hunger do his work for him.'

'You think correctly,' said Caesar. 'He has supplies, a secure position, and time on his side. Why risk battle when delay serves his purpose? Anything else?'

'The bridge he holds is the key. If we can cross the Sicoris, we can threaten his supply lines from the east. But the bridge is too well defended to take by direct assault. However, there is a ford three miles upstream. I heard the scouts discussing it. The water is lower there, crossable by men on foot when the river drops another two feet. It is watched, but not as heavily as the bridge.'

Caesar and Balbus exchanged glances.

'The scouts reported that ford,' said Balbus. 'But you heard them discuss it and understood its significance.'

'I understand that rivers are barriers, and barriers that can be crossed stop being barriers. If your legions can ford upstream, they can flank the defenders at the bridge.'

'You learn quickly,' said Caesar. 'Too quickly for a shepherd boy. Who taught you to think tactically?'

'No one taught me. I watch how you solve problems and I see patterns. When the Alps blocked the road, you found another path. When the river trapped you, you built bridges. When supplies ran low, you sent foragers. You always find solutions rather than accepting obstacles. I learn from watching solutions.'

The simplicity of the statement was almost profound

and Caesar smiled, the genuine expression that appeared when something pleased him beyond mere utility.

'Continue watching, Gavius and continue learning, but also continue your duties, such as they are. Marcus, ensure the boy is not punished for initiative that serves the army's interest. Intelligence from unexpected sources is still intelligence.'

They were dismissed, and Marcus walked with Gavius back through the camp, neither speaking until they were beyond the command area.

'You impressed him again,' said Marcus finally.

'I told him what I know. Whether that impressed him or not is his concern, not mine.' Gavius adjusted the too-large cloak he wore against the Spanish sun. 'The five denarii bonus was unexpected but I truly will save it. I have twelve and a half denarii now and by the end of the campaign, I will have twenty if I continue to prove useful. That is more money than I would have earned in five years of shepherding.

'Do you calculate everything in terms of survival and profit?'

'What else is there? Survival keeps you alive, profit gives you options. Everything else is luxury for those who have already secured both.'

It was a philosophy born of hard experience and Marcus could not entirely disagree with it. The boy had lost everything and rebuilt from nothing through intelligence and opportunism. The fact that he did so without sentiment or illusion was perhaps inevitable.

The bridges were completed on the eighth day after the rains stopped, sturdy structures that would serve until the war moved elsewhere and the first supply wagons crossed immediately, bringing grain and wine and the small luxuries that made campaign life bearable. The army's collective mood improved with full meals, and the sense of being trapped evaporated with the knowledge that the route to Gaul was once again open.

In the meantime, Afranius remained secure in Ilerda, his position too strong to assault directly, his supplies adequate to outlast any siege Caesar could maintain, and the strategic stalemate continued, both sides watching and waiting for the opportunity that would break the deadlock.

When it came, it did so from an unexpected direction and the ford Gavius had mentioned, three miles upstream, became the focus of Caesar's attention. Scouts confirmed that the water level had dropped enough to make crossing possible and if enough men could cross there quickly and establish a bridgehead on the northern bank, they could threaten Ilerda from a new direction.

Caesar called a council to discuss the plan.

'The ford is crossable,' said Caesar, pointing to the location on his map. 'But barely. The current remains strong, and our men will need to link arms to maintain footing. Our men will cross at dawn with cavalry supporting from the southern bank to cover their movement. Once across, they establish defensive positions and hold until reinforcements arrive.'

'Afranius will oppose the crossing,' said Labienus. 'His cavalry can reach the ford within an hour of our first movement. We will be vulnerable whilst crossing, caught between the river and an enemy that has solid ground.'

'Which is why we cross in force,' said Caesar, 'and we cross fast. Four cohorts in the first wave, with more following as soon as they can. The cavalry provides cover, and we use the terrain on the northern bank to establish positions before the enemy can mass against us. The river will take its toll but fewer than we would lose trying to storm Ilerda's walls, and the tactical advantage of holding both banks is worth the risk. We break the stalemate, threaten Afranius's supply line, and force him to react on our terms rather than his.'

The plan was approved, and preparations began immediately. The cohorts selected for the crossing spent the day checking equipment and tightening straps, ensuring everything was secured for a river passage that would test courage as much as strength. Later that night, Marcus gathered the officers who would lead the cohorts.

'We will cross at dawn,' he said. 'The water will be chest-deep at the ford, and the current strong enough to sweep away anyone who loses his footing. Link arms with the man beside you and move steadily. If a man falls, the whole line stops until he regains his feet. We cross as a unit or we do not cross at all. Questions?'

'What waits on the other side?' asked one officer.

'Enemy cavalry, probably, but terrain that favours defence if we reach it quickly enough. We have crossed rivers before, and this one is no different, and when we stand on the northern bank with dry ground beneath our feet, we will have turned Caesar's plan into reality.'

The speech was nothing special, but it served its purpose. The men nodded, checked their gear again, and settled into the waiting that preceded all military action.

Gavius appeared again as evening fell, moving through the camp with his usual mixture of purpose and invisibility. He stopped near Marcus, setting down the perpetually half-empty water bucket.

'I hear you will cross tomorrow,' said the boy.

'You hear many things that you should not.'

'People talk freely around servants. They forget we have ears and memories.' Gavius looked towards the northern hills where Ilerda's walls were barely visible in the fading light. 'The ford is dangerous and the Spanish cavalry are fast. You will lose men in the crossing.'

'Possibly, but the plan is sound and the risk is acceptable.'

'I could help. If I went ahead, and crossed before dawn, I could watch the enemy patrols and signal when they are furthest from the ford to give you maximum time to cross before they respond.'

Marcus looked at the boy, seeing the calculation behind the offer.

'You would risk your life to give us a few extra minutes?'

'I would risk my life for five more denarii. A bonus for scouting ahead and providing intelligence that saves Roman lives. A fair payment for fair service.'

'You are twelve years old, Gavius. I cannot send a child into enemy territory to scout on our behalf.'

'You are not sending me, I am offering to go. There is a difference. And I am not a child, I am a survivor who happens to be young. Survival does not wait until you are old enough to qualify.' Gavius picked up his bucket. 'Five denarii if my information proves useful. Nothing if it does not. That is my offer.'

'It is insane.'

'It is practical. If I am caught or killed, Rome only loses a water carrier. But if your soldiers die in the crossing because they had no warning of enemy patrols, Rome loses trained legionaries. It is a simple calculation.'

The logic was sound even if the premise was disturbing

and Marcus found himself nodding despite every instinct that said sending a twelve-year-old to scout enemy cavalry was wrong on every level.

'If I agree to this,' he said, 'you take no unnecessary risks. The intelligence is useful only if you survive to deliver it.'

'I take only necessary risks,' replied Gavius. 'Unnecessary risks are for people who have not learned that survival requires caution.' He walked away before Marcus could reconsider, disappearing into the camp's evening bustle as though the conversation had been about routine matters rather than a child volunteering for reconnaissance behind enemy lines.

Marcus reported the offer to Caesar, who listened with the same thoughtful expression he gave all unexpected suggestions.

'The boy has courage,' said Caesar. 'Or he has such profound pragmatism that courage becomes irrelevant. Either way, if he wishes to scout the ford and can do so without being caught, the information could save lives during the crossing. Allow it, but ensure he understands that we will not risk a major operation to rescue him if he is captured. He must know the stakes.'

Marcus found Gavius and delivered Caesar's approval along with the warning about rescue. The boy nodded once, showing neither excitement nor fear, just the acceptance of terms in a negotiation he had initiated.

'I understand. I am on my own if I fail but that has always been true, so nothing changes. I will leave after midnight and if I signal, it will be from the hill east of the ford. One fire means enemy cavalry are far from the crossing. Two fires means they are close. Three fires means the danger is too immediate. No fires means I am dead or captured, and you should decide without my intelligence.'

'You have thought this through, haven't you?' said Marcus.

Gavius nodded and slung a waterskin over his shoulder.

'I will return by dawn the following day whether I succeed or fail. If I do not return, assume I am dead and do not waste time looking for me. A Roman army should not pause for a shepherd boy.'

The night passed slowly. Marcus tried to sleep but could not, his mind occupied with thoughts of river crossings and cavalry charges and twelve-year-old boys who volunteered for reconnaissance because they calculated the value of their lives in denarii and found the risk acceptable.

He rose before dawn and went to the ford where the crossing force was assembling. The men moved quietly, checking gear and weapons, speaking in whispers while above them, stars faded as the eastern sky lightened towards day.

Marcus looked east towards the hill Gavius had mentioned, seeing nothing but darkness and the vague shapes of terrain. Then, as the light grew, he saw it, a single fire burning on the hillside, small but visible, signalling that the enemy cavalry were far from the ford and the crossing could proceed.

'Signal confirmed,' said Marcus to the cohort commander.

The command to advance was given, and four cohorts moved towards the ford in disciplined columns. They entered the water in formation, linking arms as Marcus had instructed, moving against the current with the careful steps of men who knew that one mistake could sweep them downstream.

The water was cold, deeper than expected, stronger than hoped. Men struggled to maintain footing, and several stumbled but were caught by their comrades, the linked arms preventing falls that could have proved fatal.

Marcus also crossed, feeling the river's power trying to tear him loose from his men, fighting each step whilst watching the northern bank where enemy cavalry might appear at any moment, but the single fire still burned on the hill, confirmation that Gavius's intelligence remained accurate.

They reached the northern bank exhausted but intact, forming defensive positions immediately whilst more cohorts crossed behind them and by the time full light arrived, Caesar had established a solid foothold on the north side of the Sicoris, with cavalry covering the crossing and infantry digging in against the expected counterattack.

Afranius's response came within the hour, his cavalry charging from Ilerda towards the ford, but they arrived too late. The Roman positions were established, reinforced, and impossible to dislodge without the infantry support that Afranius was unwilling to commit.

The stalemate was broken and Afranius would now have to react, to fight or flee or watch his strategic position crumble as Caesar threatened his supply lines from unexpected directions.

A few days later, with reinforcements continuing to join the bridgehead, Marcus headed back to the main camp and found Gavius sitting at a fire near the supply tents, eating a rabbit he had bartered from a local and cooked himself.

'Your fires were accurate,' said Marcus, taking a seat

opposite him. 'The crossing succeeded because we had ample warning of the enemy patrols.'

'The cavalry were northwest of the ford, exactly where I said they would be,' said Gavius. 'They followed their routine patrol pattern, which made them predictable.' He took another bite of rabbit and looked at Marcus expectantly. 'You owe me five denarii.'

'Caesar has authorised payment,' replied Marcus. 'I will have the quartermaster provide it this afternoon.' He stared at the boy. 'You could have died, you know. You are just twelve years old, and went alone into enemy territory to observe cavalry that would have killed you without hesitation.'

'I could die carrying water if I trip and crack my skull on a rock. Death does not wait for age or permission. I chose a risk that paid well rather than a risk that paid nothing. That seems reasonable.'

Marcus stood to leave, then paused.

'You bargain for every coin as though your life depends on accumulating silver. Why? What do you plan to do with it?'

Gavius looked at him with eyes that seemed older than his years.

'Buy land, eventually. A farm, perhaps. Something that provides warmth and security. The silver is not wealth, it is escape from poverty. I save now so I do not need to risk my life in the future.'

It was a goal more mature than most soldiers ever articulated, a long-term plan built on the harsh understanding that survival today meant nothing without security tomorrow. Marcus nodded slowly, acknowledging the wisdom in the child's calculation.

'Then continue surviving, Gavius. The army will need your intelligence again, I suspect. And I would prefer not to report to Caesar that his cleverest scout died before collecting enough silver to buy his farm.'

'I will survive,' said Gavius with certainty. 'Because that is what I do.'

The boy returned to his duties, and the war in Hispania ground forward another day, measured in river crossings and cavalry skirmishes and the slow accumulation of small victories that would eventually break Afranius's position.

And somewhere in the midst of four legions, a shepherd boy from the Alps grew richer by five denarii, having risked his life for payment and found the exchange acceptable because survival was his profession and he was very good at his work.

Chapter Seventeen

Hispania

The river crossing proved to be the beginning rather than the culmination. Caesar consolidated his bridgehead through the following days whilst Afranius watched from Ilerda, his cavalry probing but never committing, his legions remaining behind fortifications that now protected positions rendered strategically irrelevant by Roman manoeuvre.

Afranius had built his defence around controlling the Sicoris, maintaining supply lines, and keeping Caesar bottled on the southern bank but all those calculations meant nothing now. Caesar stood on both sides of the river with four legions, threatening the very roads Afranius needed for survival.

The Pompeian commander faced an impossible choice: remain in Ilerda and watch his position erode, or abandon the town and attempt retreat towards the Ebro where reinforcements might reach him before Caesar did. Either option surrendered the initiative, and either option acknowledged that Caesar had already won the campaign's crucial manoeuvre.

Afranius chose retreat, moving northwest in marching columns, attempting to reach the Ebro before Romans could intercept. The decision was tactically sound and strategically necessary, but operationally doomed, for Caesar had anticipated exactly this response.

'He runs towards the one place he thinks offers safety,' said Caesar, studying maps whilst his officers assembled. 'The Ebro represents reinforcement, resupply, and defensive positions. Afranius knows we cannot allow him to reach it, knows we must pursue, and hopes his head start will prove sufficient.'

'Will it?' asked Antonius, who commanded the cavalry now that Curio had departed for Sicily.

'No, because we are not pursuing him to the Ebro but to whatever ground we can force him to stop on, preferably ground without water, and we will do so faster than he expects.'

Caesar issued his orders. Six cohorts would garrison Ilerda whilst the remaining legions would move at forced march to intercept Afranius before the Ebro came within reach.

The pursuit began that afternoon and Marcus marched with his command in columns that moved faster than was really sustainable, eating the distance whilst the Spanish sun hammered down and dust rose from thousands of caligae striking the baked earth. They marched through the night when the heat relented, following roads by starlight and the glow of the torches carried by scouts who ranged ahead seeking signs of the enemy.

Afranius was fast, but Caesar was faster. The Pompeian forces were burdened by baggage trains and camp followers, while Caesar's legions travelled light, carrying minimal supplies, accepting discomfort in exchange for speed.

The gap closed with each day, measured by the freshness of abandoned campfires and the increasing desperation visible in enemy supply dumps left behind to lighten the march.

On the fourth day, Caesar's cavalry caught the enemy rearguard at a place where the road crossed broken ground unsuitable for quick withdrawal. The engagement was brief and brutal. The Pompeian cavalry were routed, their infantry cohorts forced to halt and form defensive positions whilst the main column continued northwest. Marcus watched from a hillside as his gallic horsemen circled the stranded infantry, not attacking but simply maintaining the pressure, forcing the cohorts to remain in formation rather than resume marching.

'They sacrificed their rearguard to buy time for the main force,' observed Corvinus.

'Those cohorts will surrender before nightfall,' said Marcus. 'Afranius will learn of it tomorrow, and his men will know that Caesar is close enough to destroy isolated forces, which means the column must remain concentrated, which means we close the gap further.'

The reality of the pursuit was unavoidable. Each gain by Caesar's men compounded the enemy's problems, and each enemy response created new vulnerabilities. Afranius was not incompetent, his decisions were reasonable given his circumstances, but reasonableness proved insufficient against an opponent who moved faster, thought clearer, and possessed the moral authority to demand inhuman effort from legions who trusted his genius completely.

By the sixth day, Afranius had covered only fifty miles from Ilerda and Caesar's forces were close enough to see dust from the enemy column.

The following day, Afranius made camp on a valley floor near a stream that provided the water essential for survival in this heat. He was still two days march from the Ebro, but his position was defensible, chosen more for necessity than advantage.

Caesar did not make camp opposite the enemy. Instead, his legions continued past the valley, moving northwest to positions that blocked the road ahead and when Afranius woke on the eighth morning, he discovered Caesar's men both behind and before him, surrounding him completely.

Marcus stood in the pre-dawn darkness, watching Pompeian scouts approach and then retreat, carrying news that would reach Afranius within the hour. The route north was blocked, the route south was blocked, and continuing in either direction meant fighting through Roman positions chosen specifically to make such fighting suicidal.

It was elegant in its simplicity. Afranius occupied a valley with one stream whilst Caesar controlled access to an entire river system. The Pompeian forces could ration water, enforce discipline, and hope for rain, but none of those measures would change the facts. Time favoured Caesar absolutely.

Pompeian cavalry attempted a breakthrough on the second day, a desperate charge against Caesar's positions that achieved nothing except additional casualties and worsened morale. The survivors retreated to their camp, and no further attempts followed.

Marcus walked the perimeter that night, checking sentries and observing the enemy campfires across the valley. They burned lower than previous nights, suggesting fuel conservation. Water discipline would follow, then food rationing, then the collapse of discipline itself as men realised their commanders had led them into a trap with no escape.

'How long do you think?' asked Corvinus, joining him at an observation post.

'Three days, perhaps four. Longer if Afranius maintains control, but men facing death from thirst will eventually ignore orders and attempt individual surrender, and once that begins, the collapse accelerates.'

'Caesar truly does not want to fight them?'

'Caesar wants them to join him, or at minimum to not reinforce Pompey. Dead Romans serve neither purpose, whilst surrendered Romans might be persuaded that the Senate's cause is less compelling than survival.'

'And if they refuse surrender and fight to the end?'

'Then we will oblige them, but Caesar will ensure the responsibility for Roman blood rests totally with Afranius and Petreius.'

On the fourth day, the stream dried completely. Whether through natural causes or Roman engineering conducted upstream hardly mattered, the effect was identical: Pompeian forces had no water except what they had stored, which would sustain them perhaps one more day in this heat.

Deserters began appearing that evening, individuals and small groups approaching Roman lines with hands raised and weapons discarded, begging for water and mercy. Caesar granted both, ostentatiously providing full rations and treating the deserters as valued recruits rather than defeated enemies. The message was clear to the guards who watched from the Pompeian lines, surrender brought immediate relief rather than punishment.

By the fifth morning, the trickle of deserters became a flood and entire cohorts approached Roman positions in formation, their centurions negotiating terms whilst their men waited in ranks. Caesar received each group personally, offering water, praising their courage in recognizing reality, and suggesting that Rome needed such practical men more than Pompey needed dead martyrs.

'Your commander made unfortunate choices,' said

Caesar to the assembled Pompeian officers. 'You served him with honour appropriate to Roman soldiers, but that service is now concluded. You may now choose to serve Rome herself, whose interests lie not with civil war but with stability under competent leadership. I require only that you acknowledge this campaign is finished and that further resistance serves no Roman interest.'

One of the officers finished drinking, wiped his mouth, and studied Caesar with a wary eye.

'What terms for officers who surrender?'

'The same terms I offer common soldiers: service under new command, or discharge with safe passage to wherever you wish to go. I do not punish men for following orders, particularly orders that were tactically doomed. Rome wastes enough of her sons without executing skilled officers for losing battles.'

'And Afranius?'

'Afranius may negotiate directly if he wishes. I bear him no personal enmity, for he defended Pompey's interests with competence and lost to a superior position. That deserves respect, not crucifixion.'

The officer nodded slowly, then made the practical calculation that Marcus had seen in dozens of surrenders. Continued resistance meant death, surrender meant survival, and no cause justified choosing the former when the latter remained available.

'The men I command will accept these terms. I cannot speak for Afranius, but I suspect he recognises the situation as clearly as I do.'

By afternoon, two-thirds of Afranius's force had surrendered. The remainder stayed in camp, presumably awaiting orders from commanders who were negotiating their own terms or making final preparations for whatever dignity could be preserved in comprehensive defeat.

Marcus found Caesar later that evening reviewing lists of surrendered units, calculating how many could be integrated into his legions and how many should be discharged to avoid overwhelming his command structure.

'Hispania is yours,' said Marcus.

'Hispania was always mine,' said Caesar, but yes, the formal acknowledgement is satisfying.' Caesar set down the lists and looked towards the Pompeian camp. 'Afranius will surrender tomorrow and will do so with terms that allow him to claim he negotiated honourable conditions rather than fled in disorder. I will grant him those terms because the alternative is fighting battles I have already won, which would be wasteful.'

'And then?'

'Then we settle Hispania's administration, ensure the province remains secure, and return to Italia. This campaign cost us three months, so Pompey has had three extra months to prepare. The next stage will be more difficult.'

Marcus considered the months ahead: Marching back o Italia, sailing to Greece and probably fighting battles that would make Ilerda seem trivial by comparison. The war was far from finished.

'I wonder if the rest of this campaign be this bloodless?' said Marcus.

'I doubt it,' replied Caesar, 'Afranius and Petreius are pragmatists who understood their position was untenable, but Pompey surrounds himself with senators who believe compromise equals betrayal and defeat equals dishonour. When we face them, they will fight until we kill them, and we will oblige because leaving enemies alive becomes dangerous when those enemies prefer death to reason.'

'That seems wasteful.'

'Civil war is wasteful. I merely try to minimize the waste where possible and inflict it where necessary.' Caesar returned to his lists, marking cohorts for integration and officers for discharge. 'Go and rest, Marcus. Tomorrow we accept their formal surrender, then begins the tedious work of turning victory into stability. You have earned your sleep.'

Marcus left the command tent and returned to his command. They had crossed a flooded river, pursued an enemy across fifty miles of Spanish hills, and forced surrender through position rather than bloodshed.

It was, Marcus thought, a very Caesar way to win a war, minimal casualties, maximum effect, and strategic brilliance that meant opponents discovered they had been defeated before realizing they were fighting.

Afranius arrived at Caesar's command tent at dawn, accompanied by Petreius and a small escort of officers. Their faces were gaunt from days without water, but they walked like generals, not prisoners.

Marcus stood near the tent's entrance, watching. Afranius moved with the bearing of a man who'd lost a campaign but kept his dignity. Petreius looked older, harder, like he was still calculating whether there was a way out of this.

Caesar received them standing. He gestured to chairs that had been arranged in a circle rather than across from each other.

'Gentlemen,' said Caesar. 'I trust your men have received adequate water and provisions?'

'They have,' said Afranius. 'Your generosity is noted. We're here to discuss terms.'

'Straight to the point?' said Caesar. 'So be it. My offer is simple, either you serve under my command, or you are discharged with safe passage and silver enough to reach wherever you're going. Those are the terms. Same for officers as for common soldiers.'

Petreius leaned forward.

'No oaths? No conditions?'

'None. You're free to go where you want, do what you want. If you fight me again later, I'll defeat you again, but I won't punish you for serving Pompey when he was your lawful commander.'

'Why?' asked Petreius. 'You could demand anything. Why let us walk away?'

'Because dead Romans serve no purpose, and imprisoned Romans make dangerous enemies.'

Afranius nodded slowly.

'Accepted. I'll take discharge and I believe most of my officers will do the same. Some might join your legions, those who have no families to return to in Italia.'

'They're welcome,' said Caesar. 'I judge men by what they can do, not who they served before.'

The negotiations took until afternoon and the details were settled, discharge procedures, transport, integration of soldiers who wanted to switch sides.

Marcus watched the Pompeian standards being lowered in the formal ceremony, thousands of men, beaten but not broken, being sent home with provisions and travel money.

'What troubles you?' said Corvinus, joining him.

'He treats them like potential recruits, not enemies who a few days ago would gladly have killed us without question.'

'He's being merciful.'

'He's being strategic. Big difference.'

One of the Pompeian centurions walked past and caught Marcus's eye.

'Your general's either a saint or a serpent. I haven't decided which.'

'He's Caesar,' said Marcus. 'That's its own category.'

The centurion laughed.

'Well, this particular Caesar just freed me to go home and tell my wife I lost to a man who thought killing me was wasteful. She'll have opinions about my career.'

'Tell her you survived. That's more than most manage.'

'That's what worries me. I think she'll make me take up farming.'

Three days later, word came that Varro had surrendered in southern Hispania without a fight. Two more legions, their auxiliaries, and the naval forces at Gades, all of it handed over when they heard what happened to Afranius.

'Seven legions,' said Caesar when Marcus brought the news. 'Four months, and fewer casualties than a Gallic skirmish. I call that more than satisfactory.'

'Varro surrendered because he heard you let Afranius walk free. Your reputation's spreading.'

'Good. It encourages people to be reasonable. I prefer enemies who surrender intelligently to enemies who die stubbornly.'

Letters from Italia arrived while Caesar was settling the provincial administration. Marcus watched him read them, saw his expression shift from neutral to cold.

'They're refusing my latest offers of peace,' said Caesar, setting down the latest scroll. 'Cato says compromise with tyranny legitimises tyranny and Pompey says he'll only accept my complete surrender.

'And the senate, do they have an opinion?'

'Aye, they do. The Senate says my clemency proves I'm weak.'

'What will you do?'

'Keep winning until they understand the difference between Caesar offering peace and Caesar imposing it.' His voice had gone flat. 'I tried mercy and they're calling it cowardice. Now they can have the alternative.'

The integration of Pompeian soldiers into the legions went about as well as could be expected, which meant badly at first.

'They wanted to kill us three weeks ago,' said Pullo when Marcus brought two new recruits to one of the contubernia. 'Now I'm supposed to trust them at my back?'

'They surrendered and Caesar pardoned them so treat them with respect. You don't have to trust them today, but you can't abuse them. Clear?'

'Clear, Praefect.'

The two new men, Gaius Albinus and Titus Memor, stood there looking uncomfortable.

'You're assigned to the second contubernium,' Marcus told them and you have a chance to prove yourselves. What happened before doesn't matter. What happens now does.'

'Understood, Praefect,' said Albinus. 'We served Afranius well and we'll serve Caesar the same. Politics are above our pay grade.'

Pullo showed them to their tent positions without warmth but without hostility. Professional courtesy, nothing more. Trust would come later, or it wouldn't. Either way, discipline would hold.

Marcus found Gavius in the quartermaster's office two days later, surrounded by supply tallies.

'I thought you'd take the discharge,' said Marcus.

'And go where? I've got no family. The army pays me to count things so why would I leave?'

'Because soldiers die in battles.'

'Civilians die from disease, bandits, starvation, and a dozen other things. At least soldiers eat regularly.' Gavius didn't look up from his wax tablet. 'Besides, I'm good at not dying.'

Marcus almost smiled.

'How are the Pompeian soldiers adapting to supply work?'

'Better than in the combat units. Nobody in logistics cares which general you served. We count food, distribute gear, and manage inventories. Politics matter less than arithmetic.'

'You've got opinions about loyalty?'

'Loyalty's a luxury for people who don't need steady wages. For people like me, loyalty is whoever pays better and wins more. Caesar does both. Simple.'

News from the east came in late August. Pompey had nine legions in Greece, forty thousand men, plus cavalry from his eastern allies. The numbers were bad.

'He used the time well,' said Caesar, studying the maps. 'Nine legions, better cavalry than ours, Senate legitimacy, the treasury, and most eastern provinces. His position's stronger than ours.'

'Can we win?' asked Marcus.

'Eventually but not immediately. We'll consolidate in Rome then cross the Adriatic and fight him wherever he has gone to ground. It'll be difficult and costly.'

'The men wanted glory. They might get it.'

'Yes. Though I suspect their enthusiasm will moderate after they watch comrades die in large numbers. Nothing cures eagerness for battle like actual battle. Send word to the Legates, Praefect, tell them to prepare their legions. We are going back to Rome.'

Chapter Eighteen

Gaul

The Alps in autumn presented different challenges than the mountains had offered during Caesar's earlier crossing. Snow dusted the highest passes, warning that winter approached and campaigning season was ending for commanders who respected traditional limitations. Caesar had never been traditional about limitations.

Marcus marched through mountain passes with his command, watching the Italian peninsula spread below them as they descended towards familiar territory. Months ago they had crossed these same mountains heading to Hispania, and now they returned as victors carrying Caesar's reputation for clemency and strategic brilliance ahead of them like the standards preceding the legions.

The political situation in Rome had shifted during their absence. The Senate in Rome, or what remained of it after the Pompeian loyalists fled east, had concluded that Caesar's military superiority required accommodation rather than continued resistance. Formal hostilities within Italia itself had ended, and what remained was the coming confrontation with Pompey's eastern forces, the decisive campaign that would determine which faction controlled the Republic's future.

Now, as Caesar's forces came down from the Alps and reached the Rubicon for the second time in a year, news reached them the Senate had appointed Caesar dictator.

The announcement carried weight beyond its immediate political implications, for dictatorship was emergency measures, temporary grants of absolute authority to address crises that normal governance could not resolve. Caesar would hold the position for the duration necessary to restore order, conduct elections, and establish stability before returning power to constitutional mechanisms.

'Dictator,' said Corvinus, testing the word.

It meant that Caesar held authority that exceeded consular power, answered to no colleague, and faced no tribune veto. He was effectively monarch until he chose to relinquish the office.

'Sulla held the same position,' observed Marcus. 'He used dictatorial power to proscribe enemies, reform the constitution, and then voluntarily retired after restoring what he considered proper governance. Caesar will presumably follow a similar pattern: use absolute authority to resolve the crisis, then step down once normal politics can resume.'

'Do you really believe that Caesar will voluntarily surrender power after experiencing what it means to command without limitation?'

Marcus did not have a confident answer. Caesar's behaviour throughout the civil war suggested pragmatism rather than rigid principle. He had crossed the Rubicon when political survival required it, shown mercy when strategic advantage recommended it, and made decisions based on effectiveness rather than on ideological consistency. Whether he would surrender dictatorship depended on whether doing so served his interests better than retaining power indefinitely.

'I think Caesar will do whatever seems most advantageous when the time comes to decide,' he said. 'For now, dictatorship provides legal authority for his actions and removes constitutional obstacles to governing whilst Pompey remains in the field.'

They reached Rome in late September, entering the city

not as conquerors but as legitimate forces under constitutional authority and Marcus walked through the Forum whilst Caesar's legions made camp outside the city walls.

Rome felt different from when they had left it, emptier, quieter, less confident. Many more prominent families had departed, taking wealth and influence east, and those who remained were either committed to Caesar's cause or pragmatic enough to accept whoever controlled Italia.

'Strange being back,' said Pullo, accompanying Marcus through streets they had not seen since their return from Brundisium. 'We left as rebels and return as legitimate forces. The Senate that declared us enemies is now meeting across the sea whilst Caesar's Senate welcomes us home.'

'Two Senates, both claiming legitimacy,' said Marcus. 'Two versions of the Republic, both insisting they represent constitutional authority. Eventually one Senate will cease to exist, probably along with many of its members.'

'You think it ends that way? With executions and proscriptions?'

'I think civil wars end when one side lacks capacity or will to continue fighting. Pompey shows no signs of losing will, and his capacity grows as the eastern provinces provide men and resources. If he cannot be defeated through battle, Caesar will need to eliminate the opposition through other means. We secured Hispania without major bloodshed, but Greece will not be so accommodating. The battles there will be brutal, the casualties substantial, and the aftermath will determine whether this civil war ends with reconciliation or with purges. I suspect the latter.'

Pullo was silent for a moment.

'The men are eager for battle. They wanted glory in Hispania and got manoeuvring instead. They think Greece will provide the combat they craved.'

'It will, and many of them will die experiencing it. Glory looks different when you are bleeding in the mud watching friends die around you.'

'You have become rather grim.'

'I have become realistic. Caesar's clemency in Hispania was possible because Afranius was pragmatic, but Pompey surrounds himself with senators who view compromise as betrayal. When we face them, there will be no reasonable surrender, no generous terms, no mercy extended or accepted. There will be Romans killing Romans in numbers that make our previous battles look trivial. The men want glory, and they will get it along with wounds, terror, and mass graves.'

They returned to camp as evening settled over the city. Marcus could see cooking fires spreading across the hills where the legions were establishing temporary quarters before moving to Brundisium for the crossing preparations.

Caesar spent three weeks in Rome consolidating his political position, appointing magistrates, and conducting elections that legitimised his authority through constitutional forms even if those forms were constrained by military reality.

Marcus attended some of these proceedings, watching Caesar navigate political complexities with the same competence he applied to military operations. The dictatorship was temporary in theory, but permanent in function, and Caesar exercised his newfound power through constitutional mechanisms that made authority appear legitimate rather than imposed.

They departed Rome in mid-October, marching south towards Brundisium whilst Caesar remained behind to complete his political arrangements. The legions moved through countryside that showed harvest season's completion, fields cleared, granaries filled, and farmers preparing for winter.

Marcus marched with the Thirteenth, watching veterans train new recruits in techniques that would keep them alive during the coming battles across the sea. The many former Pompeian soldiers, Albinus and Memor among them, had integrated adequately into their units and were accepted as competent professionals if not yet as trusted comrades.

'How do they seem?' asked Corvinus, observing training exercises where veterans demonstrated shield formations whilst recruits attempted to replicate them.

'Competent. Trust develops through shared combat experience, and we have not yet fought together yet.'

'Will they stand when battle comes?'

'Most soldiers fight for their contubernium and their century rather than for abstract causes. As long as they trust their immediate comrades, they will stand.'

'And if they do not?'

'Then they will run, and we will fill gaps with men who hold. Afterwards we will execute deserters as examples.'

Corvinus looked troubled.

'You speak of executing Roman soldiers very casually.'

'I speak of military necessity. Desertion during battle endangers everyone, and the penalty is death. That has always been true, and will remain true regardless of who commands or why we fight. War is brutal, and discipline is maintained through fear as much as through loyalty. We are going to Greece to kill Romans in numbers that will horrify everyone involved and pretending that enterprise can be conducted gently is nothing short of fantasy.

They reached Brundisium in early November and the port city bustled with activity as engineers constructed transport ships, quartermasters assembled supplies, and soldiers trained for operations that would begin once weather permitted crossing. The Adriatic in winter was notoriously dangerous, but danger could be exploited if it achieved surprise that offset any numerical disadvantage.

Within days, news arrived from Greece that Pompey had fortified Dyrrhachium and Apollonia, concentrating his nine legions in defensive positions that made supply straightforward whilst threatening any Roman crossing attempt.

The strategic situation was clearly unfavourable. Pompey held superior numbers, better positioning, and command of the sea that made reinforcement easy and invasion hazardous.

Traditional wisdom suggested waiting until circumstances improved, but Caesar was not interested in traditional wisdom. He arrived in Brundisium in late November with the final political arrangements complete and a few days later, Marcus attended the command briefing where Caesar outlined his intentions.

'Pompey has nine legions in Greece,' he said, 'perhaps forty-five thousand men, plus cavalry from eastern allies that will outnumber our Gallic horsemen significantly. He controls the Adriatic's eastern coast, holds fortified positions in major cities, and expects us to wait until spring when weather permits safer crossing and we can assemble larger forces.'

He paused, studying maps spread across the command table.

'We will, however, cross in December with whatever ships we can assemble. We will land south of Dyrrhachium, establish a beachhead before Pompey can react, and force him to respond to our presence rather than prepare at leisure for spring invasion. The crossing will be dangerous, the initial fighting will be desperate, and we will be outnumbered in hostile territory with uncertain supply lines.

The assembled officers were silent and Marcus watched their faces register what Caesar was proposing.

'This is insane,' said one of the tribunes quietly.

'This is necessary,' said Caesar. 'Pompey grows stronger each month we delay, and his position improves whilst ours remains static. We cannot win through attrition when he controls the eastern provinces and Mediterranean trade, so we must force battle before his advantages become insurmountable. That requires crossing when he does not expect it, landing where he is unprepared, and moving faster than his superior forces can respond.'

'And if we succeed?' asked another officer.

'If we succeed, we force Pompey to fight on our timeline rather than his. If we fail, we lose, the war concludes with Pompey victorious. Those are the stakes and those are the odds. We cross in three weeks.'

Caesar dismissed them to prepare their commands. Marcus walked back to his command's camp area, thinking about what he would tell his men.

Pullo was waiting.

'Bad news?' he asked.

'We cross in three weeks,' said Marcus. 'A winter assault against superior forces in defended positions.'

Pullo was quiet for a moment.

'Well, the men wanted glory and are about to receive more than they desired.'

'Yes, but make sure they understand what is coming.

This will not be manoeuvring like Hispania but desperate fighting in winter storms with limited supplies and no retreat possible.

'You want me to frighten them?'

'I want you to prepare them. Tell them the truth, that it will be brutal, and many will not survive. Then tell them that standing together gives them better chance than running alone. We are going to Greece to kill Romans and to be killed by Romans. Better they hear it from us now than discover it when they are standing in formations watching friends die around them.'

The three weeks before departure were consumed by preparations. Ships were loaded with supplies, soldiers practiced embarkation procedures, learned to maintain equipment in confined spaces, and trained for fighting immediately after disembarking from ships onto potentially hostile beaches.

Marcus watched and saw veterans teaching recruits tricks for staying alive during amphibious operations. Nothing created unit cohesion faster than knowledge that they would soon be fighting together against overwhelming odds.

Caesar addressed the assembled legions the day before departure. He stood on a raised platform where all could see him, seven legions of Roman soldiers preparing for an operation that would either win the war or lose it completely.

'Tomorrow we cross the Adriatic to attack Pompey's forces in Greece,' he said, his voice carrying across the assembled formations. 'The crossing will be dangerous, the landing will be desperate, and the fighting will be brutal. Pompey has superior numbers, consolidated positions, and control of the sea. Traditional military wisdom says we should wait until conditions favour us, so therefore we attack now, when he is unprepared, forcing him to respond to our presence rather than prepare at leisure for our eventual arrival. I will not lie to you and claim this will be easy or that casualties will be light for this will be the hardest fighting you have yet experienced, and many of your comrades will die. You will watch friends killed beside you, and you will question whether survival is possible and whether the cause justifies the cost. In those moments, remember that we fight not for abstractions but for each other, for the Republic, and for the future that will be determined by whether we stand or break when the fighting becomes desperate. You are Roman soldiers, the finest legions in the Republic, led by generals who have never lost a campaign. We will cross that sea, we will establish a beachhead, and we will defeat Pompey's forces. And we will end this civil war through superior fighting, superior discipline, and superior will. Those are not empty promises but facts based on your proven capabilities and my confidence in your courage.'

'Rest well tonight for tomorrow, we begin the final campaign of this war, and when it is finished, Rome will be united under constitutional governance, and you will be the veterans who won the Republic's civil war through extraordinary courage under impossible conditions. That is glory worth achieving. That is victory worth the cost. That is why we fight.'

He dismissed the men and Marcus watched the effect ripple through the formations, soldiers processing the reality that they were about to attempt something genuinely dangerous with uncertain outcomes and guaranteed casualties.

'He did not sweeten it,' observed Corvinus.

'He never does when stakes are genuine. Hispania

required encouragement because men were disappointed by lack of glory, but Greece requires honesty because men need to understand what is coming or they will break when reality exceeds their expectations.

'Do you think we will we win?'

'I think we will win because Caesar understands that victory in civil war comes from moving faster than your opponents expect and hitting harder than they are prepared to withstand. Do not forget that Caesar has never lost, and Pompey has never faced an opponent who refused to fight defensively. When those two realities collide, Caesar's aggression will shatter Pompey's defence, assuming, of course, enough of us survive the crossing to make that collision possible.'

Most of the ships set sail by noon the following day, the sails catching the wind that would carry them east across winter seas towards Greece.

Marcus sailed in one of the first transports, and watched the shore recede into grey distance, counting the standards still visible on the docks. Caesar had assembled twelve legions at Brundisium, but the transports could only carry seven. He could have waited months to gather more vessels, but instead he chose speed over safety, accepting the risk of sailing immediately with whatever ships were available. Four legions now remained behind, perhaps fifteen thousand men waiting their turn to be deployed.

Antonius would bring them once the empty ships returned, assuming the ships survived winter storms and Pompey's winter-harboured fleet reacted slowly enough to miss them.

The calculation was brutal and simple: seven

understrength legions against Pompey's nine, stranded in hostile territory with uncertain supply and no reinforcement until the transports made their return voyage.

If Caesar's forces did not survive the landing, Antonius would avenge them rather than reinforce them but either way, Pompey would face Roman legions before he was ready.

The gamble was insane. Caesar had calculated that surprise would offset any numerical disadvantage, and that Pompey's fleet would be slow to react during winter when most commanders kept their ships in harbour.

It was insane but if the gods were with them, it just might work.

Chapter Nineteen

The Adriatic Sea

For the next two days, the Adriatic tried to kill them and Marcus gripped the rail as another wave crashed over the bow, drenching everyone on deck in freezing spray. The transport pitched violently, timbers groaning, and somewhere below men were screaming from fear or seasickness or because they'd been thrown against bulkheads hard enough to break bones.

'Get below!' shouted the pilot, barely audible over the wind. 'You'll be washed overboard!'

Marcus ignored him. Below deck was worse. Men were packed together in darkness, vomiting, praying, and some weeping openly whilst the ship bucked and rolled. At least on deck he could see the waves coming, could brace himself, and could breathe air that didn't reek of piss and bile.

Around them in the darkness, other transports fought the same battle. He caught glimpses of them between waves, dark shapes rising and falling, lanterns swinging wildly and sails torn or reefed tight against the gale. A nearby ship had lost its mast and the crew fought desperately to keep it from capsizing whilst the soldiers aboard prepared to die.

Pullo appeared from below, staggered across the pitching deck, and vomited over the side. He stayed bent over the rail for a long moment, then straightened and wiped his mouth.

'Half the men think we're going to drown,' he said. 'The other half wish we would, just to end the misery.'

'How many are injured?'

'A dozen or so broken bones, twice that many gashed heads from being thrown around below. One man broke his arm when we hit that last wave, his bone is sticking through the skin.'

Marcus said nothing for there was nothing really to say. They were in the middle of a winter storm on the Adriatic with no physician and no way to treat serious injuries beyond binding wounds and hoping men didn't die before they reached shore.

The ship climbed another wave and at the top, Marcus could see dozens of transports scattered across dark water, the fleet spread out by wind and current, each vessel fighting its own battle against the storm. The ordered formation they'd left Brundisium in had dissolved into chaos.

'We're scattered,' said Marcus. 'Even if any ships survive, we'll land spread along miles of coastline. It'll take hours to reform the legions, assuming Pompey's forces don't hit us whilst we're still organizing on the beach.'

'Assuming we reach the beach at all,' said Pullo, 'and we don't all drown first.'

Another wave crashed over the bow and icy water surged across the deck, knee-deep, pulling at their legs. A sailor lost his grip and slid towards the rail, but two others grabbed him and hauled him back, the water draining away through the scuppers, leaving the deck glistening and treacherous.

Marcus made his way below. The hold was nightmare of sound and smell with terrified soldiers sat pressed together on benches, gripping anything they could hold whilst the ship bucked beneath them. Most looked green and many were vomiting into buckets that were already overflowing.

'How much longer, Praefect?' someone asked, as Marcus staggered past.

'Until we reach shore or sink,' said Marcus. 'Whichever comes first.'

'Helpful.'

'Do you want comforting lies?' snapped Marcus, 'or would you rather have the truth? I know which I would rather have.'

He walked on and the ship rolled hard to port. Men slid across benches, crashed into each other and someone's equipment came loose, clattering across the deck. The roll continued, kept going, the ship tilting further and further until Marcus wondered if they were going to capsize.

Then slowly, reluctantly, the transport righted itself. Men exhaled and some resumed praying. Others just sat holding whatever they could grip, waiting for the next wave.

Marcus climbed back on deck. The storm showed no signs of easing and if anything, the wind had strengthened. Waves were breaking over the bow with every swell now, sending water surging across the ship. The pilot was shouting at his crew, trying to adjust course to take the waves at a better angle.

Corvinus emerged from below, moving carefully across the wet deck. His face was grey.

'We've lost another man,' he shouted. 'He hit his head when we rolled. His skull's cracked and he's unconscious, probably dying.'

'How many does that make?'

'Three dead or dying, a few dozen or so injured, everyone else just wishing they were dead. This crossing is going to cost us men before we ever face Pompey.'

The following morning as the sun fought to break through the disappearing storm clouds, Marcus awoke on wet sand, his lungs burning, and limbs trembling from exhaustion and cold. Around him, men sprawled where they'd collapsed after dragging themselves from the surf. Some were unconscious, some were dead, he couldn't tell which without checking, and checking required moving, and moving required strength he didn't have.

He forced himself to breathe, to think, to assess.

The beach stretched in both directions, littered with wreckage. Bodies rolled in the surf, some soldiers, some sailors, impossible to tell how many. Crates and barrels drifted in the shallows alongside equipment that soldiers had dropped or lost during the landing and further down the beach, a transport lay on its side, half-submerged, rolling waves breaking over its hull.

Out at sea, ships scattered across the grey water as far as he could see. Some were intact, struggling towards the shore, while others drifted, their masts broken, the crews onboard trying desperately to regain control.

One vessel was clearly sinking, its bow already under whilst men jumped into the water rather than go down with it. Further out, barely visible through morning mist, more transports fought wind and current, blown off course, and separated from the fleet.

Marcus pushed himself to kneeling position. Around him on the beach, hundreds of Romans lay scattered like driftwood. No formation, just exhausted men who had survived the crossing and wanted nothing except to lie still and not move and not think about getting back on any ships.

He stared for a few moments longer, and as he started coming back to his senses, he realised they were too vulnerable. They were scattered along miles of coastline, disorganised with no defensive positions and no idea where they were. Pompey's forces could already be watching them and if his cavalry came over those hills right now, they would be slaughtered on the beach before they could even form ranks.

Marcus forced himself to his feet and started to walk amongst the survivors.

'On your feet,' he said to the nearest soldiers but none reacted.

He walked to the closest man, and nudged him with his boot.

'I said, get up.'

'Can't. Too tired.'

'Either get up or die here when Pompey's cavalry arrives.'

The soldier opened his eyes and stared at Marcus, then slowly, painfully, pushed himself to sitting position.

Marcus moved to the next man... and the next, pulling some to their feet, kicking others awake, and dragging a few away from the surf before waves could pull them back. His strength was returning with movement and his voice was getting stronger.

'Everyone, up on your feet. You're not dead yet but soon will be if we don't get a defensive position. Centurions, sort out your men.'

More men were stirring now. Some stood on their own, others needed help. A few didn't move at all, either already dead or too injured to respond. Marcus left those and focused on soldiers who could still fight.

A centurion appeared, soaked and limping.

'Praefect. My cohort's scattered. I've got maybe forty men I can account for.'

'It's a start,' said Marcus. Gather anyone who can still hold a sword and form them up there.' He pointed to higher ground beyond the beach. 'I want a defensive line facing inland. We'll organise properly later but right now we just need bodies between us and whatever could be hiding in those hills.'

The centurion nodded and started shouting at the men around him. Other centurions started doing the same, rallying soldiers, and forming small groups that slowly became larger groups, and slowly, the beach started coming alive with movement, men standing, grabbing weapons, and looking for their units.

Marcus kept walking, kept pulling men to their feet, kept pushing exhausted soldiers towards positions that might keep them alive if they were hit before they could properly organise. He passed bodies he recognised, men from his command who hadn't survived the landing, but he kept moving. There would be time for the dead later.

Pullo appeared, dragging two men by their equipment straps.

'I found these hiding behind that wreck,' he said, 'they're alive, just terrified.'

'Get them to the defensive line,' replied Marcus. 'Anyone who can hold a gladius holds position.'

'What about the wounded?'

'Gather them away from the surf. We'll assess any injuries once we've secured the area.' Marcus looked up to see more ships approaching the beach. 'And get men ready to help soldiers coming ashore now. Some of those transports look damaged.

Pullo moved off, shouting at soldiers he passed. The beach was transforming from chaos into something resembling organization. No proper formations yet, no cohesion, just exhausted Romans standing with weapons ready whilst they scanned the hills for signs of enemy forces.

Marcus kept moving, kept organizing, and kept building defensive positions from whatever men he could gather before putting them in positions where they could fight if necessary.

Corvinus found him before noon.

'We've located another thousand men or so beyond the headland. Hundreds more are unaccounted for but those who are alive are in a good state.'

'Put them on the northern perimeter. We're vulnerable to attack from those hills.'

'Already done, Praefect. The centurions are forming proper lines now that men have recovered enough to follow orders.'

The beach was filling with soldiers as more transports arrived. Thousands of Romans organizing into cohorts and centuries, reforming the legions that had been scattered by storm and landing. It was still chaos, but it was becoming organised chaos with men finding their units, centurions accounting for their soldiers, and tribunes establishing command posts.

Marcus climbed to higher ground where he could see the entire beach. The defensive line was growing, not strong, but ready to fight if attacked.

Out at sea, more transports were approaching and beyond them, barely visible through morning haze, a larger vessel flying standards that even at this distance were recognizable. Caesar's command ship.

The landing had been desperate and costly, but they had secured a beachhead. They were disorganised and exhausted and had lost men to storms that had nothing to do with combat, but they were in Greece, they were armed, and they were forming defensive positions before Pompey could react… and that wasn't a bad start to any campaign.

Chapter Twenty

Illyria

Later that day, Marcus watched as the last of the men stumbled ashore, half retching into the surf whilst their centurions bellowed them into formation. Two days of winter seas had turned legionaries into pale shadows, and now they had to march.

'Get them moving,' said Caesar, appearing beside Marcus without warning. 'Pompey will know we've landed within hours and we need ground between us and this beach before his cavalry arrives.'

'The men need time to recover, Imperator.'

'The men need to still be alive tomorrow,' said Caesar and turned to address the men within earshot.

'Centurions! Form your centuries. We march for Oricum at first light and any man still pissing seawater can do it whilst he walks.'

Laughter rippled through the nearest cohort, weak but genuine. Marcus had watched Caesar do this a hundred times, turning exhaustion into momentum with nothing but words and will.

The following morning, seven depleted legions trudged north along the coastal road, leaving the beach behind like a bad memory. The sun climbed into a pale winter sky, offering light but little warmth and Caesar rode near the front with the rest of his staff.

Within a few hours, one of their advance patrols rode back down the road to meet them.

'Imperator,' he said, giving Caesar a salute. 'Our scouts

report Oricum's garrison has withdrawn. The City's practically empty.'

'Empty or simply a trap?' asked Caesar

'Empty, General. Our Greek guide says the garrison commander is a man called Torquatus and values his life over loyalty.'

'Then we will take the city before he realises his mistake.' Caesar turned in his saddle, finding Marcus in the group behind him.

'Praefect. Take two centuries of the Ninth. I want Oricum's gates secured before nightfall.'

Marcus saluted and wheeled his horse around, his pulse quickening. Finally, movement instead of sailing.

The two centuries he commandeered were from the Ninth's second cohort, veteran troops who'd fought through Gaul and looked distinctly unimpressed by the Adriatic winter. Their centurion, a grizzled Campanian named Vorenus, spat into the dust when Marcus explained their orders.

'Forced march to take a city with just two centuries. Fuck me, but the man never changes.'

'Can your men do it?'

'Can they breathe?' Vorenus turned and roared at his century.

'Double time, you lazy bastards! Last man to Oricum buys wine for the whole fucking cohort!'

The men increased their pace, changing between trotting and walking at regular intervals, the steady jog that ate up the miles without them realising. Marcus urged his horse to a gentle trot, keeping pace with the front ranks whilst the coastal road unwound beneath them.

The distance was short, perhaps twenty miles, and they covered it before the winter sun began its descent. Oricum appeared ahead, perched on its natural harbour, the walls old but well-maintained, but the docks empty of warships.

Marcus called a halt and studied the approaches whilst Vorenus's men caught their breath. There was no movement on the walls and no standards flying. Either the garrison had truly fled, or they were waiting to spring whatever trap they'd prepared.

'Thoughts?' Marcus asked Vorenus.

The centurion scratched his stubbled jaw.

'The gates are shut but nobody's defending them. If they had ballistae, we'd see them. If they had archers, we'd see them. If they had anyone with balls, we'd see them. The place is empty, Praefect, or close enough.'

'So we just walk up and knock?'

'Politely, with a ram.'

They advanced in formation, shields up despite the apparent absence of defenders. The gates of Oricum stood twenty feet high, solid oak banded with iron, but when Vorenus's men put shoulders to their improvised ram, a beam torn from a dock building, the bar inside gave way with embarrassing ease.

The city beyond lay quiet, not abandoned, exactly, but subdued.

'Spread out,' Marcus ordered. 'Check the garrison barracks, the harbour and the granaries. Anyone you find, bring to the forum but no looting, the Imperator will want this city intact.'

The centuries dispersed as Marcus rode to the centre of town, where a small forum opened around a fountain decorated with faded mosaics.

An old man in military dress waited there, standing stiffly beside two Parthinian soldiers who looked ready to bolt.

'Are you Torquatus?' asked Marcus.

'I am Lucius Manlius Torquatus,' came the reply. 'Commander of this garrison, by Pompey's appointment. Or I was, until your Imperator decided January was sailing weather.'

'Where are the citizens?' asked Marcus looking around.

'Many left, but those that remained are understandably nervous and wait to see what sort of conqueror sails in the dead of winter. Those in power told me quite clearly they wouldn't fight a Roman consul, no matter what the Senate says. So here I am, Praefect, surrendering a city I was ordered to hold because the Greeks I'm defending refuse to be defended.'

'You could have fled.'

'I could have.' Torquatus straightened his shoulders. 'But I'm a Roman officer, not a coward. If Caesar wants Oricum, he can have it, along with me, if he wants that too.'

Marcus studied the older man, seeing tired dignity rather than defiance.

'The Imperator's terms are generous,' he said eventually. 'Surrender the garrison, swear an oath not to fight against him, and you're free to go.'

'That simple?'

'That simple. Caesar needs cities, not corpses.'

Relief flickered across Torquatus's face, quickly hidden.

'Then Oricum is yours, Praefect. The Parthinians will surrender their arms when Caesar stands before the gates of the city.

By the time Caesar arrived with the main column, the city already belonged to him. The Imperator rode through Oricum's gates at dusk, as his legions made camp outside the

223

city walls, their standards catching the last light. He found Marcus in the commandeered garrison headquarters, where Torquatus and his Parthinians were being processed.

'Any resistance?' asked Caesar.

'None, Imperator. Torquatus surrendered and we basically walked right in.'

'Good.' Caesar studied the map on the wall, his finger already tracing north.

'Apollonia next. It's a larger city with a better harbour, but currently occupied by a Pompeian garrison under Staberius. We'll move at first light and I want to be at their gates before they've finished breakfast. Speed, Marcus, that's what wins wars, speed and the opponent's certainty that resistance is pointless.

They marched at dawn, moving north along the coastal road, pushing hard. The distance to Apollonia was just over twenty-five miles of coastal road and winter mud, but they covered it in under a day of brutal marching that left men sleeping in their kit the moment the halt was called.

Apollonia sprawled across low hills above the Aous River, its walls rising white in the morning sun. It was larger than Oricum, more prosperous, and more defensible. Standards still flew from the gates, Pompey's standards, and Marcus could see movement along the battlements. Someone was home, and they weren't opening the gates.

Caesar called a halt outside ballista range and studied the walls through narrowed eyes. The legions spread across the plain below the city, forming a loose semicircle that cut Apollonia off from the north and east while the river protected its western flank, and the sea its south.

'Well,' said Marcus 'they're not throwing flowers.'

'No, said Caesar, staring at the walls, 'but they're not sallying out to drive us off either. Someone in there is thinking.'

They waited. An hour passed, then another and Marcus watched the walls, seeing faces appear and disappear, seeing arguments play out in gestures and pointing.

The citizens would be panicking by now, looking at seven legions and doing their own calculations about survival.

An hour later, the gates opened, not to attack or surrender, but to emit a single rider who galloped north at speed.

Marcus watched him disappear along the coastal road, heading for Dyrrachium and Pompey.

Caesar rode up beside Marcus, studying the closing gates with an expression somewhere between frustration and amusement.

'He ran,' he said. 'The bastard actually left his garrison and his city and ran for Pompey like a child for his father.'

'The garrison might still resist,' said Marcus.

'They might,' said Caesar and turned to shout up to the walls. 'I would speak with whoever commands Apollonia! Or are you all too busy watching your governor flee?'

For a few moments, there was silence until eventually, a figure appeared, an elderly Greek wearing enough gold to ransom a cohort. His voice shook when he called down, switching between Greek and heavily accented Latin.

'The garrison is gone, Imperator, and Staberius has fled! We are defenceless so if we open the gates to Caesar, we beg his mercy!'

A few moments later, the gates opened again and Caesar, protected by two centuries of legionaries, rode through.

Caesar established his headquarters in the largest

magistrate's house and immediately began organising. Marcus found himself assigned to secure the port, where a dozen ships sat at anchor, mostly merchants, but also three Pompeian quinqueremes whose crews had apparently decided switching sides beat swimming home and by nightfall, Apollonia belonged to Caesar as completely as Oricum did.

Later that night, he stood in the commandeered courtyard, maps spread across a table that had probably hosted dinner parties for Greek merchants a week ago, his staff gathered around whilst he traced lines north towards Dyrrachium.

'Three days,' said Caesar, almost to himself. 'We've been in Greece three days and we control two major cities and fifty miles of coast. Pompey has nine legions and six months of preparation behind him, and we walked through his coastal defences like they weren't there.' He looked up, finding Marcus in the crowd. 'Send word back to Brundisium. Tell Antonius to start loading the other legions. We need them here before Pompey stops reeling and starts planning.' Caesar's finger stabbed at the map. 'Dyrrachium, that's where this gets decided. If we take that, we cut him off from reinforcements and force him to fight on our terms.'

'He'll be fortifying it already,' said Labienus from across the table.

'Then we'll need to be clever.' Caesar straightened, rolling his shoulders. 'But first we consolidate what we have. Fortify both cities, and establish supply lines. Make it clear to every garrison commander from here to Dyrrachium that surrender means survival. Let Pompey figure out how to defend Greece when his own officers are looking for exits.'

Marcus left him there, still planning, still calculating, already three moves ahead whilst everyone else was still processing what they'd accomplished.

The city settled uneasily as legionaries and civilians learned to coexist, the former wanting wine and women, the latter wanting not to be robbed or murdered. Caesar's discipline held, mostly, and when two men from the Seventh were crucified for raping a young girl, the lesson stuck hard enough that Apollonia's streets stayed relatively peaceful.

January became February and the winter sun climbed higher, offering marginally more warmth, though the nights remained bitter and the seas still ran rough enough to make any crossing from Brundisium dangerous.

Caesar fortified both cities, turning them into proper bases whilst he waited for Antonius to risk the crossing with the remaining legions.

Marcus spent his days managing logistics and his nights wondering when Pompey would stop retreating and start attacking. Seven legions sounded impressive until you remembered the enemy had nine, plus superior cavalry, plus all the resources of the eastern provinces. They'd seized the initiative, but holding it would be harder.

'Praefect.' Caesar's voice cut through his thoughts. The Imperator had appeared in the harbour warehouse where Marcus was reviewing grain inventories, his presence turning administrative tedium into something more urgent. 'Walk with me.'

They walked along Apollonia's harbour wall, the winter wind cutting through their cloaks, the sea grey and hostile below. Caesar said nothing for a long while, just stared out at the horizon where the rest of their army remained trapped across the Adriatic.

'We're vulnerable,' said Caesar finally. 'And Pompey knows it. Seven legions, cut off from reinforcements, living on borrowed time until either Antonius crosses or Pompey crushes us. Everything depends on speed now. We moved fast, seized two cities, and established a position. But if we stop here, if we wait too long, Pompey will have time to concentrate his forces and turn this into the siege we can't win.'

'What do you need, Imperator?' asked Marcus.

'I need Antonius to stop being afraid of winter seas and get his arse across the Adriatic, said Caesar, 'and I need Pompey to keep hesitating. Caesar turned from the sea, his expression hard. 'And I need everyone in this army to understand that there is no going back. There's only forward, and forward means Dyrrachium.'

'When do we move?' asked Marcus, realising where the conversation was headed.

'As soon as Antonius arrives. It could be a week, it could be a month, depending on weather and whether Pompey's navy catches him.' Caesar started back towards the city. 'Until then, we prepare. Train the men, stockpile supplies, fortify our positions, and make everyone believe we're exactly where we want to be.'

'Are we?' asked Marcus.

Caesar's laugh held no humour.

'We're alive, we're in Greece, and Pompey hasn't killed us yet. That's as close to where I want to be as this war allows.'

February turned to March and the seas moderated slightly, enough that Caesar began sending urgent messages to Brundisium, demanding Antonius risk the crossing.

Pompey's cavalry appeared on the coastal road north of Apollonia, probing their defences but not attacking and the standoff continued, neither side strong enough to force a decision, both waiting for something to shift the balance.

Then, in early April, as Caesar was contemplating attacking Pompey with his existing forces, a small fleet of ships appeared on the southern horizon, approaching from the south.

'Those are our transports,' called a lookout, 'Antonius is here!'

Marcus ran for the harbour, where half the army was already gathering. But as the ships drew closer, his excitement faltered. Not dozens… six… maybe eight. A fraction of what they'd expected.

Caesar stood at the harbour's edge, watching the handful of transports approach. For once, the Imperator's mask slipped, showing something that might have been disappointment quickly masked.

'Better than none,' he said quietly.

The transports began landing that afternoon, disgorging seasick legionaries onto the timber quays throughout the dock. Perhaps a few hundred men, some cavalry and a few supply wagons. Not the three legions they'd hoped for and certainly not thousands of reinforcements Caesar needed.

A young tribune was first off the lead ship and raced up the steps with a grin that suggested he'd just accomplished something impossible. He found Caesar in the growing crowd and saluted.

'Tribune Marcus Antonius sends his regards, Imperator. The storms were a problem but we are intact.'

'So where are the rest of the fleet?' asked Caesar.

'He shouldn't be far behind us, Imperator. We were the first to set sail but he's coming.'

'How many men did you bring?'

'Five hundred legionaries, two auxiliary cohorts and supplies for a month. Not much, but Antonius sent us ahead to let you know he's on his way. He figured even a few hundred extra swords would help.'

'He figured correctly.' Caesar clasped the tribune's arm. 'Get your men fed, billeted and rested. When Antonius arrives with the main force, we'll need everyone ready to move.'

That night, Apollonia celebrated. Not the wild relief of the full army reuniting, but the cautious optimism of men who'd been given hope. Wine appeared from nowhere, songs echoed through the streets, and for a few hours the war seemed less desperate.

Marcus found himself in a tavern near the harbour, surrounded by Ninth Legion centurions and the newly arrived auxiliaries, all of them trading stories. Vorenus was demonstrating how he'd rammed Oricum's gates with nothing but a dock timber and sheer fucking will, whilst one of the new arrivals countered with his tale of slipping past Pompey's navy in the darkness.

'To Caesar,"someone shouted, raising a cup. 'The mad bastard sailed an entire army through the winter storms and we are here to tell the tale.'

'To Caesar,' the tavern roared back.

'To Antonius,' someone else shouted, raising his cup. 'May the mad bastard bring the rest of the army before Pompey figures out we're still undermanned!'

The rest of the tavern laughed but joined the toast anyway.

Marcus drank with them, feeling the wine warm his exhausted bones, but his mind stayed sharp. The extra men certainly helped, but they still faced Pompey's nine legions with only seven of their own. Everything depended on Antonius getting through with the rest.

He looked at the celebrating soldiers and hoped their optimism was justified. Because if Antonius didn't arrive soon, all the wine in Apollonia wouldn't save them from what Pompey would do.

Chapter Twenty-One

Apollonia

The celebration lasted exactly one night and Marcus woke before dawn to find the camp already stirring, centuries forming up in the pre-dawn darkness whilst centurions bellowed orders that echoed off Apollonia's walls. He stumbled from his billet, head pounding from too much wine and found Vorenus already armoured and looking disgustingly alert.

'Imperator's orders, Praefect. We march in one hour. Full kit, forced march. Someone fucked up and we're paying for it.'

'What happened?'

'Antonius landed at the wrong fucking place.' Vorenus spat into the dust. 'The storms blew him north to Lissus, fifty miles past where he is supposed to be. Now Pompey's between him and us, and the bastard's moving to crush Antonius before we can link up.'

Marcus felt his wine-fogged mind clear instantly.

'Where's Caesar?'

'Where do you think?' Vorenus jerked his thumb towards the forum. 'Planning how to march an army fifty miles before Pompey murders half our reinforcements.'

Marcus found Caesar in the commandeered magistrate's house, maps spread across every surface, his staff clustered around him.

'Praefect,' said Caesar as Marcus strode in. 'Are the Thirteenth ready to go.'

'Yes, Imperator.'

'Good, then put them in the vanguard. We leave in one

hour. Pompey's moving on Antonius and we need to be faster.'

'Can we reach him in time?'

'We'd better.' Caesar finally looked up, and Marcus saw something that might have been fear quickly hidden. 'Because if Pompey crushes four legions whilst we're still fifty miles south, this war ends today. And not in our favour.'

They marched as the sun rose, seven legions streaming north from Apollonia in columns that stretched for miles along the coastal road. Marcus rode near the front with Caesar's staff, watching the Imperator push his horse forward, and drop back to check the columns, before pushing forward again. The man never stopped moving, never stopped calculating, his mind always three problems ahead whilst his body refused to acknowledge the strain.

'Scouts!' Caesar called, as two riders appeared from the north, their horses lathered and blowing hard. 'Report.'

'Pompey's moving, Imperator, heading north along the inland road. They're between us and Lissus.'

'How far ahead?'

'Ten miles, maybe twelve. But they're moving slower with a Baggage train and full kit. They're not expecting you to catch them.'

Caesar's smile was thin and calculating.

'Then let's surprise them. Pass the word back, any man who falls out stays fallen. We don't stop for stragglers.'

The pace increased, from brutal to punishing. Legionaries ran in their armour, shield and pilum rattling, boots pounding the coastal road whilst centurions roared encouragement and threats in equal measure. Men began to drop with exhaustion or twisted ankles or simply bodies that refused to continue, and the columns flowed around them like water around stones.

Marcus pushed his horse forward, riding alongside the lead cohorts, watching veterans who'd marched across Gaul and Italy now gambling everything on reaching Antonius before Pompey did.

The sun climbed higher and the day warmed into something almost pleasant, which made the running worse. Men drank from their water skins as they ran, their sweat soaking through tunics, and their breath coming hard and fast. The coastal road unwound before them, mile after mile of Greek countryside that none of them saw because their eyes were on the ground and their minds were on survival.

By mid-afternoon, the scouts had returned again.

'Pompey's stopped,' said the lead rider, his face showing disbelief. 'He's pulled his army off the road and is making camp. We're gaining on him fast.'

Caesar turned to his staff.

'Keep moving! Pompey thinks we're sleeping off wine in Apollonia whilst he prepares to crush Antonius. Let's show him what real legionaries can do!'

They kept moving and within a few hours, the sun began its descent, the shadows lengthening across the road. Night closed in and they kept moving, the road visible only by starlight. Somewhere inland, Pompey slept in his camp, confident that Caesar remained fifty miles south while somewhere ahead, Antonius waited with four isolated legions, watching the horizon for either rescue or destruction.

Caesar pushed them through the darkness and they reached Antonius two hours before dawn.

Marcus saw the picket fires first, then the outline of marching camps, then standards flying that belonged to legions he recognised and auxiliaries from half the allied tribes of Gaul.

Caesar rode into Antonius's camp without ceremony, his staff trailing behind, his exhausted legions collapsing into whatever space they could find. Marcus followed, watching the Imperator scan the organised chaos until he spotted the big tribune emerging from his command tent.

'You're late,' said Antonius, grinning despite the circumstances. 'I was beginning to think you'd stopped for wine.'

'My men ran fifty miles in twenty hours to save your arse,' said Caesar dismounting, his joints creaking, and his face grey with exhaustion. 'Next time, land where I tell you to land.'

'The storms had other ideas,' said Antonius, 'but you made it. Now it's time to stop running and start fighting.'

'Not yet,' said Caesar, 'Pompey is near, he may even be ahead of us. But he's going to wake up to find we've slipped past him in the darkness. We can't stay here.'

Marcus blinked. They'd just run fifty miles, linked up with Antonius in darkness, and Caesar wanted to keep moving?

'The men are exhausted, Imperator.'

'The men are alive, which they wouldn't be if we'd arrived tomorrow afternoon. Pompey's whole strategy depends on that supply base. His reinforcements come through it, his grain comes through it, and his connection to the east runs through it. If we take position north of here, we cut him off from Dyrrachium and everything that keeps his army functional.'

'He'll fight to defend it,' said Antonius.

'Let him. We've got our legions now, and ground of our choosing. If he attacks, he dies on our pila. If he doesn't attack, he starves whilst we're supplied from Dyrrachium.' Caesar straightened, rolling his shoulders. 'Either way, we've turned this from a race into a siege. And I'm very good at sieges.'

They moved again before dawn, eleven legions filing north in the darkness whilst Pompey followed his own path along the inner road. Caesar pushed his men hard, gambling that exhaustion mattered less than position, and knowing that the men could rest after they'd secured the vital ground between Pompey and his supplies.

By the time the light started to fail, the legions were already building the first of their marching camps, knowing that now more than ever, they were at risk from Pompey's well-trained army.

Caesar rode the lines, his presence turning exhausted legionaries into men who found reserves they didn't know they had.

Marcus watched him work, transforming disaster into advantage through nothing but will and the absolute refusal to accept defeat but by mid-morning the following day, the scouts returned with grim news.

'Pompey reached Dyrrachium first, Imperator. He beat us by hours. He's established his main camp at Petra, south of the city, on high ground overlooking the harbour.'

Caesar's jaw tightened, the only visible sign of frustration.

'How defensible is his position?'

'Very. He's on a rocky outcrop with his back to the sea. We're cut off from Dyrrachium completely.'

'Then we don't need Dyrrachium,' said Caesar after a few moments, 'we simply need Pompey. So we build a wall around him and make him choose between attacking fortified positions or watching his army wither whilst we get stronger.'

'He's got the sea, Imperator. Ships can resupply him from the harbour.'

'They can, but it will take time to organise an efficient supply and we control everything inland. He will suffer soon enough and very day he sits there is another day his horses starve for lack of fodder or thirst for fresh water.' Caesar gestured at the terrain between their position and the distant coastal hills where Pompey's camp lay. 'Build the wall and make it long enough that he can't break out without massive casualties. Force him to attack or starve.'

'And us?' Marcus asked quietly. 'We're the ones foraging from picked-over countryside whilst he's got ships bringing grain from every Pompeian port in Greece.'

'Then we'll learn to be hungry,' said Caesar. 'We've done it before and my men are better at being hungry than Pompey's recruits are at being besieged.'

The fortifications grew over the following days, Caesar's men building an enormous circumvallation that stretched from the hills inland toward the coast, trying to encircle Pompey's position at Petra. Marcus watched the line extend and the forts rise at regular intervals, as Caesar attempted something audacious and possibly insane.

In the distance, Pompey's standards remained visible on the high ground at Petra, five miles south along the coast, the rocky outcrop giving him commanding views of both the harbour and Caesar's growing siege works. Some ships came and went from Dyrrachium's harbour, unloading supplies that kept Pompey's fifty thousand men partially fed whilst Caesar's men ventured further and further inland for diminishing returns.

'Why does he not attack?' observed Antonius, watching

the distant Pompeian camp from their position on the northern end of the siege lines. 'He's just sitting there being comfortable whilst we dig.'

'Because attacking would cost him thousands of men and he knows it,' said Marcus. He gestured at the fortifications spreading south toward the sea. 'But we're the ones starving, not him. We need to close the ring before our men collapse from hunger.'

Chapter Twenty-Two

Dyrrachium

For days, men moved across the slope in a great, ragged arc, their mattocks rising and falling as they built the immense siege walls. Marcus walked the ridge above them, his cloak gathered in one hand, his eyes tracking the sweep of the line they meant to carve into the valley.

An engineer hurried beside him, holding a wax tablet tight against his chest.

'If we shift the angle here,' he said, pointing at the edge of the ridge with his stylus, 'the ditch will catch the run of the ground rather than fight it.'

'Then shift it,' Marcus said. 'I trust your judgement.'

The man nodded and hurried off to place a new marker.

Down in the ditch two men strained at a stubborn root, grunting as the mattock heads jarred through their arms. One spat soil from his mouth and jabbed a thumb towards Marcus.

'He will have us cutting through rock next,' he muttered.

'And you will cut it,' said a nearby centurion, 'or I will use your skull as the wedge.'

The men laughed and swung again, the root coming free in a shower of dirt and as the work progressed, the bank rose in slow, patient layers.

A cart creaked around the bend, two Gauls hauling at its ropes while a legionary steadied the axle. Rough timber lay stacked high on the bed, the ends already shaped to points.

'Where are you taking that load?' asked Marcus.

'To the eastern run, Praefect,' said one of the men.

'Good. They will need it before the next watch. If the ground softens, brace the bank before you set the first posts.'

The cart moved on, leaving scuffs of fresh sap on the frosted ground. At the far end of the works a stake crew lifted their first post and four men bore the length of timber across their shoulders while a fifth guided the tip into the shallow trench cut into the crest. The ram swung in a slow, heavy arc and landed with a deep thud that travelled through the ground to Marcus's boots.

'Again,' their centurion called.

The ram rose again and the post drove deeper.

Marcus stepped over the cord that marked the walkway behind the palisade and moved to where two young soldiers were struggling with a basket that dripped mud as fast as they lifted it.

'Up with it,' he said.

Both men stiffened and hoisted the basket between them and the mud sloshed against the wicker as they staggered up the slope.

'First time on ditch work?' Marcus asked.

'Yes, Praefect,' one of them answered, breathing hard.

'You will hate it by nightfall,' Marcus said, 'but you will be better at it tomorrow.'

The man gave a faint grin.

'Is that a promise?'

'It is the curse of every soldier who lives long enough.'

He left them to it and returned to the central run where the ditch had already grown deep enough that only the tops of helmets showed above the cut. Men passed baskets hand to hand along the trench, their movements smooth, almost graceful despite the weight.

A trumpet sounded the half-day and men dragged

themselves from the trench while fresh crews stepped in.

By late light the palisade had grown into a jagged line above the rampart, each post set tight against its neighbour and men lashed ropes between the stakes, pulling them tightly together.

Marcus climbed onto the rising walkway and scanned the length of the defences where the ditch snaked across the valley floor in a dark curve. The rampart behind it had taken its full height, packed firm by hundreds of boots and smoke drifted from the camp inside the growing circle of earth and timber. Vorenus joined him on the top.

'It's coming together,' he said.

'It is,' said Marcus, 'but whether it is quickly enough, is another matter.' He gripped the top of one of the stakes. It felt solid beneath his palm, cold and strong. 'Tomorrow we finish the eastern run.'

Below them, sentries walked the freshest length of the rampart, testing the ground with measured tread as the ramparts grew beneath their feet. The valley was being shaped to Caesar's will while in the distance, beyond the stakes… Pompey watched with growing concern.

In Pompey's position, men worked on their own ramparts with renewed urgency as word spread that a patrol that had been sent north along Caesar's works to seek out any weaknesses had failed to return.

Pompey stood once more on the walkway beside the southern tower, the boards creaking softly beneath his boots. From this height the distant line of Caesar's fortifications stretched along the hills like a wound cut into the land, each section marked by the faint glimmer of torches that flickered against the falling dusk. The light was steadier now that the rain had eased, and each torch burned like an amber bead pinned against the slope.

Labienus joined him, folding his arms as he followed Pompey's gaze. The cut across his cheek had dried into a thin, dark line, though the tension at the corners of his eyes had not eased.

'Those walls look higher every hour,' he said quietly.

Pompey did not answer. He watched the ridge where the patrol had gone and counted the moments in silence.

The sky darkened into the colour of wet stone and as Pompey was about to turn away, a horn sounded from the far watchtower, one long note, then another.

'They return,' Labienus said, staring into the distance. 'Thank the gods.'

Pompey descended the walkway quickly and as the gate guards heaved aside the timbers, the patrol swept into the camp, steaming and mud-spattered.

The tribune in charge swung down, his boots sinking into the soft ground as he saluted Pompey with a sharp, urgent gesture.

'General,' he said, 'we found it.'

Pompey's voice remained level.

'Where?'

'The north ridge, beyond the marsh. Two of Caesar's redoubts stand too far apart to support one another. The ditch between them is half-cut and the rampart no higher than a man's waist. The palisade above it stands unfinished and there is ground enough for a legion to strike it head on.'

Pompey stepped closer.

'A true gap?'

'A true gap,' said the officer. Mud streaked the side of his face where he had wiped sweat from his brow. 'There were no more than thirty men holding the span. The ground dips where the marsh encroaches, and Caesar's engineers cut short rather than risk flooding their trench. They have not returned to finish it.'

'How wide is the gap?'

'Wide enough for a clean assault,' replied the officer. 'And beyond it lies a large but shallow basin. If Caesar sends reinforcements, he must either run them along the narrow ramparts or bring them over two steep rises. Either way, he gives us the advantage.'

Pompey inclined his head.

'You have done well.'

The riders dispersed to the horse lines as Pompey headed for his nearby command tent where the senators waited. Once inside, he briefed them about the situation before walking across to the map table, dragging his finger along the ridge's contour.

'Here,' he said. 'Two redoubts, both strong enough alone but useless together. It seems the marsh forced them to cut short, and the ditch shows it. If we strike with three legions, Caesar will be caught behind his own walls and his veterans cannot manoeuvre once the line collapses.'

As the information sunk in, Senator Ahenobarbus stepped forward his face almost excited at the news.

'If what you say is true,' he said, 'then you must strike immediately. That gap is ours if we move now.'

The tent filled with voices. Some senators argued to attack immediately while others demanded caution. Their excitement and fear rose until Pompey finally lifted his hand, and the noise died down.

'We do not strike merely for a breach,' he said. 'We strike to free ourselves from this valley. Once we tear open that line, we will move for the coast. We will resupply and then reform to meet him head on, as was always our plan.'

The senators stared at him in expectation and Pompey let the silence stretch as the wind pressed against the canvas, and the faint hiss of the sea drifted through the stillness. Finally, he looked again at the map, then at Labienus, then at the anxious, expectant faces of the Senate.

Finally, he made a decision and Pompey turned to Labienus.

'Prepare the legions,' he said. 'We march at last light tomorrow.'

Chapter Twenty-Three

Dyrrachium

Night settled across Pompey's eastern lines, hiding the quiet but urgent preparations being carried out by his most experienced legions as they prepared to advance. Varro, the tribune that had brought the information to Pompey the previous night now waited in the shadows between two supply wagons, one hand resting on the hilt of his short sword.

When the order finally came to advance, he gave a small nod and two Centurions, Fadius and Crispus, brought their centuries forward, each man blackened with soot and cloth-wrapped to silence the chink of armour.

'Keep tight and low,' Varro murmured, his voice barely louder than the wind. 'We'll take the goat track east of the hill, and follow it around. Once there, we'll go to ground and plan our next move.'

The men followed him out through the pickets, knowing that the whole breakout depended on whether they could force the initial breach. Behind them waited a unit of mounted engineers and beyond them, the first legion who would form the vanguard once through.

The land beyond the camp fell into deep folds of scrub, vine stumps and old terraces, illuminated by the occasional starlight that appeared from the remaining clouds blown by the retreating storm. The first few miles were relatively easy going as they were hidden from view by a small hill but as they got closer, the pace slowed and they needed to be far more careful.

Varro stopped at a gully and crouched, raising his hand as his men sank behind him. He watched as two of Caesar's sentries walked past on the unfinished ramparts, counting to himself before they reappeared, heading back the way they had come. He continued watching as they returned to repeat the process until he had finally identified the pattern and turned back to his men.

'There are two sentries on guard,' he whispered, 'and it takes about a hundred heartbeats before they turn and come back. When they next pass, we move.'

The men watched as the pair of silhouettes appeared on the crest above, their helms catching the barest hint of light. Their voices drifted faintly down, an idle conversation, one complaining of cold, the other laughing softly.

The moment their voices faded, Varro moved, climbing up the slope in a low crouch. The two centuries followed, spreading out behind him in a thin line that blended with the dark ground.

'Archers forward,' he whispered, going to ground again.

The bowmen slid past and readied their bows without a sound, checking strings and nocks by touch alone. Behind them the legionaries waited bare-headed, unshielded, their kit stripped to the essentials for silence and speed.

Varro halted beneath the bend in the palisade where the stakes were unfinished and several gaps still existed.

'As soon as we take out the guards,' he said, 'your men move onto the palisade. Take the left approach and deal with anyone you come across, quietly if possible but do not waste time. Once secure, form a position to repel any counterattack.'

Crispus nodded once and Varro turned to Fadius.

'You do the same on the right. We have to move quickly as the others will be right behind us. Any questions?'

Both men shook their heads and they took the final stretch at a slow climb, keeping their bodies low against the ground.

Moments later, the two sentries reappeared and the archers straightened up in the dark.

'Hold,' whispered Varro, '...hold... *now!*'

Twelve arrows hissed through the night sky and both sentries fell off the palisade without a sound. Two more shapes moved along the palisade towards them but the archers loosed again and they joined their dying comrades in the mud, riddled with goose-fletched arrows.

Crispus moved the instant the final volley landed, climbing fast, his men close behind. Another defender's head lifted above the walkway, eyes widening at the approaching men but before he could call out, an arrow thudded into his throat, silencing him forever.

'Advance,' said Varro, his voice louder, and the men surged forward, climbing the poorly placed stakes and onto the walkway beyond.

More defenders came running, their voices rising as they realised what was happening but it was too late and Pompey's men surged in both directions, cutting down anyone who moved without mercy. The fight ended quickly and moments later, the short section of palisade lay still.

'Get into position,' ordered Varro. 'Where's the signaller?'

A man appeared at his side and gave the tribune a shuttered lantern. Varro opened the cover to give three short flashes back towards Pompey's position and a few moments later, a faint answering light blinked across the plain. The signal had been seen.

'Now we wait,' said Varro, 'and hold the line. No movement unless ordered.'

A few minutes later, twenty mounted men appeared out of the darkness with ropes coiled across their saddles and iron grappling hooks swinging from leather straps. Varro waved the lantern again and the horsemen reined in their mounts just below the palisade.

The engineers immediately retrieved their ropes and the hooks flew upward, the iron claws spinning against the dark sky before biting deep into the timbers.

Three missed their marks and flew uselessly beyond the palisade but Varro and two of his men retrieved them and secured them to a crossbar that held three of the larger posts together.

'Secure!' Crispus called from further along the wall.

'Secure!' echoed another voice.

Varro leaned over and called into the darkness.

'Pull!'

The riders dug their heels in and the horses lunged forward, their hooves scrabbling for purchase on the slope. The ropes snapped taut and the timber groaned before the base of one tore free with a spray of dirt and splintered wood. Another followed, then two more, each pole dragging clear in a cascade of earth and broken stakes.

Other horses strained harder and within moments a section of palisade twenty paces wide had been torn completely away, leaving a gaping mouth in Caesar's defences.

Varro stared at the breach, his chest heaving. Dust hung thick in the air, and through it he could see the open ground beyond, the fires of Caesar's inner camp glowing faintly in the distance. More timbers followed and as the breach grew, a new sound rose behind him, faint at first but building quickly into a steady roar.

He turned and saw them coming across the plain,

shadows at first, then shapes, then men, hundreds of them pouring forward in tight formation with their shields raised and their helmets catching what little light remained.

Pompey's vanguard had arrived and swept past Varro's position without breaking stride. They moved through the gap in a disciplined stream, splitting left and right as they emerged on the far side, their centurions shouting orders that were swallowed by the din of marching feet and clashing equipment.

'Form the flanks!' bellowed a voice. 'Shield wall, both sides! Hold the breach!'

The first cohort wheeled left and locked their shields together in a tight line, whilst another cohort mirrored them on the right and within moments the breach was secured, a corridor of armed men standing ready to repel any counter-attack Caesar might throw at them.

The sound of hooves rose again, deeper this time, more rhythmic and Varro pressed himself against the remains of the palisade as the first of the cavalry thundered past, their spears held high and their cloaks streaming behind them like dark wings.

They burst through the gap, five hundred riders strong, then their horses snorting and tossing their heads as they accelerated into the open ground beyond.

Behind them came the legions, moving at double-time, their ranks tight and their shields catching the starlight in rippling waves of bronze and iron. The ground trembled under the weight of thousands of boots striking in unison, and the air filled with the creak of leather, the clink of mail, and the deep rhythmic breathing of men pushing themselves to their limits.

Varro watched them pour through the breach, cohort after cohort, legion after legion, an unstoppable flood of Pompey's finest troops breaking free from the trap that had held them for weeks.

The dust rose in great clouds that obscured the stars, and somewhere in the distance, the first clash of weapons echoed through the night as some of Caesar's defenders finally rallied to meet them.

'We did it,' Fadius said quietly, standing beside Varro with his sword still drawn and his face streaked with dirt.

Varro said nothing. He simply stared at the chaos he had unleashed, watching Pompey's army surge through the gap like water through a broken dam, and wondered whether history would remember this night as the moment the tide had finally turned.

A few miles away, on the higher ground, Caesar and Marcus stood on the inner walkway of their fortified camp, the cold biting through their cloaks.

Caesar looked outwards toward the darkness beyond the outer works, his expression as calm as the mask of a carved god. The lines of fatigue at the corners of his eyes were sharp in the half-light, yet his voice felt steady when he finally spoke.

'It's too quiet tonight.'

Marcus kept his own eyes on the hills.

'I suspect Pompey will try something soon,' he said.

'I agree,' said Caesar, 'he has been waiting for a weakness but will not find one.' He paused a moment, then glanced at Marcus. 'Are your men rested?'

'Tired from the construction,' said Marcus. 'But no more than that.'

Caesar gave a single nod and turned as Torquatus approached along the walkway and saluted.

'All sectors report calm, general,' he said.

Caesar nodded and looked back into the darkness,

satisfied that everything was as it should be, but as he turned away to return to his tent, somewhere far off, down along the marshy ground to the north-west, a faint sound drifted through the dark.

Marcus stepped alongside Caesar and felt the hairs rise along his arms.

'Do you hear that?' he asked quietly.

Caesar's head tilted slightly.

'I did, it sounded like a scream.'

Before Marcus could reply, a horn sounded, faint and urgent, from the north-western palisade. A single blast, then another.

'Something is wrong,' said Caesar. 'Come.'

They strode along the walkway, passing the first of the men already rousing from the ready-tents as the watch horn blared again, higher this time, edged with urgency.

As they increased speed, runner came stumbling along the rampart, his breath ragged.

'General, there is movement at the marsh gap, many men, too many to count.'

Before Caesar could respond, a worrying sound echoed up from the lower palisade, an echoing roar that rolled across the valley like a storm breaking, the sound swelling until it seemed the earth itself was groaning under the weight of an unseen army.

Voices started being raised through the camp, as sentries called men to arms and fires burst into life as watchmen thrust torches into kindling.

Another crash erupted from the dark as Pompey's vanguard clashed with Caesar's outer forces and finally they were under no illusion whatsoever.

'Sound the alarm,' said Caesar. 'We are under attack.'

A horn blared from somewhere in the darkness beyond the breach and as the sound of Pompey's legions grew louder, Marcus felt the weight of what was happening settle in his chest.

Caesar turned and moved quickly along the walkway, calling out orders as he went. Men rushed to obey and the camp erupted with activity as legions that had been sleeping just moments ago now raced to form ranks in the darkness.

A tribune stumbled up the ladder to the walkway, his face flushed and his breath coming in gasps.

'Imperator,' he said, 'the Twelfth Legion reports movement on the western approach. They request orders.'

'Western?' Caesar's head snapped around. 'Are you certain?'

'The centurion said…'

'Which centurion?' Caesar cut him off. 'Where exactly on the western line?'

The tribune hesitated, suddenly uncertain.

'He did not specify, Imperator. Only that there was movement.'

Caesar bit back whatever response rose in his throat and turned to scan the western defences, but the darkness showed him nothing and he spun back to the tribune.

'Find out what is happening. I need details. How many men, where precisely, and whether they are engaging or simply repositioning. Go!'

The tribune saluted and disappeared into the chaos as another runner arrived, this one younger, barely more than a boy. 'General! The Fourth Cohort of the Ninth asks whether they should reinforce the northern redoubt or hold position at the marsh gate.'

'The marsh gate?' Caesar stared at him. 'Who ordered them to the marsh gate?'

'I...I don't know, Imperator. They said they received orders...'

'From whom?' Caesar's voice rose despite himself. 'Who gave those orders?'

The boy's face went pale.

'Tribune Sulpicius, I think. Or perhaps it was...'

'Never mind.' Caesar waved him off. 'Tell them to hold their position until I send further word. And find Sulpicius. I want to know what other orders he has been issuing without my authority.'

A third messenger appeared, then a fourth, both speaking at once until Caesar silenced them with a sharp gesture.

'One at a time!'

'The Eighth Legion requests permission to advance from the eastern camp, General.'

'Denied. They hold position.'

'And the cavalry commander asks whether to deploy his reserve. He says he retained two squadrons for...'

'Tell him to deploy them immediately. No, wait.' Caesar paused, his mind racing through too many variables at once. 'Send them to support Torquatus at the northern sector. Or...' He stopped again, looking towards the breach where Pompey's formations were spreading wider. 'No. Have them stand ready at the centre. I may need them to plug gaps.'

The messenger hesitated.

'Which order should I...'

'The centre!' Caesar snapped. 'Tell him the centre, and make it clear this time!'

Marcus moved closer and spoke quietly.

'The men need clear direction, Caesar, too many conflicting orders will…'

'I know what they need,' snapped Caesar, and looked out at the breach again, at the enemy pouring through in numbers he could not yet count, and deploying in formations he could not yet read. For a moment he simply stood there whilst the camp erupted in confused activity around him.

Another centurion appeared on the walkway.

'Imperator, the Thirteenth reports ready, but they ask whether they should form testudo or open order.'

'Open order. No, testudo.' Caesar shook his head. 'It depends on whether Pompey sends cavalry or infantry first. Can you see which?'

The centurion squinted into the darkness.

'No Imperator. It's still too dark to see the details.'

'Then find out!' shouted Caesar, 'and send word to the artillery crews. I want every scorpion we have aimed at that breach. If they mass for a charge, I want them bloodied before they reach our line.'

'The crews are asking about range and elevation.'

'Tell them to use their judgment,' interjected Marcus. 'They are trained for this.'

The centurion saluted and left whilst two more runners arrived, and Marcus watched as Caesar dealt with each in turn, his orders coming faster now, more urgent, but also more fragmented and some contradicting what he had said only moments before.

'Marcus,' said Caesar, 'I need you to find out exactly how many men Pompey has brought through that breach. I need numbers, not guesses and in the meantime, deploy the ninth to hold him up.'

Marcus nodded and turned to go, but Caesar caught his arm.

'And Marcus? Be quick about it. We're running out of time.'

Marcus saluted and ran for the ladder whilst behind him, Caesar turned back to the breach and watched his advantage slip away into the darkness.

Marcus reached Torquatus at the far end of the camp as the Ninth Legion buckled on their armour. Men grabbed shields, tightened straps, and pulled helmets over their heads.

'To the breach!' shouted Marcus. 'Caesar wants the Ninth on the line! Move!'

The Ninth formed without hesitation and followed Marcus across the camp at a run, their boots pounding the earth, their breath steaming as they charged for the rampart where the sound of battle rose like thunder.

As they neared the breach, Marcus saw the disaster unfolding before him. Pompey's men had torn the palisade wide open and thousands were already inside the rampart, hacking left and right as Caesar's defenders fell back in tight knots, shields raised, fighting yard by yard.

A fire pot burst against the walkway, showering men in flames, and as screams of pain and terror tore the night apart, Marcus lifted his sword and headed straight towards Pompey's vanguard.

The Ninth Legion slammed into the rampaging enemy and as shields struck shields and blades clashed, the walkway became a crush of bodies. Marcus shoved forward and drove his blade into a man's ribs, before wrenching it free as another fell against him. The roar of battle closed around him and within moments, the whole world seemed to erupt into merciless, terrifying violence.

What seemed like hours later, but was probably only minutes, a horn call rose behind him, faint at first, then growing stronger as Caesar arrived with reinforcements and the men in the front lines straightened at the sight whilst their shouts rose in renewed force. But the line was already buckling and Marcus could see it in the faces of the defenders, that desperate look of men who had been holding too long against too many.

Men stumbled over each other in the chaos, shields tangling with shields whilst centurions bellowed orders that were drowned out by the roar of battle. A supply wagon had overturned near the main gate, spilling amphorae across the path and blocking reinforcements from reaching the breach and somewhere in the darkness an entire legion stood waiting for orders that never came, their commander having been killed in the initial assault and no one knowing they were there.

'Hold the line!' shouted Caesar. *'Hold!*

The Ninth pressed forward and for a brief span of heartbeats the line steadied. But then a fresh wave of Pompey's infantry surged up the ditch, smashing into the defenders like a hammer.

Marcus looked over the edge of what remained of the ramparts, only to see more men, more torches and more shields spreading out across the ground below like a dark tide that would not stop rising.

'General!' shouted Marcus. 'We cannot hold.'!'

Caesar's answer came through clenched teeth.

'We have to, Praefect, if we can hold until dawn, we can deploy our reserves.'

Marcus sensed doubt in Caesar's voice, but orders were orders and he turned away to join the men fighting for their lives in the darkness.

When dawn finally came, it brought no relief, only a momentary lull and a sense of clarity as they saw Pompey's full host pouring through the breach, a river of men flooding the basin beyond the rampart and spreading out in perfect formation.

The valley shook beneath their advance and their standards rose high whilst trumpets blared in synchronized calls that echoed off the hillsides. Cohort after cohort emerged through the gap, each taking position with the discipline of troops who had been waiting weeks for this moment.

One of Caesar's junior officers stared down at the sight, his face white with fear.

'Gods help us... they have broken the ring.'

Caesar did not blink. His jaw tightened and his hand gripped the rail until his knuckles showed white, but his voice remained steady when he spoke.

'Signal every cohort. Prepare to fall back.'

The order rippled down the line and the withdrawal began, but it was nothing like the controlled retreats they had practiced in Gaul. Men fell back in ragged clusters, some units maintaining formation whilst others broke and ran. A century of the Tenth held their ground too long, refusing to abandon the breach, and were cut off and surrounded before their centurion finally ordered them to fight their way clear. None emerged alive.

The Thirteenth formed the rearguard, their shields locked tight as they backed away step by step whilst Pompey's vanguard pressed against them. Javelins hissed through the morning air and every few paces a man would fall and the line would close around the gap. They made Pompey pay for every foot of ground, but they gave ground, nonetheless.

Caesar rode behind them on a horse someone had brought forward, directing the retreat with sharp gestures and shouted commands that cut through the confusion.

'The Ninth falls back to the second ridge! Twelfth Legion, form on the left flank! Keep the line dressed!'

But the line would not dress properly. Units became separated in the broken terrain and some centuries lost contact with their parent cohorts entirely. Officers shouted themselves hoarse trying to maintain order whilst their men stumbled backwards over ground they had fortified weeks ago and now abandoned to the enemy.

Marcus fought with the retreating ninth, his shield taking blow after blow as Pompey's men pressed relentlessly forward. His sword arm ached and his legs trembled with exhaustion, but he kept the men moving, one step at a time away from the breach that had swallowed their advantage.

A trumpet sounded from the main camp, the signal for the final withdrawal, and as soon as there was another lull in the fighting, the rearguard turned and ran. Not a rout, not quite, but close enough that Marcus felt shame burning in his chest even as his legs carried him towards the relative safety of the eastern ridge.

Behind them, the last of Pompey's army poured through the shattered fortifications and joined their comrades amongst Caesar's shattered positions. Pompey had finally broken free

----

Chapter Twenty-Four

Dyrrachium,

A few days later, several miles to the west, the first trumpet sounded before the sky had fully lightened, a long mournful call that rolled through the makeshift camps and pulled men from whatever shallow, broken sleep they had managed to grab. Marcus opened his eyes with a dull ache in every muscle, then pushed himself upright as another call answered from further along the line.

All across the hill, voices rose in harsh, tired shouts and somewhere close by, a man retched into the mud.

Men moved slowly through the grey half-light, reluctant to face what the new day brought but knew there was no other choice.

Marcus slung on his harness, feeling the familiar weight settle across his shoulders, then took his helmet under his arm and walked towards the heavily manned outer lines.

At the crossroads, the first cohort of the Tenth joined him, their shields held low and spears slanted over their backs. Their Primus Pilus, an old Gaul veteran with a scar like a white cord across his nose, saluted as Marcus approached.

'Praefect.'

'You have your orders?' said Marcus.

'Aye. We guard the rear of the column and will be the last to leave. 'If Pompey makes an appearance, we deal with it.'

'If they do appear,' said Marcus, 'you hold until the last man behind you is clear.'

The man's mouth twitched in something close to a smile.

'I have not let you down yet and do not intend to start

now.'

Marcus clapped his arm, then moved on.

Caesar's tent stood with its sides half open, as if the fabric itself had sagged with exhaustion. Inside, the Imperator stood over a table that had been stripped of all but a rough map and a few scattered stones marking positions. His cloak hung open, and dried blood stained one sleeve where a bandage had slipped. Torquatus stood opposite him, helmet under his arm, his eyes ringed by dark hollows. Caesar looked up as Marcus entered.

'Are the legions forming?' he asked.

'The Thirteenth is already on the road, the Seventh and Eighth behind them,' said Marcus. 'The rest will follow.'

Caesar nodded.

'Good. There is no time to waste.'

Torquatus shifted his grip on the helmet.

'Pompey had the chance to finish us yesterday,' he said. 'He did not take it.'

'He believed the gods had done the work for him,' said Caesar. 'Men who grow fat on prophecy forget how to use a sword. Come, I need to speak to the men.' He stepped out of the tent, and both officers fell in behind him.

The men outside parted as he walked, and he gave each cohort a glance, weighing their stance, their faces, the way their shields sat in their hands. They were tired, hollow-eyed, and stained with blood, smoke and dirt, yet the line of their shoulders still spoke of men who would answer a call and hold. He reached a rock embedded into the soil and climbed up so he could be seen by as many as possible.

'Legionaries,' he called, his voice carrying through the cold morning air, 'a few days ago you faced the worst that fortune could throw at you, and you did not break. You stood when others would have turned and you held firm when the ground itself betrayed us. Remember that. Hold it close for no man in this army has anything to be ashamed of.'

He paused, letting the words settle into them, letting them feel the weight of his gaze.

'Today we leave this valley behind us, and we will take only what we can carry in our hands and on our backs. The rest we will rebuild, with speed, with discipline, and with the skill that marks us as soldiers of Rome. What we lack we shall replace and what we have lost we shall reclaim.'

He leaned forward slightly, voice growing stronger.

'Pompey thinks he has crippled us. Let him think it. Let him cling to his hill and call it a victory. But hear me now: he has taken nothing that cannot be made anew. And he has given us something far greater in return, he has shown us the measure of his courage and the measure of his fear. That is worth more than any wagon of grain or pile of equipment.'

Several men shifted, glancing at one another.

'When we have rebuilt, and we will rebuild swiftly, you and I will march from these mountains and choose the ground of his reckoning. We will dictate the hour, not him, and we will finally end this war once and for all.'

The murmuring rose again, shoulders lifting, backs straightening. He raised his voice again, letting it ring across the assembled ranks.

'You survived the worst and that is why the best is still within your grasp. Stand with me now, and I swear to you: before this campaign ends, Pompey will look upon the eagles he once abandoned, and he will know the truth, that Rome belongs to the men who endure, not to those who hide behind the privilege of their birth.'

The murmurs were thicker now, rolling through the cohorts like a strengthening tide. Men squared their shoulders; heads lifted and shields settled more firmly on forearms as Caesar drew himself up.

'So hear me, soldiers of Rome. Today we march, not in retreat, but in preparation. Today we rebuild, not because we are broken, but because we are unbowed and when the time comes, we will stride out of these mountains with sharpened steel and renewed strength, and Pompey will feel the tread of an army that refuses to yield.' He swept an arm out over them. 'So I say this. Gather your packs, pick up your weapons and tighten your straps. This campaign is far from over, and when the battle horns sound again, it will be *we* who advance. The next blow will be ours!'

A roar broke from the ranks, rising from cohort to cohort as men slammed fists against shields, some shouting Caesar's name, others calling for Pompey's blood. The sound rolled across the valley walls and echoed back upon them, louder each time, until the morning air shook with it.

Officers moved along the lines, signalling the march and the cohorts shifted into motion, boots thudding, packs hoisted, and the formations tightening as the legions began to snake out of the valley, no longer a battered remnant but a force gathering itself anew.

Caesar stepped down from the rock as the last ranks moved past, the roar still fading on the cold air. When the noise had settled into the steady rhythm of marching feet, he turned to Marcus, who had remained at his shoulder throughout.

'Come,' said Caesar quietly, though the steel had not yet left his voice. 'There is work to do.'

Chapter Twenty-Five

Dyrrachium

The sun climbed higher over the ridge as Pompey's army spread across the valley floor.

Marcus Petreius, one of Pompey's senior legates, rode along the eastern perimeter where the Sixth Legion had already begun digging their section of the defensive ditch. The earth was soft here, easier to work than the rocky ground they had endured inside Caesar's ring, and the men moved quickly, their spades biting deep whilst spoil piled up behind them in neat ramparts.

'Keep the stakes close,' Petreius called to a centurion overseeing his century. 'Caesar may be running, but he is not yet defeated.'

The centurion nodded and turned to bark orders at his men as Petreius continued his circuit. Everywhere he looked, the camp took shape with the disciplined efficiency that had made Rome's legions masters of the known world. Tents rose in ordered rows, cook fires were lit in designated areas, and the sound of hammers driving stakes into the ground created a steady rhythm that spoke of normalcy returning after weeks of chaos.

But beneath the routine lay tension. The men worked faster than usual, their eyes flicking towards the western hills where Caesar's army had disappeared only hours before. They knew better than to celebrate too soon. Veterans remembered other battles where victory had turned to disaster in the space of a single poor decision, and no one wanted to be caught unprepared if Caesar found his courage and returned.

Labienus rode up beside Petreius, his horse still streaked

with mud from the morning's fighting.

'The northern approaches are secure. I have placed the Third Legion on the high ground with orders to maintain full watch rotations through the night.'

'Good,' said Petreius. 'What about the cavalry?'

'Screening our flanks and scouting the western road. If Caesar attempts to circle back, we will know hours before he arrives.' Labienus paused, watching the men dig. 'They are nervous.'

'They should be. Caesar is wounded, not dead, and wounded animals are dangerous.'

The two men rode in silence for a moment, observing the camp's progress. The outer ditch was nearly complete along the eastern side, and the rampart behind it already stood waist-high. Within the hour, the palisade stakes would be set and the gates positioned, and by nightfall, Pompey's army would sit behind defences that would make any counterattack costly.

'How many did we lose?' asked Petreius.

'Fewer than I expected,' said Labienus. 'Perhaps three hundred dead, twice that wounded. Most of the casualties came from the vanguard when they first broke through. After that, it was more pursuit than battle.'

Petreius nodded.

'And Caesar's losses?'

'Difficult to say. A thousand at least, maybe more. We counted thirty-two centurions among the dead, which tells you how hard they fought to hold that line.' Labienus gestured towards the western hills. 'He left bodies all along the ridge. His men carried away what they could, but there was not time to collect them all.'

They reached the southern gate where engineers were setting the timber framework into place, and Petreius reined in to watch them work. The gate would be crude, built for function rather than permanence, but it would serve its purpose.

'The senators will want to speak with Pompey,' said Labienus.

Petreius snorted.

'What they want is to congratulate themselves on a victory they watched from three miles away.'

'Nevertheless, they will want their moment. And Pompey will give it to them, because that is what politics requires.'

'Politics.' Petreius spat the word like a curse. 'We just won a battle. Can they not wait until the bodies are cold before they start planning their triumphs?'

Labienus smiled grimly.

'You have been a soldier too long if you think victory is only about the fighting. The Senate needs to believe they are still relevant, and Pompey needs them to believe it.' He gathered his reins. 'I am returning to the command tent. The council will gather within the hour.'

Petreius watched him ride away, then turned his horse back towards the perimeter. Around him, Pompey's legions continued their work, building walls that would protect them through the night whilst the western horizon remained empty and threatening.

The command tent stood at the centre of the camp, larger than the others and marked by Pompey's personal standard that snapped in the wind above it. Guards flanked the entrance, and inside, lamps had been lit against the dimness despite the afternoon sun that filtered through the canvas.

Pompey stood beside a table covered with maps, his

armour removed but his military belt still cinched around his tunic. He looked tired, the lines at the corners of his eyes deeper than they had been that morning, but his bearing remained steady. This was his tent, his army, his victory, and he would receive the Senate on his terms.

Labienus entered first and moved to stand beside the table without ceremony. Petreius followed, then a handful of other senior officers who had commanded the cohorts during the breakout. They arranged themselves in a loose semicircle, leaving space for the senators who would arrive momentarily. They did not have to wait long.

Lentulus entered with the kind of stride that suggested he believed himself the master of any room he occupied. Behind him came Scipio, then Ahenobarbus, then a cluster of other senators whose names carried weight in Rome but meant little on a battlefield.

Cato entered last, his expression as severe as always, his plain tunic unchanged from that morning despite the dust. He took his place at the edge of the gathered senators and said nothing.

'Magnus,' said Lentulus, his voice warm with congratulation. 'A victory for the Republic at last. The Senate owes you its gratitude.'

Pompey inclined his head slightly but did not smile.

'The Senate owes the legions their gratitude,' he said, 'not me. They are the ones who broke Caesar's ring.'

'Of course, of course,' Lentulus said quickly. 'But it was your leadership that made it possible. Your strategy, your timing, your…'

'My good fortune that Caesar's defences were incomplete,' said Pompey, cutting through the flattery. 'We won because Caesar made mistakes, not because we executed a brilliant plan. Let us be clear about that.'

The tent fell silent. Several senators exchanged glances, uncertain whether Pompey was being modest or making a point. Labienus stood motionless beside the table, his expression revealing nothing.

Scipio cleared his throat.

'Regardless of the circumstances, the result stands. Caesar has been defeated and driven from the field. The question now is what we do next.'

'We pursue him, of course,' said Ahenobarbus immediately. 'We have the momentum and we have the victory. We chase him down and end this war before he has time to regroup.'

'Agreed,' said another senator. 'Every hour we delay gives Caesar time to rebuild his strength. We must press the advantage while we still have it.'

Cato finally spoke, his voice cutting through the growing enthusiasm.

'And if we pursue recklessly and walk into a trap? Caesar is wounded, but he is not broken. Desperation makes men dangerous.'

'Desperation makes men weak,' Ahenobarbus countered. 'He is running so we must follow. It is that simple.'

Pompey remained silent, his eyes moving from face to face whilst the arguments built around him.

'Labienus,' he said finally, turning to his most experienced commander. 'What do you advise?'

Labienus stepped forward, his hands resting on the edge of the map table.

'Caesar has retreated west towards Thessaly. Our scouts report his army is intact but disordered. He will be gathering supplies and attempting to regroup, but his men are exhausted and their morale is broken. If we move now, we can catch him before he recovers. However, if we move now, we also risk extending our supply lines into hostile territory whilst chasing an enemy who knows he has nothing left to lose. Caesar is most dangerous when cornered.'

'Then what do you propose?' asked Ahenobarbus, his voice sharp with frustration. 'That we sit here and wait for him to gather his strength? That we allow him to rebuild his army whilst we celebrate our victory?'

'I propose that we consolidate our position,' interjected Pompey. 'We have broken his siege and have driven him from the field. That is enough for now.'

The tent erupted with protests. Senators spoke over each other, their voices rising until Pompey raised his hand for silence. The gesture took longer to work than it once had, and when quiet finally returned, the tension in the tent had thickened considerably.

'The war is not won by a single battle,' said Pompey. 'Caesar still commands his legions and he is still the most capable general Rome has produced in a generation. I will not throw away our advantage by rushing after him like a fool.'

Lentulus opened his mouth to respond, but Cato spoke first.

'Noone is asking you to rush, Magnus, but neither can we afford to wait. Every day we delay is another day Caesar uses to repair his fortunes. The question is not whether to pursue, but when.'

Pompey looked at Cato for a long moment, and something passed between them that the others could not quite read. Finally, Pompey nodded once, though the gesture carried more resignation than agreement.

'We will discuss this further once I have consulted with

my officers and received more detailed intelligence from the scouts. For now, the legions will rest and resupply. That is all.'

The dismissal was clear, but the senators were slow to leave. They filed out one by one, their conversations continuing in low murmurs that carried back through the tent flap long after they had gone. Only Labienus remained behind, standing beside the map table with his arms crossed.

'You know they will not let this rest,' said Labienus quietly.

'I know,' said Pompey. 'And they are not entirely wrong. Caesar is vulnerable. Perhaps more vulnerable than he has ever been.' He moved to the tent entrance and looked out at the camp beyond, where his legions continued their work in the fading afternoon light.

'I won the battle because Caesar made mistakes,' he said, 'I will not win the war by making the same ones.'

Over the next three days, the senators came to Pompey's tent in pairs and small groups, each delegation pressing the same argument with different words. They spoke of duty to the Republic, of the opportunity that would never come again, of the disgrace that would follow if they allowed Caesar to escape. Some appealed to his honour, others to his ambition, and a few simply stated the political reality that Pompey could not afford to ignore.

'The Senate expects action,' Lentulus said during one such visit, his tone leaving no room for misunderstanding. 'You have won a great victory, Magnus, but victories mean nothing if they are not followed through.'

'I am aware of what the senate expects,' said Pompey.

'Then why do we still sit here?' demanded Lentulus. 'Every hour we waste is another hour Caesar uses to slip further from our grasp.'

On the evening of the third day, Cato came to the command tent alone. He did not bring arguments or appeals, he simply sat across from Pompey whilst the lamps burned low and said what no one else had been willing to say.

'You are afraid of him.'

Pompey looked up sharply, but Cato's expression held no judgment, only observation.

'Not afraid,' said Pompey carefully. 'Cautious.'

'Call it what you will, the result is the same. You hesitate because you know Caesar is capable of turning defeat into victory, and you do not want to be the general who gave him that opportunity.' Cato leaned forward slightly. 'But consider this, Magnus. If you do not pursue him now, you will spend the rest of this war reacting to his movements instead of dictating your own. He will choose the ground and he will choose the timing. And when the next battle comes, it will be on his terms, not yours.'

Pompey said nothing for a long moment. Outside the tent, the camp settled into the quiet rhythms of evening watch, and somewhere in the distance, a legionary called out the hour.

'Go you think I should chase him,' asked Pompey finally.

'I think you have no choice,' said Cato. 'Not anymore.' He stood and moved towards the tent entrance, pausing only to look back at Pompey one last time. 'The Republic needs you to finish this. Not next month, or next year, but now, whilst Caesar is still reeling from his defeat. If you wait, he will recover, and when he does, you may not get another chance.'

Cato left without waiting for a response, and Pompey sat alone in the lamplight, staring at the maps spread across his table whilst the weight of expectation pressed down on him from all sides.

The following morning, Labienus was inspecting the northern perimeter when a runner found him with word that Pompey wanted to see him immediately. He rode back to the command tent to find the senior officers already assembled.

Pompey stood beside the map table.

'We march in two days,' he said without preamble. 'The Seventh Legion will form the vanguard and the cavalry will screen our flanks as we pursue Caesar into Thessaly.'

The tent filled with murmurs of approval, and Labienus let out a silent sigh. This was the decision he had been waiting for, the commitment that would finally end the war.

'What of the baggage train?' asked one of the officers.

'It follows at its own pace with a guard of auxiliaries. We travel light and fast. I want to cover at least twenty miles a day until we close the distance.' Pompey looked around at his officers. 'Caesar has a head start so we will need to move quickly if we hope to catch him before he reaches fortified ground.'

'And when we catch him?' asked Petreius.

'We force him to fight,' said Pompey. 'He cannot run forever, and his men are exhausted. Sooner or later, he will have to turn and face us, and when he does, we will finish what we started here.'

The officers saluted and began filing out to carry the orders to their legions, but Labienus remained behind. When the tent had emptied, he moved closer to Pompey and spoke quietly.

'You are certain about this?'

Pompey did not answer immediately. He looked down

at the map, at the roads that led west into Thessaly, and at the marks that showed Caesar's likely route.

'No,' he said finally. 'But certainty is a luxury I no longer have.'

Within hours, the camp transformed from a place of rest into a hive of purposeful activity. Legionaries packed their kit, centurions barked orders about march formations, and engineers began breaking down the fortifications that had been built only days before. The cavalry assembled in the southern fields, their horses groomed and ready, whilst the supply officers counted grain sacks and calculated rations for the march ahead.

The senators moved through the camp with renewed energy, speaking to anyone who would listen about the great victory that awaited them in Thessaly. Some had already begun composing the speeches they would give when they returned to Rome in triumph, and more than one discussed which honours they would claim for their role in ending Caesar's tyranny.

Pompey watched it all from outside his tent. Labienus joined him there as the sun began to set.

'The men are ready,' said Labienus. 'They want this as much as the Senate does.'

'Do they?' Pompey asked quietly. 'Or do they simply want it to be over?'

'Does it matter?'

Pompey did not answer. He simply stood there, watching his army prepare to march, whilst the western horizon swallowed the last of the daylight and left only darkness in its wake.

Chapter Twenty-Six

The Road to Thessaly

The road south ran through country that offered nothing but bare hills stretching away on either side, their slopes covered with scrub and stones that provided no shelter and less sustenance. The few villages they passed stood empty, their grain stores cleaned out and their wells filled with dirt by inhabitants who had fled days before Caesar's army arrived. The land had been picked clean, either by Pompey's foraging parties or by locals who knew what happened when armies passed through their territory.

Marcus rode near the head of the column, watching the legionaries march with the steady rhythm of men who had learned long ago that complaining changed nothing. Their faces were drawn, their cheeks hollow beneath the rim of their helmets, and their eyes held the flat exhaustion that came from too many days with too little food. Some had tightened their belts another notch that morning. Others had stopped tightening them because there were no more notches left to use.

The baggage train followed at a distance, lighter now than it had been at Dyrrachium, reduced to the essentials because there was little left to carry. The cavalry screened their flanks, but even the horses looked gaunt, their ribs showing through dull coats that had lost the sheen of health.

Caesar rode at the front with Antonius beside him, the two of them conferring quietly whilst the miles passed beneath their horses' hooves. Marcus could not hear their conversation from where he rode, but he could read their postures well enough. Caesar sat straight in his saddle despite the heat and the hunger, his bearing giving nothing away to the men who watched him for signs of weakness. Antonius gestured occasionally towards the hills, probably discussing routes and water sources, his tone pragmatic rather than optimistic.

A centurion from the Ninth Legion rode up alongside Marcus, his face red from the sun and his voice hoarse when he spoke.

'Praefect, the men are asking about tonight's rations.'

'What about them?' asked Marcus, though he already knew the answer.

'Whether there will be any.'

Marcus looked back at the column, at the thousands of men who had followed Caesar away from Dyrrachium and now marched through hostile country with empty bellies and diminishing hope.

'Tell them there will be grain tonight. Not much, but enough.'

'Is that true?'

'It will be,' said Marcus, though he had no idea how he would make it so. 'And make sure the officers keep the men in formation. I don't want any foraging parties breaking off without permission. If we lose cohesion, we lose everything.'

The centurion saluted and rode back to his unit whilst Marcus urged his horse forward towards Caesar. He caught up with the general and Antonius just as they were discussing the very problem he had come to report.

'The supply wagons have enough grain for three more days at quarter rations,' Antonius was saying. 'After that, we are dependent on what we can find or take from the countryside.'

'And the countryside offers nothing,' said Caesar. 'Pompey's foragers have been thorough.'

'Not everywhere,' said Antonius. 'There are towns ahead that may still have stores. Gomphi lies two days' march to the south-east. It is a substantial settlement and may not have been stripped yet.'

Marcus cleared his throat and both men turned to look at him.

'The men are also asking about rations, Imperator. I told them there would be grain tonight.'

Caesar's expression did not change, but something flickered behind his eyes.

'Then we will need to make sure you were not lying to them. Antonius, send riders ahead to Gomphi. Offer to pay for supplies and make it clear we are willing to negotiate.'

'And if they refuse?' asked Antonius.

'Then we negotiate more persuasively.'

Antonius nodded and spurred his horse forward to find the cavalry scouts, leaving Marcus alone with Caesar. They rode in silence for a moment, the only sound the steady thud of hooves and the creak of leather and the distant murmur of thousands of men marching in column.

'How bad is it?' asked Caesar quietly.

Marcus knew better than to soften the truth.

'Bad enough that we will start seeing desertions if we do not feed them soon. The veterans will hold, but some of the newer recruits are already talking about slipping away at night. The centurions are keeping watch, but hungry men make poor decisions.'

'And discipline?'

'Holding, but only just. There was a fight yesterday between men from the Ninth and the Twelfth over a stolen loaf. The officers broke it up before it spread, but the tension is there.'

Caesar absorbed this without visible reaction.

'We cannot slow down,' he said eventually, 'Pompey is

behind us, and every day we delay is another day he gains ground. But we also cannot march the men into the ground. They need food, they need rest, and they need to believe that this march has a purpose beyond simple survival.'

'What do you want me to tell them?'

'Tell them we are marching to meet allies in Thessaly who will provide supplies and reinforcements. Tell them that once we reach friendly territory, we will have everything we need to turn and face Pompey on ground of our choosing. And tell them that I have not forgotten what they did at Dyrrachium, and that their loyalty will be rewarded.'

'Will it?' asked Marcus, and immediately regretted the question. But Caesar did not take offense. He simply looked at Marcus with tired eyes that had seen too much and promised too little.

'If we survive this, yes. If we do not, then the question becomes irrelevant.'

A shout rose from somewhere in the middle of the column, and both men turned to see a legionary had collapsed in the road, his shield and pack scattered around him whilst his comrades tried to lift him back to his feet. The man's legs would not hold him, and after a moment, two of his friends simply picked him up and carried him between them, their own steps slowing under the extra weight.

'How many is that today?' asked Caesar.

'Five that I have seen,' said Marcus. 'Probably more that I have not.'

Caesar watched the collapsed legionary being carried along by his companions, and something in his expression hardened.

'Double the watch tonight. I want sentries on every approach to the camp, and I want officers walking the lines throughout the night. If men are going to desert, they will do it in the darkness, and I will not make it easy for them.'

'And tomorrow?'

'Tomorrow we march faster. We reach Gomphi by tomorrow night, or we start losing the army one man at a time.'

The column continued its slow progress through the barren hills whilst the sun climbed higher and turned the road into a furnace. Men stumbled, recovered, and kept walking because there was no alternative. The standards dipped and rose with each uneven step, but they did not fall, and somewhere in that simple fact lay the difference between an army in retreat and a mob in flight.

Marcus dropped back and as he passed along the column, he saw the same scene repeated again and again. Men marching with empty eyes and hollow cheeks, their hands gripping their pila more from habit than strength, their feet moving because they had been moving for so long that stopping would feel like death.

The veterans showed nothing, their faces blank masks that revealed neither fear nor hope. The younger men looked worse, their inexperience showing in the way they glanced back over their shoulders as if expecting Pompey's cavalry to appear on the horizon at any moment.

A boy who could not have been more than eighteen stumbled past Marcus, his shield scraping the ground because he no longer had the strength to carry it properly. Marcus reached down and caught his arm, steadying him.

'Keep your shield up, soldier.'

The boy looked at him with eyes that seemed too old for his face.

'Yes, Praefect.'

'How long have you been with the legion?'

'I joined just before we crossed into Greece, Praefect.'

'Then you have not seen the worst yet,' said Marcus, releasing his arm. 'This is just a march. When the real fighting comes, you will wish you were this tired and this hungry, because at least you will still be alive to feel it.'

The boy nodded, hoisted his shield back onto his shoulder, and continued marching. Marcus watched him go, wondering how many boys like that would still be with the army when they finally stopped running and turned to face Pompey.

The sun reached its peak and began its slow descent towards the western hills. Water skins were nearly empty, and rationed to a few swallows each hour, and the few streams they passed ran too low to provide relief for an entire army.

By the time Caesar called a halt for the evening, the column had covered fifteen miles through some of the most inhospitable country Marcus had ever seen and the men dropped where they stood without bothering to set up tents.

Marcus moved through the camp as the sun set, checking on the men and speaking quietly with the centurions who held the army together through force of will and hard-earned respect. Everywhere he went, he saw the same exhaustion, the same hunger, the same quiet determination that defined Caesar's legions even in their worst moments.

And everywhere he went, he heard the same question repeated in different words. How much further?

He had no answer. None of them did. All they could do was wake up the next morning and march again, and hope that Gomphi held supplies, that Thessaly held allies, and that somewhere ahead on this barren road lay the ground where they would finally stop running and make their stand.

The walls of Gomphi appeared on the third day and Marcus rode with the advance party, fifty cavalry who looked more like scarecrows than soldiers, their armour hanging loose on frames that had grown thin from hunger.

Caesar had sent riders ahead two days before with messages of friendship and offers of silver for grain, but the gates remained closed as the column approached, and men lined the walls with spears visible above the ramparts. That told Marcus everything he needed to know about how this negotiation would proceed.

Antonius rode at the head of the cavalry, his face showing the strain of days without proper sleep. He raised his hand to halt the column whilst still beyond arrow range, and Marcus moved his horse alongside.

'They have made their choice,' said Marcus quietly.

'So it seems,' said Antonius. 'But we will give them one more chance to reconsider.'

They stopped fifty paces from the gate and the lead tribune called out in a voice trained to carry across battlefields.

'We come in peace, seeking only supplies for which we will pay fairly. Open your gates and let us trade as friends.'

Silence answered him as the men on the walls stood motionless, their spears gleaming in the afternoon sun.

The tribune tried again.

'Caesar offers silver and guarantees the safety of your town. We want only grain and meat, nothing more. There is no need for conflict.'

This time a voice answered from the walls.

'We know what happened at Dyrrachium and that Caesar runs from Pompey like a dog with its tail between its legs, so why should we feed an army that cannot feed itself?'

'Because we are asking nicely,' the tribune called back. 'And because the alternative will be less pleasant for everyone.'

'Pompey will be here within days and when he arrives, he will reward those who stood against Caesar and punish those who helped him. We choose to stand.'

The tribune looked back at Marcus, who shook his head slightly. The negotiation was over before it had properly begun.

The delegation rode back to the column and Caesar listened to their report without expression.

'How many defenders?' he asked finally.

'Perhaps three hundred,' said the tribune. 'Maybe less. Most will be local militia, not trained soldiers.'

'And the walls?'

'Old but intact. There is a weak section on the eastern side where the stone has crumbled, but it would still take time to breach.'

Caesar looked at the sun, calculating how many hours of daylight remained.

'We do not have time for a proper siege. Antonius, bring up the rams. Marcus, form assault parties on three sides. I want ladders against those walls before nightfall tomorrow.'

Antonius opened his mouth as if to say something, then closed it again and rode back to organise the attack. Marcus followed, gathering centurions and explaining what would be required. The men received the orders with grim acceptance. They were hungry enough that the promise of food inside those walls made the prospect of climbing ladders under arrow fire seem almost reasonable.

The assault began at noon the following day. Rams

were brought forward under cover of shields whilst archers loosed volleys at the defenders to keep their heads down. The ladders came next, crude things knocked together from timber scavenged along the march, and they slammed against the walls with crashes that echoed across the plain.

Marcus led one of the assault parties himself because asking men to do what he would not do seemed wrong. He climbed a ladder with his shield raised above his head whilst stones and arrows clattered against it, and when he reached the top, he found a young militiaman waiting with a spear. The man thrust awkwardly, more afraid than skilled, and Marcus batted the point aside with his shield before driving his gladius into the man's chest. The militiaman fell backwards with a sound that was more surprise than pain, and Marcus stepped onto the walkway.

Others followed him up, and within moments the wall was contested along its entire length. The defenders fought harder than Marcus had expected, their desperation lending strength to arms that lacked training, but they were outnumbered and outmatched. One by one they fell or fled, and when the gates finally opened from the inside, a full cohort of Caesar's battle-hardened veterans poured inside.

What followed was ugly but brief. The soldiers went straight for the grain stores whilst the inhabitants fled to their homes and barred their doors. There was some looting, and some violence that the officers could not prevent or chose not to see, but mostly there was just hungry men finding food, each desperate to take their frustration out on anyone they could find.

An hour later, Marcus found Caesar in the town's central square, standing beside a fountain whilst legionaries filled their water skins and drank until their bellies hurt.

'Three hundred defenders dead,' he said as Marcus approached. 'We lost eighteen. The grain stores will feed the army for five days if we ration carefully. Tell the centurions to restore order and anyone found harming civilians will be flogged. We needed supplies, not enemies.' Caesar looked around at the chaos slowly resolving into order as officers reasserted control. 'Set a watch on all approaches. Pompey's scouts may be close, and I want warning if they come looking.'

Marcus saluted and moved off to carry out the orders whilst behind him, Caesar stood alone in the square and watched his army feed itself on another town's misfortune.

Two days later they reached Metropolis, a smaller settlement but one that had heard what happened at Gomphi. The gates opened before Caesar's army even came into sight, and a delegation of town elders rode out with white banners and expressions that mixed fear with pragmatism.

'We offer supplies freely,' said the eldest, a man whose white beard reached halfway down his chest. 'Grain, wine, livestock, whatever you require. Only spare our town the fate of Gomphi.'

Caesar received them with courtesy, though the silver he offered was worth less than half what the supplies would fetch in peacetime. The elders accepted without complaint because complaint would have changed nothing, and Caesar's army restocked its dwindling reserves whilst the townspeople watched from doorways and windows.

Marcus oversaw the loading of the supply wagons, ensuring that the legionaries did not wander beyond the areas designated for their use. The men were in better spirits now, their bellies full for the first time in days, and the desperate edge that had marked their march from Dyrrachium had softened into something more manageable.

A local farmer approached Marcus as he was watching the grain count, his hat in his hands and his eyes fixed on the ground.

'Praefect, will there be more armies coming through?'

'Pompey follows us,' said Marcus. 'How far behind, I cannot say.'

'And when he comes, will he take supplies as well?'

'Probably.'

The farmer nodded as if this confirmed what he had already known.

'Then we will have nothing left for winter.'

Marcus had no answer for that. He simply returned to watching the count whilst the farmer walked away, and the wagons continued to fill with grain that would feed Caesar's army whilst Thessalian families faced hunger in the months ahead.

They stayed in Metropolis only one night, long enough for the men to rest and for the horses to recover some of their strength. At dawn, the army formed up and marched again, leaving behind a town that was lighter by several tons of food but slightly richer in in silver.

Other towns came and went over the following days. Some opened their gates like Metropolis, calculating that cooperation was cheaper than resistance. Others barred themselves tight and had to be convinced through demonstrations of force, though none required the full assault that Gomphi had demanded. A few simply fled, their inhabitants vanishing into the hills with whatever they could carry, leaving behind empty granaries and wells that had been poisoned rather than surrendered.

By the end of the second week, Caesar's supply situation had stabilized enough that the immediate crisis had passed. The men were no longer starving, discipline had been restored, and the column marched with renewed purpose towards whatever ground Caesar had chosen for his stand against Pompey.

But Marcus noticed something else as well. The men no longer asked how much further. They had stopped looking back over their shoulders for signs of pursuit and marched with the steady confidence of soldiers who believed their general knew what he was doing, even if they did not understand his plan.

Somehow, despite everything, Caesar had bought himself time and given his army back its faith. Whether that would be enough when Pompey finally caught up to them remained to be seen.

Caesar called the assembly on the morning of the fifteenth day, when the army had finally stopped running and established a proper camp on high ground overlooking a river valley. The location had been chosen carefully, a place where the terrain favoured defence if Pompey arrived before Caesar was ready to give battle on his own terms.

The legions formed up in the wide field below the camp, arranged in their cohorts with standards planted in neat rows that stretched across the valley floor. Marcus stood with the other officers to one side of the makeshift platform that had been erected overnight, a simple wooden structure that would allow Caesar to be seen and heard by thousands of men at once.

The morning was cool, the sky clear, and the army waited in silence that felt more anticipatory than anxious. Word had spread through the camp that Caesar would speak, and the men understood this would be more than a routine address.

Caesar emerged from his tent wearing his general's cloak and full armour, the red fabric bright against the dull browns and greys of the camp. He walked to the platform without hesitation, climbed the steps, and stood looking out at his army whilst they looked back at him.

For a long moment he said nothing. He simply let them see him, let them remember that despite Dyrrachium and the long retreat and the hunger and the fear, he was still here, still leading them, still believing in whatever vision had brought them to this valley in the middle of Thessaly.

When he finally spoke, his voice carried across the field with the clarity of a man who had spent decades addressing soldiers.

'Fellow Romans,' he called out. 'You marched with me across the Rubicon when Rome called us criminals. You fought beside me through Italy when the Senate fled rather than face us and you sailed with me to Greece despite the weather and many believing that Pompey's numbers could drive us back into the sea.' He paused, letting the words settle. 'And when our brothers, led by Antonius were isolated, driven off course by the gods of the seas, did you fear that we were outnumbered, did you hesitate, no you marched to their aid, for that is who we are. You should be proud of everything that passed to that moment for you were magnificent.'

He paused before the next part, knowing it was going to be difficult.

'And then came the siege at Dyrrachium. I will not lie to you about what happened there. We were outmanoeuvred, we were caught unprepared and we lost good men, brave men, soldiers who deserved better than the death they received. And we retreated because staying would have meant annihilation.'

Caesar's voice hardened slightly.

'But retreat is not defeat. Not unless we allow it to become so.'

He stepped forward to the edge of the platform.

'You have marched through hostile country with empty bellies and dry water bottles. You have carried your wounds with little complaint and even less sleep. And you have watched towns close their gates against us and heard men who should be our allies declare for Pompey instead. You have endured mockery and doubt and the whispers that say Caesar's luck has finally run out.'

The silence deepened and Marcus could see faces in the crowd now, individual men totally focussed on what Caesar was saying.

'Let them whisper,' said Caesar. 'Let them declare for Pompey and let them believe that one setback erases years of victory. Because when we meet Pompey on the field, when we face his legions in open battle, those whispers will die in their throats.'

A murmur ran through the assembled cohorts, not quite agreement but something approaching it.

'I promised you glory all those years ago, and I have delivered. Gaul, Germania, Britannia, places that existed only in legend until you made them real. I promised you wealth, and you have taken it from every corner of the Republic. But now I promise you something more.'

He let the pause stretch, letting the anticipation build until the entire valley seemed to hold its breath.

'I promise you that the men who fled from you in Rome, the same men who jeered as we marched away from Dyrrachium, the senators who called you traitors and criminals, the aristocrats who believed the Republic belonged to them alone, I promise you now, that they will kneel before you. Not because we ask them to, but because when this war ends, there will be no other choice.'

The murmur grew louder. Some men nodded. Others glanced at their neighbours, checking to see if they were hearing the same thing.

'And when they kneel, when Rome is ours by right of conquest here in Thessaly, I promise you this as well. Every man who stands here today will receive land. Not the scraps that the Senate throws to veterans when it remembers they exist, but real land, good land, enough to build a life that does not depend on another's generosity.'

The noise increased again, more animated now, and Marcus saw something change in the faces around him. Men who had been hollow-eyed and exhausted an hour ago now stood with shoulders back and heads raised.

'You followed me into Gaul and I made you rich. You followed me across the Rubicon and I made you part of history. Now follow me to victory here in Thessaly, and I will make you masters of your own fate. No more begging the Senate for what you have earned. No more watching patricians grow fat on the glory you won for them and when this war ends, Rome will belong to its soldiers, and its soldiers will never be forgotten again.'

The cheering started in the front ranks and spread backwards like a wave breaking on a beach. It built slowly at first, individual voices joining together, then swelling into a roar that echoed across the valley and sent birds scattering from the trees along the river.

Caesar stood motionless on the platform, letting the sound wash over him, and when he raised his hand for silence, it took longer than usual for the men to quiet down. When they finally did, he spoke again, his voice lower now, more intimate despite the distance.

'Pompey believes he has won because he drove us from Dyrrachium. He believes his numbers give him the advantage and the Senate's blessing makes his cause righteous.' Caesar smiled. 'He believes many things, but here, in Thessaly, we are going to teach him how wrong he is.'

More cheering, louder this time, and Caesar let it continue for several heartbeats before raising his hand again.

'We will meet him soon and when we do, I want you to remember what you have endured to reach that moment. I want you to remember the hunger, the exhaustion, the towns that turned us away, the men we lost at Dyrrachium. I want you to remember all of it, because that memory will turn your gladius into something more than iron. Pompey has his numbers, but we have our fury. Pompey has the Senate's approval but we have the knowledge that everything we have built will be destroyed if we lose. Pompey fights to preserve the old order but we fight to create a new one.'

The valley fell silent again, but it was a different kind of silence now, charged with something that had not been there before.

'In camp tonight, and every night going forward, rest when you can, eat well, train hard, and when the day comes and the trumpets sound and the standards advance, show Pompey and his Senate and all of Rome what Caesar's legions can do when they have something to fight for.'

He descended from the platform whilst the cheering erupted again, and this time he did not wait for it to fade. He simply walked back towards his tent whilst behind him, the army celebrated its renewed sense of purpose with voices that carried for miles.

Marcus found him an hour later, sitting alone in his command tent with the usual maps spread across the table and a cup of wine sitting untouched beside them. Caesar looked up when Marcus entered, his expression returning from wherever it had been.

'They believed you,' said Marcus.

'They wanted to believe me,' said Caesar. 'There is a difference.'

'Is there? They are ready to fight now. Before your speech, they were ready to survive. That is not a small thing.'

Caesar picked up the cup but did not drink from it.

'They are ready to fight because I promised them things I may not be able to deliver. Land, glory, revenge, all of it depends on us winning a battle against an army that outnumbers us by thousands.'

'You have won battles against worse odds.'

'In Gaul, yes. And against the Germans and the Belgae who fought with courage but not discipline. But Pompey's legions are Roman. They know our tactics because they are the same tactics. They know our strengths because they are the same strengths. And they have more of everything that matters in a pitched battle.'

Marcus moved closer to the table.

'Then why did you promise them victory?'

'Because the alternative was watching them break apart one desertion at a time until nothing remained but a memory of what we might have accomplished.' Caesar finally drank from the cup, a small sip that he barely seemed to taste. 'Sometimes a general's most important weapon is not his strategy or his tactics, it is the belief his men have that he knows something they do not.'

'And do you?'

Caesar smiled.

'I know that Pompey is cautious and I know that his senators will pressure him to end this quickly. I also know that his legions are well-fed and well-rested but have not fought a real battle in years. And I know that my men are angry and have nothing to lose.' He set the cup down and looked at Marcus directly. 'Is that enough? I have no idea. But it is what we have, and so it will have to be.'

Outside the tent, the sounds of the camp continued their usual rhythms. Men laughed, officers barked orders, and smiths hammered at damaged armour, and somewhere in the distance, a cohort sang a marching song that had been old when their grandfathers were young.

The army had stopped running. It had found its ground and recovered its spirit. And now, for better or worse, it would wait for Pompey to arrive and discover whether Caesar's promises had been prophecy or fantasy.

Chapter Twenty-Seven

Thessaly

The dust from Pompey's legions hung in the air like a brown curtain, visible for miles across the Thessalian plain. They had been marching for days, maintaining the pace that Labienus had insisted upon and that Pompey had finally accepted as necessary. Twenty miles a day through country that offered good roads and better sightlines, closing the distance between hunter and prey with methodical determination.

Marcus Varus rode with the vanguard cavalry, five hundred horsemen under the command of a Gallic chieftain named Verco who had sworn loyalty to Pompey years before. They ranged ahead of the main column, scouting the roads and bringing back reports on Caesar's position, and with each day, those reports described an enemy that was closer than before.

'Two days ahead of us now,' Verco said as they crested a ridge that overlooked a river valley. 'Maybe less if they stop to rest.'

'Will they?' asked Varus.

'Caesar does not strike me as a man who rests when being chased.' Verco pointed towards the horizon where a faint smudge of dust marked another army's passage. 'But his men are exhausted, and exhausted men make mistakes. Sooner or later, he will have to slow down.'

Behind them, Pompey's army stretched back along the road in tight formation, the standards rising above cohort after cohort whilst the baggage train followed at a steady pace. The men marched with the confidence of soldiers who believed victory was inevitable, their spirits high despite the forced pace, and their voices carried across the plain in snatches of song and conversation.

Labienus rode up alongside Varus and Verco, his horse streaked with sweat from another reconnaissance ride.

'The scouts report Caesar is establishing a camp near the Enipeus River. It looks like he intends to stop and fortify.'

'How far?' asked Verco.

'A few day's ride, perhaps less.' Labienus looked at the Gallic chieftain. 'Take your cavalry forward. I want you to harass his supply lines, and hit his foraging parties, make it expensive for him to stay in one place. Nothing that risks a major engagement, but enough to keep him off balance.'

Verco's teeth showed in a smile that had nothing to do with humour.

'My men have been waiting for this.'

'Then stop waiting and start riding. I want results before nightfall.'

Verco gathered his captains and within moments, the cavalry had split into smaller groups that spread across the plain like fingers reaching towards Caesar's position. Varus rode with Verco's main force, fifty riders who moved at a canter to conserve their horses whilst still covering ground quickly.

They found their first target a few hours later, a foraging party from Caesar's army scattered across a field that had somehow escaped the ravages of war. Twenty legionaries with sacks and baskets, guarded by perhaps a dozen more with shields and spears, all of them focused on gathering what little grain remained rather than watching for threats.

'Easy,' said Verco quietly, and his riders spread out in a line that would encircle the foragers before they knew what was happening.

The attack was brief and brutal. The cavalry swept

across the field at full gallop, spears lowering as they closed the distance, and the foragers barely had time to drop their sacks before the first riders were among them. Some tried to run, others attempted to form a defensive position, but cavalry against scattered infantry in open ground was not a fight with any question about its outcome.

Varus found himself in the middle of the chaos, his spear thrusting at a legionary who raised his shield too slowly, and then they were through the other side and circling back whilst the survivors fled towards the tree line. Verco's men did not pursue, they simply regrouped and rode towards the next opportunity, leaving behind bodies and abandoned supplies in the churned dirt.

'How many?' asked Varus, his hands shaking slightly from the sudden violence.

'Enough,' said Verco. 'And we are just beginning.'

They struck three more times that day, hitting supply carts and isolated detachments. Each time, they appeared from unexpected directions, inflicted casualties, and vanished before Caesar's veterans could organise an effective response. Each time, they left behind burning wagons and bodies that would need to be collected and buried.

By evening, when they regrouped on a hill overlooking Caesar's camp, Verco's cavalry had lost only four men whilst killing or wounding perhaps fifty of Caesar's soldiers and destroying supplies that could not easily be replaced. It was not a decisive blow, but it was the kind of persistent damage that accumulated into something more serious over time.

Varus could see Caesar's camp from their vantage point, the fortifications already taking shape as legionaries dug ditches and raised ramparts. Fires burned within the perimeter, small and carefully controlled, and sentries walked the walls in pairs whilst the camp settled into evening routines.

'They work fast,' said Varus.

'They are afraid,' said Verco, so they dig, because digging makes them feel safer.'

'Does it work?'

Verco shrugged.

'Walls stop arrows and slow charges. They do not stop fear.' He turned his horse away from the overlook. 'Come. We report to Pompey, and tomorrow we do this again. And the day after that until Caesar is too tired and too hungry and too scared to run anymore.'

They rode back through the darkness, following roads they had memorized during daylight, and reached Pompey's camp as the late watch was being called. The general received them in his command tent where maps covered every surface and lamps burned against the night.

Pompey listened to Verco's report without interruption, his expression revealing nothing whilst the Gallic chieftain described each attack in economical detail. When Verco finished, Pompey looked at Labienus, who stood beside the map table with his arms crossed.

'Effective,' said Labienus. 'But not decisive.'

'It does not need to be decisive,' said Pompey. 'It needs to be constant. If Caesar cannot forage, he cannot feed his army. If he cannot feed his army, he cannot stay in one place. And if he cannot stay in one place, he will eventually have to turn and face us on ground we choose rather than ground he prepares.'

'And if he chooses to fortify where he is and dare us to attack him?'

'Then we besiege him until his supplies run out.'

Pompey traced a line on the map with his finger. 'But I do not think he will do that. Caesar is too aggressive to sit behind walls whilst we control the countryside around him. He will move again, and when he does, we will be ready.'

Labienus studied the map, his eyes following the marks that showed Caesar's position and the routes he might take.

'How close do you want to get before we force the engagement?'

'Close enough that he has no choice but to fight. Far enough that we can choose the ground.' Pompey looked up from the map. 'Continue the harassment. Double the cavalry patrols tomorrow, and if Caesar sends out foraging parties, I want them destroyed. Make him burn through his remaining supplies faster than he can replace them.'

'And the legions?'

'We continue to close the distance. By the end of the week, I want our camps within sight of each other. Then we will see whether Caesar's nerve holds or breaks.'

Verco and Varus were dismissed, and as they left the tent, Varus glanced back to see Pompey still studying the map whilst Labienus spoke quietly beside him.

Outside, the camp hummed with activity despite the late hour. Officers moved between tents carrying orders, sentries called out challenges and responses, and somewhere in the distance, a century drilled in darkness, their caligae striking the ground in perfect unison. It was the sound of an army that believed itself on the verge of victory, and as Varus walked back to his own tent, he wondered if Caesar's camp sounded the same or if the men there knew they were being hunted.

Marcus was inspecting the evening watch when the alarm came, a single trumpet blast from the southern perimeter followed by shouts that carried across the camp with unmistakable urgency. He grabbed his helmet and ran towards the commotion, arriving at the wall to find a century already forming up whilst a wounded legionary was being carried inside by two of his comrades.

'What happened?' Marcus demanded of the nearest centurion.

'Cavalry, Praefect. They hit one of our water parties at the stream. Killed six and wounded four more.' The centurion pointed towards the dying light. 'They rode south before we could respond.'

Marcus climbed the rampart and looked out across the plain. The stream lay perhaps half a mile distant, marked by a line of scrub that provided the only cover for miles. Nothing moved now except the wind pushing across the grass, but he could see the bodies lying near the water's edge, dark shapes that would need to be collected before nightfall.

'How many riders?' he asked.

'Thirty, maybe forty. They came fast and left before we could send a response.'

Marcus turned to find more officers arriving, drawn by the alarm, and made his decision quickly.

'I need two centuries, and a cart. We are going out to bring our brothers back.'

Within the hour, Marcus and his temporary command reached the stream and stared at the aftermath of the attack.

Six men lay dead, their bodies showing spear wounds that told of a fight that had lasted only moments. Four others had crawled or been dragged into the scrub where they bled from injuries that would kill some and cripple others.

'Bury the dead,' said Marcus. 'And get the wounded

onto the cart. We are too exposed here.'

The legionaries moved quickly, their eyes scanning the plain whilst they worked. Marcus dismounted and walked to where the bodies lay, studying the wounds and the ground around them. The cavalry had come from the south-east, hit hard, and retreated the same way. Professional work, nothing wasted, nothing personal, just soldiers doing their job.

A shout from one of the sentries Marcus had posted made him look up as riders appeared on the southern ridge. They sat on their horses watching the scene below, and Marcus felt his heartbeat increase.

'Form up,' he ordered.

The legionaries placed the last of the wounded on the cart and formed into a loose line facing the ridge.

For a long moment, nothing happened. The riders remained motionless, and Marcus's men waited with hands on weapons and eyes fixed on the enemy. Then the riders turned and disappeared and Marcus released a breath he had not realised he was holding.

'Back to camp,' he said. 'Double time.'

They made it halfway before the cavalry returned, appearing from a different direction and moving faster this time. Marcus saw them coming and knew immediately that running would be fatal.

'Form a square,' shouted Marcus, 'and put the cart at the centre.'

The legionaries stopped and formed up in a tight defensive position, shields facing outward and spears braced as the cavalry swept past on both sides, testing for weaknesses.

A spear flew from the circling riders and struck a legionary's shield, punching through the wood but stopping short of the man behind it. Another followed, then a scatter of arrows that clattered against raised shields, but the legionaries held formation without breaking, veterans who understood that panic meant death.

'Hold!' Marcus shouted. 'And wait for my command!'

The cavalry circled again, tighter this time, and Marcus saw what they were doing. Trying to draw his men out of formation and provoke a charge that would break the square. He kept his men still, kept them disciplined, and waited for the moment that would decide whether they lived or died.

It came when the cavalry leader, perhaps frustrated by the lack of response, led a charge straight at one face of the square. Twenty riders at full gallop, spears lowering as the thunder of hooves drowned out everything else. Marcus waited until they were thirty paces away.

'Front rank, pila! *Now!*'

Twenty javelins flew as one, the heavy iron points designed to punch through shields and armour at close range. Three riders went down immediately, their horses screaming as they tumbled. Two more were unhorsed when their mounts took pila in the chest and the charge broke apart, the riders swerving to avoid the carnage. And in that moment of confusion, Marcus saw his chance.

'Charge! Drive them back!'

The legionaries surged forward, breaking formation because staying in the square now meant waiting to be picked apart. They ran at the scattered cavalry with the fury of men who had been hunted and were now hunting back, and the riders, caught between reforming and retreating, made the mistake of doing neither quickly enough.

Marcus found himself facing a Gallic rider who was trying to wheel his horse around. He grabbed the man's leg and pulled, using his weight to drag the rider from his saddle. They hit the ground together, rolling in the dirt, and Marcus's gladius found the gap between the rider's mail and his helmet. The man went still, and Marcus pushed himself up, already looking for the next threat.

But the cavalry were retreating, pulling back to a safe distance whilst Marcus's men regrouped and counted their losses. Two dead and five wounded. Against that, perhaps seven enemy cavalry dead or dying, and the knowledge that Caesar's men could still fight when pressed.

'Back into formation,' Marcus ordered, his voice hoarse from shouting. 'Get the wounded onto the cart. We move now before they decide to try again.'

They made it back to camp as full darkness fell, and Caesar was waiting at the gate when they rode through. The general took in the scene with a single glance, the dead and wounded laying side by side on the cart, and the experienced survivors who had survived another skirmish that would not appear in any official history.

'How bad?' Caesar asked quietly.

'Bad enough,' said Marcus. 'They are hitting us every time we send men outside the walls. Water parties, foraging details, even scouting patrols. We cannot move without being harried.'

'Can you stop them?'

'Not with what we have. They are faster, better mounted, and they choose when to engage. We can hurt them when we catch them, but we cannot catch them often enough to matter.'

Caesar watched the wounded being taken to the medical tents.

'Then we adapt,' he said. 'No more small parties. Water

details will go out in century strength with cavalry escort and foraging is done by full cohorts, and they go armed for combat. We make it expensive enough that Pompey's riders will think twice before attacking.'

'That will slow everything down. It will take twice as long to gather supplies, and we are already running low.'

'I know,' said Caesar, 'but losing men is worse than moving slowly. We'll conserve our strength until the battle comes, and when it does, I want every soldier we have left standing.'

Three days later, the pattern repeated itself with worse results. A cohort sent to gather wood from a forest five miles east of camp was caught between two cavalry forces that had coordinated their attack with professional precision. The cohort formed square and held as they had been trained, but cavalry with bows kept them pinned whilst other riders burned the carts they had brought for carrying timber.

Marcus received word of the attack and led a relief force at double time, but by the time they arrived, the cavalry had withdrawn and the cohort was battered. Fifteen dead, twenty wounded, and nothing to show for the expedition except empty carts and the knowledge that Pompey's harassment was getting more sophisticated.

The cohort commander, a grizzled centurion named Salvius, stood beside Marcus and looked at his reduced command with eyes that had seen too much.

'They knew where we were going. They were waiting for us.'

'They have scouts watching every approach,' said Marcus. 'Probably locals who know the country and get paid in silver for information.'

'So what do we do?'

Marcus had no answer. The strategic situation was deteriorating with each passing day, and no amount of tactical skill could change the fundamental problem that Pompey had more men, more cavalry, and control of the countryside whilst Caesar's army slowly consumed itself.

They were gathering the wounded when a rider came galloping from the direction of camp, his horse lathered and his face urgent. He reined in beside Marcus and spoke between gasping breaths.

'Praefect, another cohort is under attack three miles out. Caesar is already riding to support them, and he wants every available man to follow.'

Marcus looked at Salvius.

'Can your men march?'

'They can march,' said Salvius grimly. 'Whether they can fight when they get there is another question.'

'Then we find out together. Form up, double time. Those are our brothers out there.'

They ran across the plain with the afternoon sun beating down on them, and Marcus pushed his men harder than was wise because Caesar was ahead of them and the general did not ride into danger to watch from safety.

They heard the fighting before they saw it, the clash of weapons and the screams of men and horses carrying across the open ground.

The cohort that had been attacked was surrounded, their square compressed into a tight defensive position whilst cavalry circled and struck and circled again. Bodies lay scattered around the formation, some in Roman red, others in the mixed colours of Pompey's auxiliary cavalry. It was the kind of fight that had no victor, just survivors and corpses.

Caesar arrived from the north with his cavalry escort, and the sight of the general's red cloak seemed to energize both sides. The surrounded cohort straightened and pushed outward whilst Pompey's cavalry hesitated, suddenly aware that what had been an easy harassment had become something more dangerous.

Marcus led his relief force in from the east, hitting the enemy cavalry in the flank. The impact scattered the riders, and suddenly the surrounded cohort had room to breathe and reform.

Caesar drove straight through the centre, his cavalry escort clearing a path with spears and swords, and when he reached the cohort commander, he dismounted and stood with the men as if daring Pompey's cavalry to come close enough to strike.

They did not. They had done what they came to do and now withdrew whilst Caesar's forces consolidated their position.

The ride back to camp was quiet. The rescued cohort had lost twenty men, Marcus's relief force had lost five more, and Caesar's cavalry escort had taken casualties as well. It was not a defeat, but it was not a victory either. Just another day of bleeding whilst Pompey closed the distance and waited for Caesar to make the mistake that would end everything.

Pompey received the reports in his tent each evening, and with each report, the pattern grew clearer. Caesar was no longer moving with the speed that had marked his retreat from Dyrrachium. His army stayed in camp for days at a time, venturing out only in large formations that moved cautiously and returned quickly. Foraging parties that had once ranged freely now clustered close to their fortifications, and when Pompey's cavalry struck at them, they formed defensive squares and waited for rescue rather than counterattacking with the aggression that had defined Caesar's legions for a decade.

'He is afraid,' said Labienus, standing beside the map table where markers showed the positions of both armies. 'Look at the pattern. Every engagement, he pulls back. Every skirmish, he chooses defence over attack. This is not the Caesar who conquered Gaul.'

Pompey studied the map without responding. The distance between their camps had shrunk to less than five miles now, close enough that scouts could observe each other's fortifications and count the standards that rose above the ramparts. Caesar had chosen good ground, a position near the Enipeus River that offered water and some protection from cavalry, but he had made no move to advance or threaten Pompey's supply lines. He simply sat behind his walls and waited.

'Or he is conserving his strength,' said Pompey finally. 'Waiting for us to make a mistake.'

'What mistake? We have superior numbers, better supply lines, and control of the countryside. He grows weaker every day whilst we grow stronger. If he truly wanted to fight, he would march out and give battle before his position deteriorates further.' Labienus moved one of the markers on the map, pushing it closer to Caesar's position. 'But he does not march out. He sits in his camp like a man who knows he has already lost.'

One of his officers who had been listening quietly from the corner of the tent, cleared his throat.

'The men believe the same thing, General. They see Caesar refusing to engage, and they interpret it as weakness. Morale is high, perhaps higher than it has been since we broke out at Dyrrachium.'

'And if Caesar is not weak?' asked Pompey. 'If he is simply waiting for terrain or timing that favours him?'

'Then we do not give him the choice,' said the officer. 'We force him to fight on our terms, when we are ready and where we choose. Every day we delay is another day he uses to prepare defences or receive reinforcements that may be marching to join him.'

'What reinforcements? His allies in Thessaly have been cowed by our presence and the local towns have learned what happens to those who support him. He is isolated and running out of options.'

Pompey walked to the tent entrance and looked out at his camp. His legions moved through their evening routines with the confidence of men who believed victory was inevitable, and their voices carried across the camp in songs that celebrated battles not yet fought.

'The Senate wants to speak with me again,' he said not turning around. 'That's the third time this week.'

'Let them speak,' said Labienus. 'But do not let them dictate strategy.'

'Apparently, they do not dictate, they advise.' Pompey's tone suggested he found the distinction less meaningful than he wished it to be. 'And their advice is always the same. End this quickly, return to Rome in triumph, restore the Republic to its proper order.'

'For once, the Senate is correct.'

Pompey finally turned back to face his officers.

'Increase the cavalry harassment. I want Caesar's men exhausted and desperate. And send scouts to find ground suitable for battle, somewhere that favours our numbers and negates whatever advantages his veterans might still possess. We will give Caesar his battle, but it will be on our terms and in our time.'

The officers saluted and departed, leaving Pompey alone with his maps and his doubts. He traced the line of the Enipeus River with his finger, following it to where Caesar's camp sat like a fortress that dared him to attack. Everything Labienus said made sense. Everything the scouts reported suggested Caesar was weakening. But Pompey had fought too many battles to trust what seemed obvious, and Caesar had survived too many desperate situations to be dismissed as beaten before the final blow fell.

The senators arrived the following morning, a delegation led by Lentulus and including Cato, Scipio, and half a dozen others whose faces showed varying degrees of impatience.

'Magnus,' said Lentulus, 'the army is ready, the men are ready, and Rome is ready. When do we finish this?'

'When the time is right,' said Pompey.

'The time is right now,' Lentulus insisted. 'Caesar cowers behind his fortifications whilst we grow stronger. Every day we wait is another day the people of Rome wonder why their Senate cannot end a rebellion led by a single man.'

Cato spoke more carefully.

'No one questions your judgment, Imperator, but there is a political reality that cannot be ignored. The longer this war continues, the more damage it does to the Republic's institutions. A swift victory restores stability while a prolonged campaign breeds the kind of uncertainty that ambitious men exploit.'

'I am aware of the political reality,' said Pompey. 'I am also aware of the military reality, which is that rushing into battle before proper preparation has cost more generals their lives than caution ever has.'

'Caesar would not hesitate,' said Scipio. 'If our positions were reversed, he would attack immediately.'

'If our positions were reversed, we would already be dead,' Pompey replied bluntly. 'Caesar attacks when he has nothing to lose. We have everything to lose, which is why we move carefully.'

Lentulus opened his mouth to argue further, but Cato raised a hand to stop him.

'What do you need in order to be satisfied that the time is right?'

'Ground that favours our numerical advantage, confirmation that no reinforcements are marching to join him, and weather that allows cavalry operations without the mud that would negate their mobility.' Pompey looked at each senator in turn. 'Give me those things, and I will give you your battle.'

The senators exchanged glances, and Lentulus's expression showed he wanted to press harder but recognised he had extracted all the commitment he was likely to receive.

'Then we will pray the gods provide them soon. Rome cannot afford much more waiting.'

They filed out, and Pompey watched them go with the weariness of a man who had spent his entire career balancing military necessity against political expectation. Labienus, who had been standing outside during the meeting, entered as the senators departed.

'They grow restless,' said Labienus unnecessarily.

'They have been restless since Dyrrachium.' Pompey returned to his map table. 'But they are not wrong about the timing. Caesar is vulnerable now in ways he may not be later. If we are going to strike, it should be soon. Next week at the absolute latest.'

Labienus planted both hands on the table.

'Give me permission to probe his defences. Let me test his response with something more substantial than cavalry raids. If he is as weak as he appears, a proper assault might crack him open without needing a full battle.'

'And if he is not as weak as he appears, you will have wasted men and shown him our intentions.' Pompey shook his head. 'No. We wait for the right ground and the right moment. But soon. Very soon.'

The army continued its slow advance over the following days, closing the distance until the camps were near enough that sentries could see each other's fires at night. The cavalry harassment intensified, and Caesar's responses grew more defensive, more cautious, more indicative of an army that had lost its edge.

But the pursuit was complicated by the Senate's presence. Where a military force could move quickly with minimal baggage, the senators travelled with wagons full of personal effects, servants to attend them, and demands for accommodations that slowed the entire column. They held councils that delayed marching orders, debated strategy with men who had never commanded troops, and generally made themselves present in ways that reminded everyone that this was not merely a military campaign but a political crusade.

Pompey tolerated it because he had no choice. The Senate's blessing gave his cause legitimacy that force of arms alone could not provide, and alienating them now would create problems that would outlast whatever happened on the battlefield.

'They want to be part of the victory,' Labienus observed

one evening as they watched the senatorial wagons being positioned for yet another night's camp. 'They want to stand on the field after Caesar falls and claim they were instrumental in preserving the Republic.'

'Let them claim whatever they wish,' said Pompey. 'As long as they stay out of the way when the fighting starts.'

He turned and walked back to his tent, leaving Labienus standing alone in the darkness, watching the distant glow of Caesar's campfires and wondering whether they marked the position of a defeated enemy or a trap that had not yet sprung.

Chapter Twenty-Eight

Pharsalus

The plains of Pharsalus stretched before them like an open invitation, broad and flat and offering no obvious advantage to either side. Marcus stood beside Caesar on the low rise that overlooked the field, watching as the army filed past below and began the work of establishing what might be their final camp of the campaign.

'It looks exposed,' said Marcus.

'It is exposed,' Caesar replied. He gestured across the plain towards the distant hills where Pompey's scouts had been visible since dawn. 'No high ground to anchor our flanks. No forests to hide reserves and no rivers deep enough to protect our rear. Just open ground where numbers will tell more than tactics.'

'Then why here?'

Caesar did not answer immediately. He simply stood looking at the field, as if seeing something others could not.

'Because Pompey will look at this field and see the same things you do. He will see open ground that favours his cavalry. He will see space for his superior numbers to deploy and manoeuvre and that confidence will make him careless.'

'And what do you see?'

'I see ground that gives me room to do what must be done.' Caesar pointed to the right flank where the land rose slightly towards a line of low hills. 'There. That is where Pompey will place his cavalry. It is the obvious choice, the only choice really, and he will mass them there because he believes numbers decide cavalry battles.'

Marcus studied the terrain, trying to understand what

Caesar saw that made bad ground seem acceptable.

'And our cavalry?'

'Will be outnumbered three to one, possibly worse and they will not hold against Pompey's charge.' Caesar turned to look at Marcus directly. 'Which is why we will not rely on them to hold.'

'Then what?'

'Come. I will show you where this battle will be won or lost.'

They rode down from the rise with a small escort, leaving the main army to continue establishing camp whilst they examined the ground that could soon be soaked in Roman blood. Caesar moved methodically, stopping at various points to pace distances and test the footing, occasionally dismounting to dig at the earth with his boot and check how the soil would hold under the weight of thousands of men.

Marcus followed, making mental notes of what Caesar examined and trying to anticipate the plan that was forming behind the general's careful inspection. They reached the right flank where the ground rose gently, and Caesar spent long moments studying the approaches and the angles.

'Pompey's cavalry will come from here,' he said, pointing towards the open ground that stretched between their position and where Pompey's camp would likely be established. 'They will deploy in mass and they will charge straight at our right flank with the intention of rolling it up and collapsing our entire line from the side.'

'Can we stop them?'

'Not with cavalry alone. But we do not need to stop them with cavalry.' Caesar remounted and rode along the slight rise, gesturing as he spoke. 'This elevation is minor, barely noticeable unless you are looking for it, but it will slow a cavalry charge just enough to matter. Not much, perhaps a few heartbeat's worth of momentum lost, but battles are decided by heartbeats.'

They continued along the right flank until they reached a position roughly four hundred paces from where Caesar estimated their main battle line would form. Here the ground was even, unremarkable, offering no natural advantage except that it was slightly behind and to the side of where the cavalry engagement would occur.

'Here,' said Caesar, dismounting again. 'This is where we place our reserve.'

Marcus looked around at the empty field, seeing nothing special about this particular patch of grass. 'What reserve? We barely have enough men to form a proper battle line. If we hold back reserves, we weaken the centre.'

'We will weaken the centre by six cohorts. Three thousand battle hardened veterans taken from across all our legions.' Caesar walked in a small circle, measuring distances with his paces. 'Those men will wait here, out of sight behind our main line and when Pompey's cavalry charges and drives back our horsemen, when they begin to wheel around our flank to attack the rear of our legions, these men will advance at the double and hit the cavalry in their moment of victory.'

Marcus tried to visualize what Caesar described, imagining the flow of battle and the timing required.

'Infantry against cavalry in open ground?' It is a big risk.'

'Everything is a risk. The question is whether the risk is worth the potential gain.' Caesar remounted. 'If our centre holds and our right flank collapses, we lose the battle and probably the war. If our centre holds and our right flank holds just long enough for this reserve to do its work, we break

Pompey's cavalry and turn his advantage into ours.'

They rode back towards the main army, and Marcus found himself both impressed by the audacity of Caesar's plan and troubled by how much depended on precise timing and the discipline of men who would need to wait whilst their comrades were being slaughtered around them.

'Who commands the reserve?' Marcus asked.

Caesar stopped and met his eyes.

'I need someone who will wait until the timing is exactly right, who will not advance too soon or too late, and who will not lose his nerve when he sees Pompey's cavalry bearing down on our flank. Can you do that?'

Marcus thought about all the battles he had seen, all the chaos and confusion and the impossibility of knowing what the right moment was until it had already passed. He thought about all those men trusting him to make that decision, and Caesar trusting him to make it correctly.

'Yes,' he said finally. 'I can do that.'

'Good. Then when we return to camp, you will select six cohorts from different legions. Choose the best we have, men who understand discipline and will not break when cavalry charges past them. Brief the centurions on what will be required, but keep the details of the plan quiet. The fewer people who know our intentions, the less chance Pompey's spies learn what we are preparing.'

They reached the camp as the sun climbed towards its peak, and the fortifications were already taking shape. The standards rose above the ramparts, marking the positions of each legion, and the sound of hammers and voices filled the air.

Caesar rode to his command tent whilst Marcus remained on his horse looking out at the plain that would soon become a battlefield. Somewhere across that empty ground,

Pompey was making his own plans and his own preparations, confident in his superior numbers and his cavalry advantage.

Marcus hoped Caesar's confidence was as well-founded as Pompey's appeared to be, because if the plan failed, if the timing was wrong or the reserve broke or any of a hundred things went differently than expected, there would be no second chance and no retreat. Just defeat, and everything that followed from it.

Pompey's camp rose on the opposite side of the plain, larger than Caesar's by half. The standards of his eleven legions flew above the ramparts, each one representing five thousand men or close to it, and the cavalry corrals stretched for hundreds of paces along the eastern perimeter where nearly seven thousand horsemen tended mounts that were well-fed and fresh.

Labienus stood on the rampart watching Caesar's smaller camp take shape in the distance, and the smile that crossed his face was one of pure satisfaction.

'Look at them. They may have the banners of eleven legions but they are half strength at best and cavalry that would not hold against a decent Gallic warband. This is what we have been chasing for weeks?'

One of the other officers stood beside him, less demonstrative but equally confident.

'Caesar has chosen his ground,' he said. 'He must have his reasons.'

'He has chosen open ground where numbers matter more than cleverness. That is not strategy, that is desperation.' Labienus gestured at the plain. 'There are no obstacles to hide behind, and no terrain to channel our advance, nothing that will prevent us from bringing our full strength to bear. He might as well have drawn up his men on a parade ground and invited us to march over them.'

'Perhaps that is what he wants us to think.'

'What he wants does not matter anymore. What he has is a broken army that has been run to exhaustion, and what we have is the strongest force the Republic has fielded in a generation. Tomorrow, or the day after at the latest, we will give him the battle he has been avoiding, and it will end exactly as everyone knows it must.'

Below them, the camp hummed with activity as Pompey's legions settled into position and officers moved between units carrying orders and confirmations. The mood was celebratory despite the lack of fighting, with soldiers laughing and placing bets on how long Caesar's lines would hold and which legion would claim the honour of breaking them first.

Pompey emerged from his command tent and climbed the rampart to join his officers. He looked across at Caesar's camp without expression.

'Their fortifications are solid,' he observed.

'They are building their own tomb,' said Labienus. 'Let them dig it as deep as they wish.'

Pompey did not reply immediately. He simply watched whilst the distant figures moved like ants across the plain. When he finally spoke, his voice carried none of Labienus's certainty.

'Caesar has fought too many battles to choose ground this poor by accident. There will be something, some trick or deception that we are not seeing.'

'There is nothing,' Labienus insisted. 'We have scouted every approach, examined every fold in the terrain. This is flat, open ground that favours cavalry and numbers. Caesar has no cavalry worth mentioning and his numbers are half of ours.

What trick could possibly overcome those disadvantages?'

'I do not know. Which is precisely why I am cautious.'

The senators arrived before the evening meal, a final delegation that included all the most senior members who had travelled with the army.

'Magnus,' said Lentulus, his voice carrying across the tent. 'Tomorrow, yes? We give battle tomorrow and end this charade?'

'When the time is right,' said Pompey, not looking up from the map.

'The time is right whenever you give the order. Caesar sits across that plain with barely enough men to form a proper battle line, and you have assembled the greatest army the Republic has seen since Sulla. What are we waiting for?'

'Intelligence on his exact dispositions, confirmation that he has no reinforcements approaching and weather that will allow cavalry operations without complication.' Pompey straightened and looked at Lentulus directly. 'The same things I stated the last time you asked.'

'You already have all of those things,' Lentulus protested. 'Our scouts have ranged for miles in every direction and found nothing. The weather is clear, and as for his dispositions, what does it matter how he arranges his men when he has so few of them?' He moved closer to the table. 'The army is ready, Magnus. The officers are ready and Rome is ready. Every day we delay is another day we tell our men that we fear Caesar, and that fear will erode the confidence we have built since Dyrrachium.'

'I do not fear Caesar,' said Pompey quietly. 'I respect his capabilities, which is different. And that respect tells me to be thorough in my preparations.'

Cato spoke from the edge of the group, his voice cutting through the growing argument with measured deliberation.

'No one questions your judgment as a commander. But there is a political dimension that cannot be ignored. The Republic needs to see that its Senate can act decisively when required. A swift victory here restores faith in our institutions. A prolonged siege or drawn-out campaign breeds cynicism and provides opportunities for future ambitious men to claim that the Senate is weak.'

'The Senate is weak,' said Pompey bluntly. 'It has been weak for decades, which is why we are fighting this war in the first place. One battle will not change that.'

The tent fell silent. Several senators exchanged uncomfortable glances whilst Lentulus opened and closed his mouth without finding words. Finally, Ahenobarbus stepped forward.

'Regardless of the Senate's *perceived* weaknesses,' he said, 'we are here now, with an army that can end Caesar's rebellion once and for all. Tomorrow we should deploy for battle. If Caesar refuses to engage, we have lost nothing. If he accepts, we finish this once and for all.'

Pompey looked around at the assembled senators, at their faces that showed varying degrees of impatience, expectation and entitlement, and he felt the real weight of political necessity pressing against military caution. They were not wrong about the army's readiness or about the opportunity that lay before them. They were simply incapable of understanding that opportunities could also be traps.

'Very well,' he said finally. 'Tomorrow at dawn, we deploy for battle. The legions will form up in three lines, cavalry on the higher ground on the left flank, auxiliaries screening the right. If Caesar comes out to fight, we give him the battle he has been avoiding. If he does not, we reassess based on his response.'

The senators erupted in approval, their voices overlapping in expressions of satisfaction and relief. Lentulus clapped Pompey on the shoulder with inappropriate familiarity, and Scipio began discussing which vantage point would provide the best view of the coming victory.

After they had filed out, still talking amongst themselves, Labienus moved closer to Pompey.

'You made the right decision General.'

'I made the necessary decision. Whether it is right remains to be seen.'

'What concerns you? We have every advantage. Numbers, cavalry, supply lines, morale. Caesar has nothing except reputation, and reputation does not stop pila.'

Pompey returned his attention to the map, studying the plain where tomorrow his army would deploy and where the question that had hung over Rome for years would finally be answered.

'Caesar has survived more desperate situations than this. Alesia was desperate. The crossing into Britannia was desperate and half his campaigns in Gaul involved odds worse than what he faces tomorrow. And yet here we are, still chasing him.'

'This time it is different. This time he has nowhere to run and no trick that will save him.' Labienus tapped the map where Caesar's camp was marked. 'Tomorrow we end it. Tomorrow Rome gets its Republic back.'

Pompey said nothing. He simply looked at the map whilst outside his tent, his men started the preparations needed to go into battle. Not far away, the plains of Pharsalus lay quiet under the fading light, waiting for the dawn that would bring over forty thousand men into collision and one way or another, decide the fate of the Republic.

In the cavalry lines, Verco walked among his riders checking equipment and offering words of encouragement. The Gallic chieftain had fought for Pompey for years, had led raids and skirmishes across half the known world, but tomorrow would be different. Tomorrow would not be harassment or reconnaissance but a full cavalry charge against an enemy that was outnumbered and outmatched.

'How many do they have?' asked one of his captains.

'Perhaps six hundred riders, maybe less. Most of their cavalry deserted or died during the retreat. What remains is barely a screening force.' Verco checked the girth on his horse with practiced hands. 'We will outnumber them three to one, possibly four to one. It will not be a fight, it will be a slaughter.'

'And after we break their cavalry?'

'We wheel around their flank and hit the rear of their infantry. Legionaries cannot form a square when they are already engaged to their front. We will roll up their line like a scroll, and the battle will be over before noon.'

The captain nodded, satisfied, and moved off to relay the information to his squadron. Verco finished with his horse and stood looking across the plain towards Caesar's distant camp. Somewhere over there, Caesar's cavalry commanders were making their own preparations, knowing what tomorrow would bring and knowing they had no realistic chance of stopping it.

He allowed himself a small smile at that thought, then turned back to continue his preparations, never once considering that Caesar might be counting on exactly that kind of confidence.

In Caesar's camp, Marcus stood near the eastern gate where six cohorts had assembled quietly, their officers speaking in low voices whilst the men checked their equipment without the usual noise that accompanied military formations.

'These are your men,' said Caesar, gesturing at the assembled cohorts, 'all veterans, chosen because their centurions trust them and they trust their centurions. Tomorrow they will decide the battle.'

Marcus looked at the faces barely visible in the torchlight. Hard faces, experienced faces, men who had survived Gaul and Germania and the civil war's opening campaigns. They stood without speaking, waiting for orders but knowing that questions would be answered when necessary and not before.

'Brief the centurions now,' said Caesar. 'Tell them what will be required. Make certain they understand the timing and the positioning but keep it among the officers tonight. The men will be told in the morning, when there is no time for word to spread beyond those who need to know.'

Marcus gathered the centurions away from their men and in the shadows beside the rampart, he explained what Caesar intended. They listened without interruption, their expressions showing nothing except concentration, and when he finished, the oldest of them, a grey-haired veteran named Titus who had been with Caesar since the Helvetii campaign, asked the question Marcus had been expecting.

'So we wait behind the line whilst Pompey's cavalry charges our flank?'

'Yes.'

'And we do nothing whilst our own cavalry gets destroyed?'

'We do nothing until the moment is right. Then we

advance at the double and hit Pompey's cavalry with pila whilst they are disordered and celebrating.'

Titus considered the tactic, his scarred face thoughtful.

'Infantry against cavalry in open ground is suicide unless the timing is perfect.'

'The timing will be perfect,' said Marcus, hoping he sounded more confident than he felt. 'You will know the moment when it comes because you have fought enough battles to recognise when cavalry has overextended and made itself vulnerable.'

The centurions exchanged glances, and something passed between them that needed no words. Finally, Titus nodded again.

'Where do we position before the battle?'

Marcus led them to the edge of the camp and pointed across the dark plain towards where the right flank would form. 'Four hundred paces behind our main battle line, angled slightly to the right. You will be out of sight from Pompey's position, hidden by our deployed legions. When his cavalry charges, you will see them pass, but they will not see you until you are amongst them.'

'And our own cavalry? Do they know we will be there?'

'They do and will not stand and fight. Instead they will retreat past your formation and leave the field clear for you to advance.'

The second centurion, younger but no less experienced, spoke for the first time.

'The men will want to help when they see our cavalry being slaughtered. Holding them back whilst brothers die will test discipline.'

'Which is why I chose veterans who understand that battles are won by following orders, not by individual courage.'

Marcus looked at each centurion in turn. 'Can your men do this?'

'They can do it,' said Titus. 'Whether we should do it is a different question, but that is above our rank to decide. Caesar has the plan and we execute it. That is how this works.'

Marcus dismissed them and they dispersed into the darkness whilst he stood looking out at the plain that would become a battlefield when the sun rose. The weight of what he had been given pressed down on him, and for a moment, he allowed himself to doubt whether he was capable of making the judgment that might decide everything.

Caesar appeared beside him without announcement. The general stood silent for a moment, looking at the same empty darkness, before speaking.

'You are questioning the plan.'

'I am questioning whether I can execute it properly. There is a difference.'

'Not from where I stand. If you doubt yourself, the men will sense it, and doubt spreads faster than plague in an army the night before battle.' Caesar turned to face him. 'So I will tell you what I know, and you will decide whether to believe it or not.'

Marcus waited whilst Caesar chose his words, and in that moment, he saw past the general's mask to something more human underneath. Not fear exactly, but recognition of consequences that would outlive whatever happened tomorrow.

'Pompey has more men than we do. His cavalry outnumbers ours by thousands and his supplies are secure whilst ours are nearly exhausted. And his legions are rested whilst ours are worn down from weeks of retreat and harassment.' Caesar's voice remained steady, listing facts without emotion. 'By every measure that matters in conventional warfare, we should lose tomorrow's battle. We should lose badly, decisively, and that defeat should end not just this war but any hope of reforming the Republic into something worth preserving.'

'Then why fight here? Why not retreat further, find better ground, and wait for circumstances to improve?'

'Because circumstances will not improve. They will only deteriorate. Each day we delay is another day Pompey grows stronger whilst we grow weaker. Each town that closes its gates against us is another resource denied whilst Pompey swims in abundance. We have reached the point where retreat is no longer strategy but desperation, and armies in desperation make mistakes that get them destroyed without even fighting.' Caesar looked back at the plain. 'So we fight here, tomorrow, and we fight with the only advantage we have left. Surprise and precision. What I need from you is judgment about when the moment has come, and the nerve to act on that judgment even when everything around you suggests you are wrong.'

'And if my judgment is misguided?'

'Then we lose, and history will record that Caesar's final gamble failed. But history will not record your name, and the loss will be laid at my feet where it belongs, because I chose the strategy and I chose you to execute it.' Caesar's expression softened slightly. 'But you will not make a mistake, Marcus. You have survived too many battles to suddenly lose your ability to read them now.'

Marcus wanted to believe that. He wanted to feel the confidence Caesar projected, the certainty that the plan would work because it had to work. But all he felt was the weight of thousands of men whose lives would depend on his decision, and the knowledge that even Caesar's genius could not guarantee success against odds this steep.

'I will not fail you,' he said finally, because there was nothing else to say.

'I know. Which is why I gave you this command.' Caesar clapped him on the shoulder, a brief gesture that carried more meaning than words. 'Get some sleep, old friend. Tomorrow will be long, and you will need clarity when the moment comes.'

Caesar walked away, back towards his tent where maps and plans and the weight of command waited. Marcus remained on the rampart, watching the darkness and thinking about timing and cavalry charges and the narrow space between victory and destruction that he would need to navigate when the sun rose.

In the camp below, the six cohorts settled into their designated area, their tents pitched in positions that would allow rapid deployment when morning came. The men sensed something different, could feel it in the way their officers moved and spoke, but discipline held and questions remained unasked.

Titus walked among his men checking equipment, not because it needed checking but because it gave him something to do with his hands whilst his mind worked through what would be required. He had fought in more battles than he could count, had survived wounds that should have killed him and situations that should have ended differently, but tomorrow felt heavier somehow, as if the weight of everything balanced on a knife edge that could tip either way.

Around him, the camp gradually quieted as men sought whatever rest they could find before the battle. Some slept easily, veterans who had learned to take rest when it was available regardless of what dawn might bring. Others lay awake, staring at the stars and thinking about home, family, and the possibility that tomorrow might be their last sunrise.

Titus found his own tent and sat down heavily on his bedroll, his joints aching from decades of campaigning and his thoughts already focused on the timing that would matter more than anything tomorrow. Four hundred paces behind the line, wait for the cavalry charge, and advance at exactly the right moment. Simple instructions that carried the weight of an entire army's survival.

He closed his eyes and tried to sleep, knowing it would not come easily, knowing that when dawn arrived, everything would depend on judgment and discipline and the hope that Caesar's genius had not finally reached its limit on the plain of Pharsalus.

Chapter Twenty-Nine

Pharsalus

The sun rose over the plain of Pharsalus, and forty thousand men emerged from their camps to take their places on the field that would decide the fate of Rome. Marcus stood with the three reserve cohorts four hundred paces behind Caesar's main battle line, watching as both armies deployed.

Caesar's nine legions formed three lines, each depleted from weeks of retreat and fighting. The right flank looked desperately weak, Caesar's six hundred cavalry forming a screen that would not hold against any serious assault. Behind them, the infantry line bent slightly back, refusing the flank in a way that made it appear even more vulnerable. Which was exactly what Caesar intended.

Across the plain, Pompey's nine legions deployed in waves that stretched far beyond Caesar's flanks. The standards seemed endless, and on Pompey's left flank, seven thousand cavalry assembled in a mass that made Caesar's horsemen look like a scouting party.

Marcus felt his stomach tighten watching them deploy. Even knowing Caesar's plan, the sight of that cavalry force made him question whether three thousand men with pila could possibly stop what was coming.

'They have committed everything to that flank,' said Titus beside him. 'If we break their cavalry, their entire strategy collapses.'

'And if we do not break them, we die.'

The deployments completed, and for a moment, the air fell silent. Every man on the field stared across at those they were about to face. They were all united under the name of

Rome, but they didn't fight for different ideologies, for Rome would emerge the victor no matter who won. No, they fought for their generals, their centurions and the men they stood alongside. It was kill or be killed, as simple as that.

A horn echoed across the field and with a tremendous roar, Caesar's army surged forward at a run, closing the distance with speed that caught Pompey's forces unprepared. The front line advanced in tight formation, covering ground so quickly that Pompey's officers barely had time to react before Caesar's veterans were halfway across the field.

Marcus understood immediately. By advancing at speed, Caesar gave Pompey less time to coordinate his superior numbers, and less space for his longer line to envelop the flanks.

Pompey's response came with parade-ground precision. His front line stood firm, not advancing but setting themselves to receive the charge, shields locked and spears braced.

'He is making them stand,' Titus observed. 'He's not advancing.'

'Caesar is forcing the pace,' said Marcus. 'Our men will hit his line whilst running, but our momentum might carry us through before Pompey's reserves can react.'

The distance closed to fifty paces, then twenty, and at the last moment, Caesar's front line released their pila. Thousands of heavy javelins flew in a dark cloud, punching through shields and bringing down men who had been standing firm moments before.

Within seconds, Caesar's front line hit Pompey's stationary ranks, thousands of running men slamming into thousands of standing men, and the plain erupted as shields struck shields like hammers on anvils and blades found fellow-Roman flesh.

Men pushed forward or were driven back, and along a

front that stretched for half a mile, two Roman armies tore into each other with fury that had nothing to do with politics and everything to do with survival.

Marcus watched the standards dipping and rising as combat swayed back and forth without clear advantage. But the main battle was not his concern. His concern was the cavalry massing on Pompey's left flank.

Within moments, Verco raised his spear high, and seven thousand cavalry began their advance. They started at a trot, building speed, and the ground trembled beneath horses and armoured men moving in unison. The charge built momentum, a wall of horseflesh and iron bearing down on Caesar's pathetically thin cavalry screen with the inevitability of an avalanche.

Caesar's cavalry stood their ground longer than Marcus expected, but when Pompey's charge closed to fifty paces, discipline broke and they fled. Not in panic, but in controlled retreat through the gap Marcus's cohorts had left for exactly this purpose.

Pompey's cavalry thundered past like a storm, their attention fixed on pursuing Caesar's fleeing horsemen, and not one looked to where three thousand infantry lay flat in the depression.

'Hold,' Marcus said, his voice steady despite the fear that threatened to choke him. 'Wait for the wheel.'

The cavalry continued their charge, pursuing deeper into the field, and Marcus counted heartbeats whilst judging when they would begin the manoeuvre that would make them vulnerable. Finally, he watched them turn with practiced precision, reforming whilst maintaining momentum, and preparing to crash into the rear of Caesar's infantry line.

Marcus swallowed hard as the moment crystallized. Too soon and his cohorts would be exposed whilst the cavalry could respond. Too late and they would be irrelevant. He glanced upwards to the gods and taking a deep breath, gave the command they had been waiting for.

'*Now,*' he roared and over three thousand men surged up from the depression like demons emerging from the underworld, forming their battle line as they ran, their shields coming together through instinct and training.

The cavalry saw them too late and horror dawned on their faces as they realised what was happening.

Verco shouted his frantic orders, trying to reform, but cavalry needed space and time, and Marcus's cohorts gave them neither. They closed to thirty paces, still running.

'*Pila! Loose!*' roared Marcus and six hundred heavy javelins flew in a massed volley, iron points spinning through air to fall on the turning cavalry. Horses screamed and went down thrashing and riders fell with javelins through their chests.

'Second rank, pila! *Loose!*' shouted Marcus and another volley flew through the air, killing men and horses alike. A third volley followed and the charge that should have broken Caesar's army fell apart against infantry that had appeared from nowhere.

The cohorts surged forward, and what had been a cavalry charge became a confused melee where infantry with shields and short swords had every advantage. Marcus found himself in the thick of it, his shield catching a spear thrust from a rider trying to control his panicking horse. He stepped inside the rider's reach, and drove his gladius into the man's thigh before dragging him from his horse and plunging his Gladius into the terrified man's face.

Dust rose in choking clouds as thousands of hooves

churned the earth, and as visibility dropped to a few paces, Marcus lost track of everything except immediate threats appearing from the murk. A horse slammed into him from the side, cracking ribs, but he stayed on his feet because falling meant being trampled.

Around him, his men worked in pairs, supporting each other whilst cavalry tried and failed to use their mobility in the terrible conditions.

The dust began to settle, and Marcus could see more of the field. Pompey's cavalry was scattered across hundreds of paces, some riders still trying to reform, others fleeing back towards their own lines, many lying dead amongst their horses.

Titus appeared, blood streaming from a cut above his eye.

'We broke them, Praefect.'

'For now,' replied Marcus, 'but they still have numbers.'

Verco reformed his cavalry slower than he wanted, his remaining riders scattered and shaken from an engagement that should have been straightforward. He rode among them shouting orders, trying to restore confidence that had evaporated when Marcus's cohorts emerged from nowhere.

Labienus appeared on a lathered horse with barely controlled fury in his voice.

'What happened? Why is the flank not broken?'

'We were attacked by infantry hidden behind their main line. They hit us during the wheel.'

'How many?'

'Enough to stop us.'

Labienus stared at where Marcus's cohorts stood reformed.

'Caesar kept reserves hidden,' he said, 'he planned this.'

His face showed disbelief warring with rage. 'Reform and charge again. We still have over a thousand riders against a few hundred infantry.'

'My riders have seen what pila do to cavalry. Some will not charge a second time.'

'Then kill any man who refuses. We still have the numbers.'

The reformation took time, and Marcus used it to reposition his own cohorts more defensively, creating gaps that would channel cavalry charges into killing zones. Looking at his dispositions, he knew they would extract a heavy price from any cavalry that came at them, but he also knew it would not be enough. The numbers were too uneven but before Pompey's horsemen could charge again, Caesar's centre pushed hard against Pompey's front ranks, driving them back through sheer pressure. The movement created a pivot that swung Caesar's battle line like a door opening, and suddenly Pompey's forces found themselves compressed from an unexpected angle.

More importantly, Caesar himself appeared at the front of the advance, his red cloak visible even through the dust. The veterans saw him and roared, and Pompey's soldiers saw him too, saw their enemy's general where no general should be, fighting with his soldiers instead of observing from safety. The psychological impact was devastating.

Pompey's front line, which had been holding steady, began to buckle. Not everywhere, but in key positions where Caesar's presence turned discipline into panic.

Across the field, Verco's cavalry charge, when it finally came, was half-hearted, maintaining formation but lacking momentum and when Marcus's cohorts loosed another volley of pila, the charge broke before the javelins even landed.

Riders pulled up, wheeled away, and scattered back

towards their own lines in ones and twos that became dozens and then hundreds. Verco tried to rally them, but cavalry that has lost its nerve cannot be restored through orders. They fled, and Verco finally abandoned his attempt, riding back towards Pompey's camp.

Labienus appeared at the edge of the rout, trying to stem the tide, but even his authority could not turn men who had decided that charging infantry pila was suicide. He sat on his horse and watched his cavalry dissolve, watched the flank that should have won the battle collapse into scattered remnants, and the realization finally dawned that Caesar's hidden reserves had broken more than just a charge, they had broken the entire cavalry wing.

Marcus saw the disintegration and gave the order his cohorts had been waiting for.

'Advance! Threaten their flank!'

They moved forward in tight formation, not chasing fleeing cavalry but positioning themselves to attack the exposed flank of Pompey's infantry, advancing across ground littered with cavalry casualties.

Pompey's infantry tried to refuse their flank, pulling units out to face this new threat, but the manoeuvre was complicated in the middle of combat. Some cohorts turned, others remained engaged to their front, and the gaps that opened were exactly what well-trained infantry exploited.

Marcus led his men into those gaps with pila first, then shields and gladii, and what had been a strong position dissolved into isolated fights where experience mattered more than numbers.

Labienus slowly realised battle was lost. He could see it in the way Pompey's formations were breaking apart, in the way the cavalry had fled, and in the way Caesar's smaller army was dominating through tactical superiority. He turned his horse and galloped back towards the main camp.

Pompey, watching from his command position, saw the same things and gave orders for a fighting withdrawal. But armies that start to break rarely stop until they have fled completely and the collapse spread like fire through dry grass.

Pompey's right flank, already battered, also began pulling back and the withdrawal became a rout as men dropped their shields to run faster, abandoning their wounded comrades where they had fallen. Standards fell as bearers were trampled, and without standards to rally around, his cohorts dissolved into mobs running for their lives.

Finally, Caesar gave the order his army had been desperate to hear for so many months on both sides of the Adriatic.

'Advance! Drive them from the field!'

The trumpets sounded, and Caesar's legions surged forward. They were exhausted from the fighting, many wounded, but they could almost smell victory and that scent gave them strength they should not have possessed.

Marcus reformed his cohorts and joined the advance, moving across ground churned to mud from blood and trampling feet. Bodies lay everywhere, piled thickest where the main lines had ground against each other but his men stepped over them, professional enough not to waste time on casualties whilst live enemies remained.

Scattered groups tried to make stands, buying time for comrades to flee, but Caesar's veterans broke through each position with merciless efficiency and men died in their hundreds.

They reached Pompey's camp and found it in chaos. Servants fled carrying whatever they could grab, officers shouted contradictory orders that no one followed, and wagons overturned creating barriers that slowed the evacuation and turned confusion into panic. Caesar's forces poured through and what little resistance remained collapsed completely.

Marcus followed with his cohorts, moving carefully because camps were dangerous during an assault, but Pompey's camp offered no resistance. It had been abandoned so quickly that food still sat on tables and the tents stood intact.

'Secure the camp,' Marcus ordered. 'Search for holdouts but do not pursue beyond the perimeter.'

Beyond the camp, the pursuit continued with savage efficiency as Caesar's cavalry ranged across the countryside hunting stragglers and cutting down any man who tried to escape. The killing was indiscriminate and unstoppable and they caught the rear guard three miles east, where desperate men had tried to form a defensive position on a low hill. What followed was slaughter, not battle and by the time it ended, another two hundred of Pompey's soldiers lay dead under the burning sun.

Several hours later, on the main battlefield, Caesar's army started dealing with the aftermath as legionaries moved across the field collecting the wounded, stripping bodies of equipment, and occasionally killing enemy wounded too badly hurt to save. Medical tents overflowed with casualties, and the surgeons worked furiously to save who they could.

Caesar walked the field with Marcus and a small escort, stopping occasionally to speak with wounded soldiers. He showed no expression, no triumph, just blank focus. He reached the position where Marcus's cohorts had stopped the cavalry charge, and stood there looking at ground churned by horses' hooves and stained with blood.

'Your cohorts executed the plan perfectly,' said Caesar. 'Perfect timing, perfect formation.' He turned to survey the field. 'Do you know how many we killed today?'

'Fifteen thousand? Perhaps more?'

'At least that many. Possibly twenty thousand. We lost perhaps three hundred killed and a thousand wounded.' Caesar gestured at the field stretching towards the horizon. 'This is what happens when tactics overcome numbers, and when timing defeats strength.'

Marcus said nothing. Victory on this scale should have felt triumphant, but standing among bodies of men who had been alive that morning, all he felt was exhaustion.

'Pompey escaped,' Caesar continued. 'My cavalry pursued him but lost him somewhere east. Labienus also escaped, along with most senior officers and several thousand troops. The senators scattered in every direction.'

'So it is not yet over.'

'Not yet. Pompey has the remnants of an army left and the senators have some forces to protect them. But what remains is pursuit and consolidation, not battle.' Caesar's voice was flat. 'We won today, Marcus. We won completely.'

To the east, Pompey rode hard with a hundred cavalry, all that remained of his personal guard. His horse stumbled, pushed beyond endurance, and behind him the sounds of pursuit had faded, though whether because Caesar's cavalry had given up or simply lost the trail, he could not say.

They halted in an olive grove ten miles from the battlefield, the horses too exhausted to continue. Pompey dismounted heavily and leaned against a tree whilst trying to process what had happened.

A few moments later, Labienus appeared, his face dark with fury.

'How? We had every advantage.'

'Caesar's hidden reserves,' said Pompey quietly. 'The cohorts that hit our cavalry during the wheel. He positioned them exactly where they would have maximum effect and deployed them at exactly the right moment.'

'A few cohorts should not have mattered against so many cavalry.'

'We were outgeneralled, Labienus,' said Pompey, 'the only question is what we do next.'

More riders appeared, scattered remnants who had found each other during the flight. They arrived exhausted and demoralized, each bringing reports of more casualties and widespread collapses of command.

'We need to regroup,' said Labienus finally, 'and establish new positions further east or in Macedonia. Caesar won this battle, but the war continues.'

'With what army?' asked Pompey, looking up. 'We lost fifteen thousand men, possibly more and the remaining legions are destroyed or scattered. The cavalry have fled and our supplies captured. What exactly do we regroup with?'

'Whatever remains,' said Labienus. 'However many men still believe in the Republic. We find them, arm them, and continue fighting.'

Pompey saw the fury that drove Labienus, the conviction that the fight must continue regardless of circumstances. It was admirable, but divorced from reality.

'I am riding to the coast,' said Pompey. 'I will take ship to Egypt or Africa, anywhere Caesar cannot immediately follow. Those who wish to continue fighting can do so under your command. But I will not sacrifice more Roman lives in a cause that ended today.'

'You are abandoning the Republic?'

'The Republic died long before today, probably when Sulla marched on Rome Caesar did not kill the Republic, he buried a corpse that had been rotting for decades.' Pompey moved towards his horse. 'But you are correct that I am abandoning the fight. Someone else can carry the standard from here.'

He mounted and turned towards the coast without looking back. A dozen cavalry followed him, men whose loyalty remained personal, and they rode into the gathering darkness.

Labienus watched him disappear, then addressed the men who remained. Perhaps three hundred cavalry and infantry, battered but still armed.

'Pompey has given up,' he said, 'but we have not. The Republic stands as long as we defend it. Caesar won through deception, but that does not change that he is a traitor who must be opposed.' His voice carried across the grove. 'I am riding to Dyrrachium to gather whatever forces remain. Those who wish to continue will come with me.'

Half the group mounted to follow but the rest sat down where they were and waited for whatever fate would find them.

Elsewhere, the senators scattered like leaves in wind. Lentulus rode north with twenty bodyguards, his face pale, his hands shaking. Scipio turned south towards the coast while Cato continued east towards ports that might offer passage to Africa, each choosing the route that seemed to offer their best chance of escape.

By dawn, they were scattered across three provinces, hunted by Caesar's forces, and united only by the knowledge that the Republic they had sworn to defend had ended that day on an isolated field in Thessaly.

The sun set over Pharsalus in shades of red and orange that seemed too beautiful for a field soaked in blood. Marcus walked among the dead whilst collection details continued their grim work, separating Roman from Roman and friend from foe, though the distinction seemed meaningless now.

The casualties stretched for miles, and bodies lay in positions that told stories of their final moments. Some clutched weapons they had never used, others sprawled in attitudes of flight, and still others locked together in death grips that continued past the moment both men had stopped breathing.

Marcus recognised men he had trained with, eaten with, and shared watches with during the long march from Dyrrachium. All gone now, their stories ended on this field, to be remembered only in letters that would reach their families, if anyone bothered to write them.

He stopped at a cluster of bodies where one of his centuries had made a stand. Perhaps thirty legionaries, shields still locked in the defensive formation they had maintained until being overwhelmed. The centre held a standard, still gripped by the bearer who had died defending it, and around him lay men who had chosen death over abandoning their brothers.

'They held the line,' said Titus behind him, his face exhausted and left arm useless in blood-soaked bandages.

'They held until they were all dead. That is what we ask of them.'

Titus looked at the standard gripped by dead hands.

'That is what makes them Rome's finest. Not that they win, but that they still stand when standing means dying.'

They continued walking as light failed and collection

details lit torches to work into the night.

The wounded had been gathered in the captured camp, organised by severity. Those who would survive lay in neat rows whilst surgeons moved between them with needles and bandages. Those too badly wounded to save had been separated to a different area where they were given wine and what comfort could be offered whilst they died.

Marcus walked through both sections, stopping to speak with men from his cohorts, offering words that felt inadequate. Some asked whether they had won, whether it had mattered. Others asked about their units, or who would carry word to their families. A few said nothing, simply looked at him with eyes that had seen too much.

One young legionary, chest wrapped in bandages already soaked through, caught Marcus's hand.

'Praefect, did we win?'

'Yes,' he replied quietly. 'We won. The war is over.'

'Good. That is good.' The grip weakened. 'Tell my mother I died well, Praefect. Tell her it mattered.'

Marcus promised he would, though he had no idea who the boy's mother was, and by the time he looked for a surgeon, the legionary had stopped breathing.

He emerged from the medical area as darkness fell, and found Caesar standing alone near his command tent, looking out at torches marking the collection details. The general's face showed nothing except exhaustion.

They stood together in silence whilst around them the camp settled into routines that felt obscene in their normalcy. Men ate rations, officers gave orders about tomorrow's march, and life continued as if fifteen thousand men had not died that morning.

'Do you know what I thought about during the battle?' Caesar asked finally.

Marcus waited.

'I thought about all the men I have led into combat over the years,' continued Caesar. 'I thought about how many died because I chose strategies that required their sacrifice, how many families received letters explaining their sons had fallen serving Rome.' Caesar turned to Marcus. 'And I realised the difference between a successful general and a failed one is not tactics or courage or genius. It is willingness to make decisions that cost other people their lives and then live with those decisions afterward.'

'You make it sound cold.'

'It is cold. War is mathematics with blood. You count your men, calculate odds, and make decisions that maximize victory whilst minimizing losses. The fact that each number represents a person with a family is something you acknowledge but cannot dwell on.' Caesar looked back at the field. 'I risked three thousand men today by placing them where they would be exposed to cavalry. Was that justified? Yes, because it saved the army and won the battle. But tell that to the mothers of the men who died.'

'They followed you willingly and understood the risks.'

'Did they? Or did they obey because they had no choice except to follow orders or be executed for desertion?' Caesar's voice carried bitterness Marcus had never heard. 'I am very good at making men believe they are choosing freely when in fact they are following the only path I have left open.'

Marcus had no answer, because Caesar was not wrong.

'What happens now?' he asked eventually.

'Now we pursue Pompey and his scattered remnants. We hunt down senators and offer them terms or justice, but eventually, we will return to Rome.' His voice hardened. 'The Republic is dead, Marcus. It died today, though it has been dying for decades. What replaces it will be different, possibly better, certainly more efficient. But it will not be what those men died believing they were defending.'

He walked away, leaving Marcus alone in darkness whilst around him torches marked where the dead lay waiting for burial or burning. Victory was complete, the enemy scattered, and the path back to Rome open. But standing on that battlefield whilst the smell of death filled the air and the cries of wounded echoed through the night, victory felt less like triumph and more like tragedy.

Chapter Thirty

Pharsalus

Caesar's command tent had been erected in what remained of Pompey's camp, a deliberate choice that sent a message to anyone who cared to notice. The maps spread across the table no longer showed Thessaly but the eastern Mediterranean, coastal routes marked in red, ports circled, distances calculated in days of march and days of sailing.

Marcus stood with the other senior officers, watching Caesar trace his finger along the coast from Greece to Egypt. The general looked much older than he had before Pharsalus, the lines at his eyes deeper, but his voice carried the same certainty it always had when he made decisions that others would execute.

'Pompey has fled east,' said Caesar without preamble. 'My cavalry lost him past Larissa, but the reports from coastal towns confirm he is making for the sea.'

'Where will he go?' asked Antonius.

'Egypt, most likely. He has connections there, favours owed to him from when he supported the Ptolemies. He will believe they will grant him sanctuary and possibly troops to continue the war.'

Labienus, who had been captured two days after the battle whilst trying to rally scattered forces near Dyrrachium, stood silent in the corner under guard. Caesar had insisted he be present for this council, though whether as humiliation or courtesy, Marcus could not determine.

'What are your orders, Imperator?' asked Torquatus.

'We march to the coast with all speed. Light kit, forced pace, twenty-five miles a day until we reach ports where ships can be commandeered. I want a fleet assembled within the week, enough to transport myself and a guard force to Egypt. The main army will follow as soon as transport becomes available.' Caesar looked around at the assembled officers. 'Some of you have been with me since Gaul and know how I operate. We have won a great victory at Pharsalus, but victory means nothing if we allow our enemy to escape and rebuild. While Pompey still lives, the war continues. Is that clear?'

The officers nodded, though Marcus saw exhaustion in their faces that mirrored what he felt in his bones. They had marched and fought for months, suffered defeat at Dyrrachium, won at Pharsalus, and now they were being asked to march again before they had time to bury all their dead or treat all their wounded.

But that was Caesar's way. He never stopped, never rested, and never allowed circumstances to dictate his actions. He drove forward with relentless determination, and those who followed him either matched his pace or were left behind.

'Antonius,' said Caesar, 'you will command the advance force. Take three legions and whatever cavalry can be spared. Move fast, secure the ports, and begin commandeering ships. I want to be at sea within ten days.'

Antonius saluted, and Caesar turned his attention to a map showing Egypt and the Nile delta.

'When we reach Alexandria, we will be operating in foreign territory with questionable local support. The Egyptians are pragmatic and will side with whoever they believe will win, which means we must project strength from the moment we arrive. There will be no hesitation, no negotiation, and no suggestion that we are anything except the inevitable victors of this war.' He looked up from the map, his eyes moving from face to face. 'Pompey believes he is fleeing to safety and Egypt will protect him because he once did them favours. But he does not understand that favours mean nothing when weighed against survival. The Egyptians must see that we have won, and that Pompey has lost.

'Do you want him taken alive?' asked Torquatus.

'I want him taken before he can establish a new base of operations. Whether that means alive or dead is secondary to ensuring he cannot continue the war, but yes, alive would be preferable. Pompey deserves better than assassination by foreign kings, he deserves to face Roman justice, and I would prefer to be the one who decides what that justice looks like.'

Labienus spoke from his position in the corner, his voice bitter.

'Roman justice. Is that what you call it when you hunt an old friend across the world and force foreign powers to choose between betraying him or facing your legions?'

Caesar turned to look at him, and the tent fell silent.

'I call it the consequence of choices made. Pompey chose to ally with the Senate against me. He chose to fight at Pharsalus despite knowing the risks and he chose to flee rather than negotiate terms. Each choice led to the next, and now he is running out of places to run. That is not injustice, Labienus. That is inevitability.'

'It is tyranny dressed in legal language.'

'Perhaps. But it is also victory, which is the only language that matters when the fighting is done.' Caesar gestured to the guards. 'Take him back to his quarters. Make sure he is comfortable, but watched. He has earned that much courtesy.'

The guards escorted Labienus out, and Caesar returned his attention to the assembled officers.

'What about the prisoners?' asked Antonius. 'We have

several thousand, and more are being brought in daily. What do we do with them?"

'Offer them terms. Those willing to swear loyalty to me will be integrated into our legions, those who refuse will be held until we can arrange transport back to Italia where they can be discharged. No executions, no punishments beyond confinement. These are fellow Romans who followed orders, as our men did. The fact that they followed Pompey's orders instead of mine does not make them traitors.'

The officers exchanged glances, and Marcus saw surprise in some faces. Caesar's clemency towards defeated enemies was not new, but offering to integrate Pompey's soldiers into his own legions was generous beyond what most generals would consider.

'We march at dawn,' said Caesar, 'and we do not stop until Pompey is accounted for and this war is finished. Dismissed,'

The officers filed out, already calling for their subordinates to begin the work of breaking camp and preparing for another forced march. Marcus remained behind, and after the tent had cleared, and Caesar looked at him with something approaching weariness.

'You have a question?'

'Why offer clemency to Pompey's soldiers but pursue Pompey himself so relentlessly? Why not offer him the same terms?'

'Because Pompey is not a soldier following orders. He is a general who made choices that led to this war, and those choices must have consequences. If I allow him to escape to Egypt and rebuild, if I let him rally opposition and continue fighting, then everything we won at Pharsalus means nothing. The war continues, more men die and Rome suffers longer. I do not pursue Pompey because I hate him. I pursue him because I respect him. The alternative is letting this war drag on for years, and I will not allow that.'

'And when you catch him? When he has nowhere left to run?'

'Then I will offer him an honourable surrender, a trial in Rome, and a chance to live out his remaining years in exile with his dignity intact. He will refuse, because Pompey is proud and stubborn and cannot imagine accepting mercy from someone he considers beneath him.'

Caesar turned back to his maps.

'Go. Make sure the men are ready to march. Egypt is six weeks away, perhaps less if we push hard.

Marcus saluted and left the tent, and as he walked away, he felt the weight of inevitability settling over him. They had won at Pharsalus, but winning meant nothing except the right to keep marching, keep fighting, and keep pursuing until there were no enemies left to chase.

Near the supply wagons, he paused and watched as a boy sat on the back of a wagon, counting grain sacks and marking his tally. It was Gavius, the shepherd boy from the mountains who had come a long way from demanding a single denarius for his knowledge. Now he tracked the supplies that kept an army alive, and he did it well.

Marcus paused and walked over before reaching beneath his cloak and retrieving his purse. He bounced it up and down in his hand before tossing it over to Gavius.

'What's that for?' asked Gavius, hearing the denarii clinking inside. 'I carried out no errands to earn such a sum.'

'Put it towards buying that farm,' said Marcus. 'But just make sure you stay alive long enough to spend it.'

'I will,' said Gavius with a grin, 'after all, it's the one

thing I am good at.'

'You certainly are, Gavius,' said Marcus, 'you certainly are,' and as Gavius tucked the purse beneath his tunic, he turned away to seek the rest of the day.

The army marched east ten days after Pharsalus, leaving behind a plain still marked by pyres and mass graves where fifteen thousand of Pompey's soldiers had been buried or burned. The column stretched for miles, standards rising above each legion, but the formations were thinner than they had been when they left Rome and the men who marched bore the marks of too many battles fought too close together.

Marcus rode near the front of the column, watching men who no longer thought about marching because their bodies did it automatically, but the energy that had driven them through Gaul and across Italia was gone, replaced by something harder and colder.

Titus walked beside Marcus's horse, his left arm still in a sling but otherwise recovered enough to keep pace.

'The men are asking how much further.'

'To where?'

'To anywhere that is not marching. To rest, to home, to whatever comes after this.' Titus adjusted his sling. 'They fought at Pharsalus because they believed it would end the war. Now we tell them we are marching to Egypt, and after Egypt, who knows where. They are tired, Praefect. More tired than I have ever seen them.'

'I know. But Caesar will not stop until Pompey is dealt with, and we follow Caesar. That is how this works.'

'And when Pompey is dealt with? When there are no more enemies to chase and no more battles to fight? What then?'

Marcus had no answer, because he had been asking himself the same question. Rome seemed like a dream, something that existed only in memory, and the idea of returning there felt almost as foreign as the eastern lands they now marched towards.

Later that night, the sun set over the Greek countryside, painting the sky in shades of red that reminded Marcus of Pharsalus and blood and pyres burning. The army once again made camp for the night in a field beside the road, and the familiar sounds of entrenchment and meal preparation filled the evening whilst sentries took their positions and officers made their rounds.

Marcus stood at the edge of the camp looking east, towards the coast and Egypt and whatever waited there. The war was ending, whether any of them were ready for it or not. And when it did end, when the last enemy was defeated and the last battle fought, they would all have to discover who they were in a world where Caesar's word was law and the Republic was just a memory.

He turned back towards his tent, and as he walked through the camp, he watched the men settling in for the night. They talked quietly, sharing what food they had, tending wounds that would not fully heal, preparing for another day of marching towards a destination that kept receding further into the distance.

They were good soldiers, these men. They deserved better than endless marching and distant wars, but they were Caesar's soldiers, and Caesar never stopped, never rested, never allowed the possibility that there might be peace somewhere down the road.

Marcus reached his tent and lay down on his bedroll,

too tired to remove his armour, too aware of tomorrow's march to sleep properly.

Around him, the camp settled into the routines of night watch and in the darkness, the army that had won the greatest victory in Roman history, rested before marching towards the next battle, and the next, and the next, until there were no more battles to fight… or no more soldiers left to fight them.

Epilogue

Rome

The letter arrived on a grey morning in Rome, carried by a courier who had sailed from Greece on the fastest ship available. Aurelia received it in the atrium of Caesar's house on the Subura, where she had lived for more years than she cared to count, and where she had waited through too many wars for news of her son.

Calpurnia stood beside her as Aurelia broke the seal, Caesar's signet ring pressed into red wax, and together they read words written in his own hand from a coast half a world away.

"To Aurelia, my mother, and to Calpurnia, my wife.

I write from the coast of Greece, where I prepare to pursue Pompey across the sea to Egypt. The battle is won, the war nearly finished, and soon I will return to Rome with the Republic's enemies defeated and its future secured."

Aurelia's hand trembled slightly as she read, and Calpurnia moved closer so they could share the papyrus between them. The words were Caesar's, unmistakably his voice even translated to ink and papyrus, but Aurelia heard something beneath them that troubled her.

"Mother, you once told me that ambition was both Rome's greatest strength and its deepest flaw. You were right, as you have been right about most things.

I have spent my life pursuing glory and power, telling myself it was for Rome's benefit, and perhaps it was. But I cannot deny that it was also for myself, for the satisfaction of proving I could do what others believed impossible."

'He sounds tired,' said Calpurnia quietly.

'He sounds old,' Aurelia replied. 'And my son does not admit to being old, which means something has changed in him.'

They continued reading whilst around them, the household moved through its morning routines, unaware that the letter they held would reshape Rome more thoroughly than any battle.

"At Pharsalus, I gambled everything on a plan that required perfect execution and absolute trust in men I had trained and led for a decade. They did not fail me. They held when they should have broken, attacked when they should have fled, and turned certain defeat into total victory.

I am often called a great general, but my greatness lies only in recognizing great soldiers and giving them orders they are capable of executing."

Aurelia paused at that passage, reading it twice. Caesar acknowledging his soldiers' role in victory was not unusual, but the tone of it was. There was something approaching humility in those words, and Caesar was not a humble man.

'He is preparing us,' she said.

'For what?'

'For the man who will return. Not the man who left, but whoever the war has made him.' Aurelia looked at her daughter-in-law. 'He knows he has changed, and he wants us to know it too before we see him again.'

"The Republic you remember from your youth is gone, Mother, if it ever truly existed. What I bring back to Rome will be different. Whether it will be better is something history will judge.

I can only promise that I have done what I believed necessary, and that the cost, though terrible, was less than the cost of allowing the Republic to continue tearing itself apart."

Calpurnia's breath caught, and Aurelia felt her own chest tighten. The Republic was gone. Caesar stating it plainly, without apology or justification beyond necessity. She had known this was coming, had seen it approaching for years, but reading the words written in her son's hand made it real in ways that rumour and speculation never had.

'He is telling us he has become what they always feared he would become,' said Calpurnia.

'No. He is telling us he has accepted what he always was, and that he will not pretend otherwise anymore.' Aurelia's voice was steady despite the weight of what she was reading. 'The Republic died long before Pharsalus. Caesar is simply willing to say so.'

"Calpurnia, I know these years of war have been hard on you, and I know that the husband who returns will not be the same man who left. War changes everyone it touches, victors and defeated alike.

But I am still the man you married, still Caesar, and when this is finally over, I will come home to you and we will build whatever peace can be built in the world we have created."

Calpurnia's eyes filled with tears, though she blinked them back quickly. Aurelia reached out and took her hand, squeezing it once, a gesture of solidarity between women who had both loved Caesar in different ways and both understood that the man they loved was also capable of things that would horrify them if they thought about them too carefully.

"I expect to be in Rome before winter. The pursuit of Pompey continues, but it will end soon, one way or another. When it does, when all threats are eliminated and all enemies defeated, I will lay down my sword and turn my attention to the harder work of governing rather than conquering.

You will hear many things about what I have done and what I intend to do. Some will be true, others will be exaggerations or outright lies. Remember that I have never acted except in what I believed to be Rome's interest, and that whatever comes next, it comes because there was no other path forward that did not lead to worse outcomes."

The letter ended with Caesar's signature, bold and unmistakable, and Aurelia set it down on the table beside her with hands that were steadier than she felt.

'He believes what he is doing is right,' said Calpurnia.

'Of course he does,' replied Aurelia, 'Caesar always believes he is right. That is both his greatest strength and his most dangerous weakness.' Aurelia looked at the letter, at her son's handwriting that had barely changed since he was a boy learning rhetoric and dreaming of glory. 'But believing something is right does not make it so, and I fear we will all pay the price for his certainty before this is finished.'

'What do we do?'

'We wait and we prepare. And when he returns, we welcome him home and try to help him become whatever Rome needs him to be, even if that is something neither of us can quite imagine yet.'

Aurelia stood, her face showing the strength that had

raised Caesar and survived his ambition. 'He is my son, and I will love him regardless of what he becomes. But I will not lie to myself about what he is becoming, and neither should you.'

Calpurnia nodded and carefully folded the letter, and together they walked from the atrium into the house that would soon become the centre of an empire that neither woman had wanted but both would have to learn to live with.

Outside, Rome continued its routines, unaware that the Republic was already dead and that the man who had killed it was writing letters home to his mother and wife, explaining himself because even Caesar needed someone to understand why he had done what he believed necessary.

On the other side of the Mediterranean, the Egyptian coast appeared through the morning haze, a thin line of yellow sand and palm trees that marked the end of Pompey's flight from Pharsalus. He stood at the prow of the merchant vessel he had commandeered in Greece, watching Alexandria's harbour grow larger as the ship approached.

Twenty men remained with him, all that was left of the personal guard that had once numbered in the hundreds.

A small boat put out from the harbour as the ship dropped anchor, and Pompey watched it approach with relief. Three men sat in it, one rowing whilst the other two remained still, dressed simply for the heat. Their boat bore no markings, but Pompey assumed they were servants sent ahead of the formal delegation.

The boat pulled alongside, and one of the men stood, cupping his hands to shout up at Pompey's ship.

'Gnaeus Pompeius Magnus, consul of Rome and commander of its eastern provinces, Pharoah Ptolemy has received your message and invites you to come ashore as his honoured guest. A proper reception awaits you in the palace, but the harbour is too shallow for your ship to dock. If you transfer to our boat, we will carry you to land.'

Pompey looked at the man who had spoken and felt reassured by his words. The invitation was warm and the fact that they had come so quickly suggested Ptolemy was eager to receive him.

'I am grateful for Pharaoh Ptolemy's hospitality,' he replied, 'take me to him.'

He climbed down into the rowing boat, and the two men shifted to make room. The boat pushed away from the ship, and Pompey watched the Egyptian coast grow closer, the palm trees and white buildings of the harbour becoming clearer with each stroke of the oars.

'Where is the reception?' Pompey asked as they began rowing towards shore.

'Ahead,' said the man who had spoken earlier. His name was Achillas, Pompey remembered now, a soldier who had served in Rome's eastern campaigns and knew Roman ways. 'Pharaoh waits to greet you properly.'

'It is good to be among friends again. The journey from Greece was difficult, and I feared we might not find safe harbour.'

'You are safe now, Magnus. Egypt remembers what you have done for us.'

Pompey nodded and looked towards the shore, thinking about what he would say to Ptolemy, and how the war might yet be turned in his favour. The sun was warm on his face, and for the first time in weeks, he allowed himself to feel something approaching hope.

His eyes closed as he turned his face upward to the sun, so did not see Achillas nod to the two men behind him. He only felt the blade plunging into his back between the ribs.

His body jerked forward with the shock and he tried to turn, tried to understand what was happening, but the blade thrust again and he fell forward onto the bottom of the boat whilst the sounds of the harbour faded into silence.

Gnaeus Pompeius Magnus, who had been Rome's greatest general before Caesar, who had conquered the east and celebrated three triumphs and commanded more legions than any man except Caesar himself, died far from Rome, far from his legions, and far from everything he had built and believed in.

His murderers took his head and left his body for the tide where a merchant found him floating in the shallows and burned him on a pyre of driftwood, the only funeral Rome's greatest son would ever receive.

Three days later, Caesar arrived in Alexandria and was presented with Pompey's head by Achillas, who expected thanks and received something else entirely. Caesar looked at the severed head of his former friend and rival, at the face he had known for decades, and his expression showed nothing except weariness.

'You have murdered a consul of Rome without trial, without dignity, and without any of the honour that was his due. And you believe I will thank you for this?'

Achillas stepped back, uncertain.

'We thought... Pharaoh believed you would want...'

'You thought wrong.' Caesar turned away from the head. 'Pompey was a worthy opponent who deserved better than assassination by foreigners seeking to curry favour. I would have offered him an honourable surrender, a trial in Rome, and a chance to live with dignity. You have denied him that, denied Rome that, and denied me the opportunity to show mercy to a man who earned it through decades of service.'

He walked out of the palace whilst Achillas stood holding the head, and outside, Marcus waited with Caesar's guard.

'Pompey is dead,' said Caesar simply. 'Murdered by Egyptians who believed I wanted him dead and thought killing him would please me.' He turned to look back at the palace.

'This war is over, Marcus. Pompey is dead, his forces are scattered, and the Republic that he fought to preserve has died with him. What remains is simply finishing the details and returning to Rome to build whatever comes next.'

The war was over.

The age of Caesar had begun.

The End

Next Book in the Series

The Ides of March

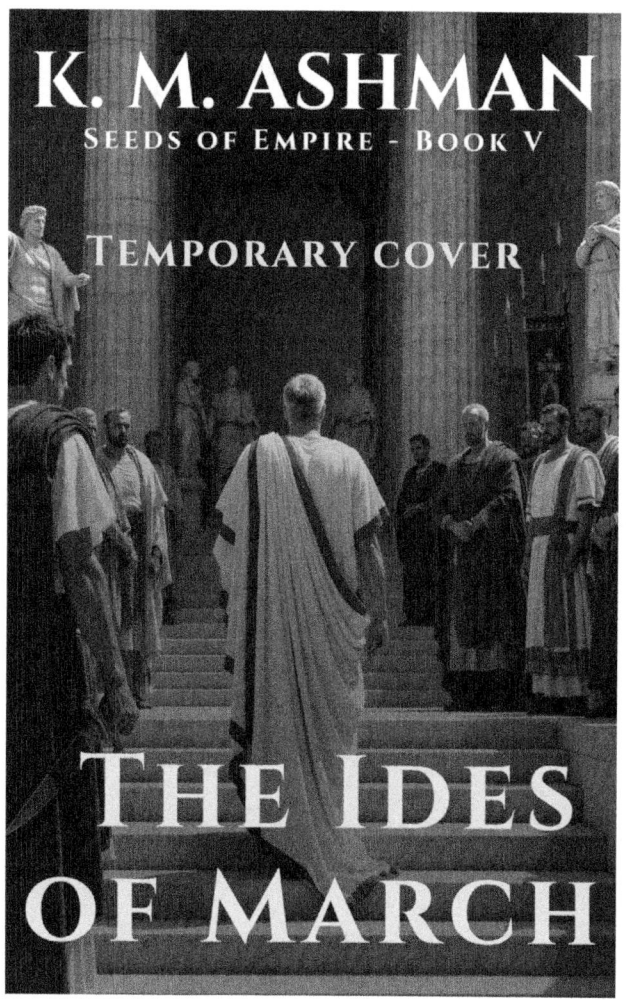

Authors Notes

The Rubicon Crossing (January 49 BC)

Caesar's famous crossing of the Rubicon River was not a grand military spectacle but rather an intimate act of treason. The Rubicon marked the boundary between Gaul (where Caesar had legal military authority) and Italia proper, where no general could bring armed troops without Senate permission.

When Caesar crossed with just one legion (the Thirteenth), he uttered the famous phrase "alea iacta est" (the die is cast), though some ancient sources suggest he actually spoke in Greek: "anerriphtho kybos."

The river itself was small and unimpressive, but the political significance was enormous. By crossing armed into Italia, Caesar became an enemy of the state, punishable by death. There was no turning back, which made his decision one of history's most consequential gambles.

Modern scholars debate the exact location of the ancient Rubicon, as several small rivers in the region could have been the historical boundary.

Pompey's Military Reputation

Gnaeus Pompeius Magnus (Pompey the Great) earned his cognomen "Magnus" at age 25, styled after Alexander the Great.

Before Caesar's rise, Pompey was Rome's most successful general, having celebrated three triumphs by the age of 45 (an unprecedented achievement). He had defeated Sertorius in Spain, cleared the Mediterranean of pirates in just three months, and conquered vast territories in the East, including Syria and Judea.

Pompey's eastern campaigns added more territory to Rome than any previous general, and he personally organised fourteen new provinces. His wealth was legendary, and his political influence dominated Rome for decades.

However, Pompey had not commanded troops in active combat for nearly a decade before the civil war, which may have contributed to his more cautious approach compared to Caesar's aggressive tactics. The rivalry between these two giants was as much personal as political.

The Senate's Flight from Rome

When news reached Rome that Caesar had crossed the Rubicon with his army, the Senate's response was panic rather than preparation. Despite Pompey's assurances that he could raise legions to defend the Republic, many senators fled Rome within days, abandoning the city to Caesar without a fight.

This mass exodus revealed the Senate's fundamental weakness: they commanded loyalty through tradition and legal authority, but when faced with military force, they had no effective response.

Pompey himself withdrew from Rome, famously declaring that "Sulla did it, why shouldn't I?" referring to Sulla's earlier march on Rome.

The Senate relocated first to Capua, then to Brundisium, and finally across the Adriatic to Greece, taking the state treasury with them.

This flight effectively ceded Italia to Caesar and demonstrated that the Republic's institutions had become hollow shells unable to defend themselves against a determined general with loyal legions.

Caesar's Clementia (Clemency)

One of Caesar's most effective political weapons was his policy of clementia, or clemency toward defeated enemies. Unlike previous civil wars where victors massacred their opponents (as Sulla had done), Caesar made a deliberate choice to pardon enemies who surrendered or were captured.

This policy served multiple purposes: it made resistance seem futile since defeat didn't mean death, it allowed him to appear merciful rather than tyrannical, and it enabled him to integrate defeated soldiers into his own legions, actually strengthening his forces.

However, this clemency was also strategic calculation. Caesar understood that Romans hated civil war and that being seen as needlessly bloodthirsty would undermine his support. His famous phrase "let us try this new method of winning, by mercy and generosity" was both genuine philosophy and brilliant propaganda.

Many senators who opposed him were pardoned multiple times, only to continue plotting against him, which ultimately contributed to his assassination in 44 BC.

The Roman Legion Structure

A Roman legion at full strength comprised approximately 5,000-6,000 men, divided into ten cohorts. Each cohort contained six centuries of about 80 men (despite the name suggesting 100). The first cohort was double-strength at 800 men and included the legion's most veteran troops.

A century was commanded by a centurion, the backbone of Roman military power. These professional officers were promoted from the ranks and provided continuity and expertise that made Roman armies so effective.

Legionaries were heavy infantry, equipped with the gladius (short sword), pilum (heavy javelin), scutum (large rectangular shield), and segmented armour. They were trained to fight in tight formations, with each man protecting his neighbour with his shield.

The pilum was ingeniously designed with a soft iron shank that would bend on impact, making enemy shields useless and preventing the javelin from being thrown back. Roman military success came not from superior technology but from superior discipline, training, and organization.

The Battle of Dyrrachium (July 48 BC)

Dyrrachium was actually one of Caesar's worst defeats, though it's often overshadowed by his later victory at Pharsalus. Caesar attempted to trap Pompey's larger army behind a massive circumvallation (a ring of fortifications stretching over 15 miles), one of the largest military engineering projects in ancient warfare.

However, Pompey discovered a weak point in Caesar's lines where construction was incomplete. In a nighttime assault, Pompey's forces broke through the fortifications, turned the tables on Caesar's siege, and inflicted significant casualties. Caesar lost approximately 1,000 men including 32 veteran centurions, while Pompey's losses were minimal.

It was a severe tactical defeat that could have ended the war. Caesar himself admitted the danger, reportedly saying "Today the victory had been the enemy's, had there been anyone among them to gain it," implying that Pompey failed to press his advantage.

Pompey's decision not to pursue Caesar's defeated army aggressively has puzzled historians for 2,000 years and proved to be his fatal mistake.

The Logistics of Ancient Warfare

Ancient armies lived off the land, which made logistics as important as tactics. A Roman legion required approximately 15 tons of grain daily, plus water, fodder for animals, and firewood. This meant that armies couldn't stay in one place long without exhausting local resources.

Caesar's retreat from Dyrrachium was partly driven by supply shortages caused by Pompey's cavalry cutting his foraging parties. The army described in the book, moving through Greece while being harassed by enemy cavalry, reflects the reality that warfare was often decided by logistics before a battle was even fought.

Towns that closed their gates against an army weren't just being defensive, they were protecting their winter food supplies from being consumed by thousands of hungry soldiers.

The sack of Gomphi described in the novel was historical fact: Caesar's starving army assaulted the town and looted it for supplies, showing how desperation could turn professional soldiers into plunderers when food was scarce.

The Battle of Pharsalus (August 9, 48 BC)

Pharsalus was one of the most decisive battles in human history, ending the Roman Republic and paving the way for the Empire.

Pompey commanded approximately 45,000 infantry and 7,000 cavalry against Caesar's 22,000 infantry and 1,000 cavalry, nearly a 2:1 numerical superiority.

Pompey's battle plan was sound: mass his cavalry on the flank, sweep away Caesar's weak cavalry, and roll up Caesar's infantry line from the rear. It should have worked.

However, Caesar secretly positioned six cohorts (approximately 2,000-3,000 men) as a fourth line behind his right flank, hidden from Pompey's view.

When Pompey's cavalry charged and drove back Caesar's horsemen, these cohorts emerged and attacked the cavalry with pila at close range.

Roman heavy infantry with javelins against cavalry in the midst of a charge was devastating. The cavalry broke and fled, exposing Pompey's left flank. Caesar then committed his reserves and won decisively.

Casualties were staggeringly one-sided: approximately 15,000 of Pompey's soldiers died versus only 200 of Caesar's. The "fourth line" tactic was Caesar's tactical masterstroke.

Pompey's Death in Egypt (September 28, 48 BC)

Pompey fled to Egypt after Pharsalus, expecting sanctuary from young Pharaoh Ptolemy XIII, whom Pompey had helped place on the throne years earlier. However, Ptolemy's advisors calculated that Caesar would win the civil war and decided to curry favour by eliminating Pompey for him.

As Pompey's boat approached the Egyptian shore, he was stabbed to death by Achillas and Septimius (a former Roman officer who had served under Pompey).

When Caesar arrived days later and was shown Pompey's severed head, he reportedly wept, whether from genuine grief for his former friend and ally, or from anger at being denied the opportunity to show clemency and appear merciful, historians debate.

Caesar ordered Pompey's assassins executed and gave

Pompey's signet ring a proper burial. The murder of Pompey, rather than settling matters, actually prolonged the civil war, as Pompey's sons and supporters continued resistance in Spain and Africa for several more years.

Other Books by K. M. Ashman

Seeds of Empire
Seeds of Empire
Rise of the Eagle
Fields of Glory
Ides of March

The Exploratores
Dark Eagle
The Hidden
Veteranus
Scarab
The Wraith
Silures
Panthera
Shadow Walker
Acheron

The Brotherhood
Templar Steel
Templar Stone
Templar Blood
Templar Fury
Templar Glory
Templar Legacy
Templar Loyalty

The India Summers Mysteries
The Vestal Conspiracies
The Treasures of Suleiman
The Mummies of the Reich

The Tomb Builders

The Roman Chronicles
The Fall of Britannia
The Rise of Caratacus
The Wrath of Boudicca
The Medieval Sagas
Blood of the Cross
In Shadows of Kings
Sword of Liberty
Ring of Steel

The Blood of Kings
A Land Divided
A Wounded Realm
Rebellion's Forge
The Warrior Princess
The Blade Bearer

The Road to Hastings
The Challenges of a King
The Promises of a King
The Fate of a King

The Otherworld Series
The Legacy Protocol
The Seventh God
The Last Citadel
Savage Eden
Vampire

Printed in Dunstable, United Kingdom